T0330142

Social Mobilisation in Post-Industrial China

This book is dedicated to all the people who have contributed to this research.

Social Mobilisation in Post-Industrial China

The Case of Rural Urbanisation

Jia Gao

Asia Institute, University of Melbourne, Australia

Yuanyuan Su

School of Social and Behavioural Sciences, Nanjing University, China

 Edward Elgar
PUBLISHING

Cheltenham, UK • Northampton, MA, USA

Published by
Edward Elgar Publishing Limited
The Lypiatts
15 Lansdown Road
Cheltenham
Glos GL50 2JA
UK

Edward Elgar Publishing, Inc.
William Pratt House
9 Dewey Court
Northampton
Massachusetts 01060
USA

A catalogue record for this book
is available from the British Library

Library of Congress Control Number: 2018958900

This book is available electronically in the **Elgar**online
Social and Political Science subject collection
DOI 10.4337/9781786432599

ISBN 978 1 78643 258 2 (cased)
ISBN 978 1 78643 259 9 (eBook)

Typeset by Servis Filmsetting Ltd, Stockport, Cheshire
Printed and bound in Great Britain by TJ International Ltd, Padstow

Contents

List of figures   vi
List of tables   vii
List of abbreviations   viii
Preface   ix
Acknowledgements   xv

1   China's current rural urbanisation and historical context   1
2   The evolving role of central decision-makers in launching policy
    initiatives   30
3   The politics of social mobilisation at the provincial level   61
4   The emerging powers of the 'invisible hand'   89
5   Mobilising policy support and resources at the prefectural
    level   111
6   The awkward roles of county and township governments in
    rural urbanisation   141
7   Participatory responses of villagers to initiatives   162
8   Towards an updated understanding of social mobilisation in
    China   184

References   201
Index   239

Figures

2.1	Location of Yantai, Shandong province	36
2.2	China's governmental structure, 2015	38
2.3	Urban–rural distribution of population in China, 1975–2015	48
2.4	China's rural–urban income gap, 1978–2006	53
2.5	China's GDP across three sectors, 1978–2015	53
2.6	Percentages of employment across three sectors, 1980–2015	54
3.1	Shandong's GDP compared to other rich provinces, 1996–2014	64
3.2	Shandong's gross industrial and agricultural output values, 1949–2015	67
3.3	Population of Shandong and rural–urban distribution	80
4.1	Numbers of sizeable domestic enterprises in Shandong, 2005–15	97
4.2	Numbers of Shandong people working in three types of sizeable domestic enterprise, 2005–15	98
5.1	The location of Laiwu, Shandong province	120
5.2	Shares of three sectors in Laiwu's GDP, 2005–15	121
7.1	The increasing occurrence of mass protests, out of 871 cases, 2000–2013	165
7.2	The growing dependence of governments on revenues from land transfer, 2006–13	166
7.3	Four types of responses and the most difficult groups	173

Tables

2.1	Reductions in the number of State Council agencies	40
2.2	China's main post-1978 financial reform efforts	42
2.3	Key strategic ideas of 'No. 1 Document' from 2004	56
3.1	Shandong's gross industrial and agricultural output (billion yuan), 1949–2015	66
3.2	Gross output values of Shandong's light and heavy industries (million yuan), 1949–2015	68
3.3	Lower-level governments under Shandong, 2015	69
3.4	Central rural work conferences and the rural land-use policy, 2004–15	73
4.1	Introduction of market forces into the Chinese economy, 1978–2004	91
4.2	Annual business turnover of three sizeable domestic enterprises in Shandong (billion yuan), 2005–15	99
6.1	Laiwu's total population and urban–rural distribution, 2005–16	145
6.2	Laiwu's rural income and public investment in rural infrastructure, 2005–15	150
6.3	Laiwu's public investment in rural infrastructure, new projects and housing units, 2009–16	156
7.1	Mass protest incidents in 17 categories, out of 871 cases, 2000–2013	164

Abbreviations

CASS	Chinese Academy of Social Sciences
CCDI	Central Commission for Discipline Inspection
CCP	Chinese Communist Party
CCTV	China Central Television
CDRF	China Development Research Foundation
CIS	Centre for Independent Studies
CNR	China National Radio
CPC	Communist Party of China (the CCP's own English translation of its name)
CSC	China Scholarship Council
GDP	Gross domestic product
HKTDC	Hong Kong Trade Development Council
IMF	International Monetary Fund
KPI	Key performance indicator
LWTJJ	Laiwu Tongjiju (Laiwu Bureau of Statistics)
NBSC	National Bureau of Statistics of China
NDRC	National Development and Reform Commission
NSSFC	National Social Science Fund of China
OECD	Organisation for Economic Co-operation and Development
PLA	People's Liberation Army (of China)
PRC	People's Republic of China
RMB	Renminbi, China's currency
SEITC	Shandong Economic and Information Technology Committee
SOE	State-Owned Enterprise
SPBS	Shandong Provincial Bureau of Statistics
TVE	Township and village enterprise
UNICEF	United Nations Children's Fund
USITC	United States International Trade Commission
VOA	Voice of America

Preface

This book seeks to fulfil the timely need for a better understanding of how social mobilisation works in present-day China, and the changes that have occurred with this important socioeconomic and socio-political mechanism since the late 1970s and early 1980s, especially since the mid-1990s, when more fundamental reforms of China's party-state system and governance have been undertaken. Social mobilisation has long been considered a key characteristic of modern Chinese life, which has been so apparent over the course of past decades that many analysts even define China as a nation of mobilisation. The existing scholarly literature on social mobilisation in China, however, is largely characterised by studies of pre-1978 Chinese socioeconomic and socio-political situations, many of which are also scattered and fragmentary. These problems have not only resulted in misjudging the crucial role of social mobilisation as a process of social change and a key analytical construct, but have also overlooked the work of many researchers in the fields of socioeconomic and socio-political activities in China, which is rather different from what we have known from the past and even what we can read in English these days.

Through careful and thorough analysis of new empirical evidence from both primary and secondary sources, this co-authored book aims to contribute to the discussion in academic literature on contemporary China in the midst of competing views. Those views cover the ways in which the social mobilisation mechanism is used at different levels of government and society at different times for different purposes, how meaningful mass socio-political participation is, and the ways and the extent to which China's governance has been transformed as a result of many fundamental shifts in its economy and politics, as well as whether China's state capacity has declined since the early 1990s.

The research focus on social mobilisation emerged in the 1960s and 1970s when waves of socio-political activism were spreading, especially in the United States, China and several European countries. China became a subject of intellectual interest and inquiry soon after the concept of social mobilisation emerged, though China closed its door to the West in the 1960s and through much of the 1970s. Despite this, there are not many big countries like China where social mobilisation has been system-atically employed as a useful and effective mechanism for socioeconomic development.

In recent decades, China has experienced rapid economic growth and many other crucial socio-political changes. China has not only trans-formed itself into a rapidly urbanising industrial economy as defined by the Organisation for Economic Co-operation and Development (OECD) (2015), but has also already quietly entered its post-industrial stage of economic development. In 2015, according to the National Bureau of Statistics of China (NBSC, 2016), the service sector in China already accounted for more than 50 per cent of its GDP (gross domestic product), about five percentage points higher than the GDP contribution from the manufacturing and construction sectors. At the same time, China's domestic political structure, political power relationships and politics have all been substantially transformed, though many have not yet fully realised it or refused to accept it, entering what researchers in China have frequently called the new era of *boyi*, political bargaining games among interest groups or various social forces (Liang, 2014, p. 119). As will be further discussed in Chapter 1 and other chapters, Chinese politics are no longer based on ideology, but on political bargaining and negotiation among various competing interest groups seeking to maximise their shares of material benefits and political power.

All these rapid and far-reaching changes in China are of immense inter-est to many researchers and observers, both in China and in other coun-tries, resulting in a growing number of academic publications on a wide range of issues relating to a rapidly changing China and the diversification of research interests and perspectives. However, China's rapid and never-ending transformations, as well as its complexity and scale, have tended to mean that much of our understanding quickly becomes outdated, and research efforts are too broadly scattered to focus on the essential clues to understanding the changes and the important enduring characteristics of Chinese life.

Social mobilisation is one such important theoretical clue and char-acteristic that is fundamental for a good understanding of present-day China, but it has also been overlooked by researchers for decades. This co-authored book distinguishes itself from other books on present-day China in the following ways.

First, this book is exclusively about social mobilisation, one of the most important and regularly used socioeconomic and socio-political mechanisms in rapidly transforming China. As mentioned, despite the broad and fundamental changes in the country, this crucial social mechanism has not been systematically studied for a few decades, and almost no book-length study on it has been published in English since the early 1990s, the only exceptions of which are those based on China's birth control (White, 2006) and the mobilisation of emotions (Perry, 2002, 2011; Y. Liu, 2010).

Second, this study presents an historical account of the changes that have taken place because of the social mobilisation mechanism in China since the early reform era after the late 1970s, including crucial changes in China's socio-political system, bureaucratic structures at different levels and politics, central–state relations and state–society interactions, and policy-making and implementation processes at different levels of government and society. Special attention is given to two parallel processes: China's decentralisation efforts of the past decades and the emerging power of its market or private economy. This specific feature of the book is important to enable readers to understand what changes have occurred in recent decades, how the mechanism of social mobilisation has been slowly transformed over the past decades, what steps have preceded and what may follow.

Third, this research book reveals a dynamic process that challenges both the oversimplified views of Chinese political life and culture and the misunderstanding of mass political participation, if not democracy, in China. To clearly present the dynamics that emerge from, as well as drive, the ongoing deep changes in China, this book also gives more attention than earlier studies to the complex interactions between top-down and bottom-up processes, and among different sets of motivations, market forces and active participation of community members. The complexity of rural urbanisation in a heavily populated country like China makes such analysis possible.

Fourth, this book will be distinguished by its interdisciplinary points of view and the richness of new empirical evidence on social mobilisation in China. This study will draw on the work of researchers from the fields of sociology, public policy and administration, political science, human and economic geography, and other applied economic disciplines. The authors' long-time research interests and experience in these areas in China – rural areas and the upper levels of bureaucracy – have made it feasible to conduct such a high-quality and comprehensive analysis.

Finally, and importantly, because of the above unique and important features, this book aims to fill the intellectual void left by few thorough studies on social mobilisation in post-Mao China and little systematic discussion of how social mobilisation has been used in China and the changes that have occurred to this crucial mechanism over the past decades. Among new data and perspectives, this book also provides a new explanation of the nature of social mobilisation in contemporary China, where there has been a trend away from ideology-based rule and social mobilisation, and toward a new politics based on shared needs, material interests and benefits. The book aims to be stimulating and rewarding.

As will be detailed below and in Chapter 1, this analysis of social mobilisation in present-day China is primarily based on its recent rural urbanisation push, which is, according to its various features, a unique and typical social mobilisation campaign that involves almost all levels of government and society. In fact, there has been no other nationwide campaign in China in recent years that can reveal more about the social mobilisation mechanism used in post-industrial China.

In general, this research is based on the idea that issues regarding social mobilisation in present-day China are in urgent need of systematic study. Social mobilisation is no longer employed in China in the ways it used to be, but is more dynamic than is often thought. Similarly, China is no longer a country that can be simply defined as communist or a centrally planned economy, but has over the past few decades been transformed beyond recognition. We can safely assume that few readers in English-speaking countries are familiar with all the recent developments in China, the changes to its governance and practices, and implications for its future, as well as that for the rest of the world. We may also safely assume that many English readers are interested in learning more about what has taken place in China, in its hierarchical socio-political system, and how its governance have been transformed. Since social mobilisation in China has not been analysed for a long time. Because this study focuses on recent empirical evidence and theoretical implications, this book will not only be able to renew our understanding of what has happened in China in the areas of governance, bureaucratic structure and political culture, policy-making and implementation, state or administration interference, private sector development, institutional capacity-building, mass protest and political participation, but will also provide readers with some new perspectives on these important issues in a rapidly changing China.

The idea of writing this book originated a few years ago, when I was first contacted by Su Yuanyuan who was recommended by Professor Zhou Xiaohong, her doctoral supervisor at Nanjing University, China, for a position as a visiting PhD scholar at the Faculty of Arts, University of Melbourne.

At the time, two of my university colleagues and I had just completed editing *Transforming Chinese Cities* (Routledge, 2014), and another edited volume entitled *Global Media and Public Diplomacy in Sino-Western Relations* (Routledge, 2016) was well underway. Through these projects, my research attention has gradually been drawn back to what has been taking place in China. My second major monograph on the new Chinese migrant community in Australia, entitled *Chinese Migrant Entrepreneurship in Australia from the 1990s* (Elsevier, 2015), was near completion, which made it possible for me to shift my attention away, at least momentarily, from the rapidly expanding, and increasingly interesting and important, new Chinese migrant community in Australia, on which I have conducted a series of research projects over many years.

What intrigued me from the time I started giving attention to what is happening in China is the research question initially put forward by Professor Zhou Xiaohong and Su Yuanyuan, which is how Chinese peasants have been mobilised in many regions to accept and move to live in new modern apartment buildings. The latter is often called *nongmin shanglou* in Chinese, referring to 'the campaign to make peasants live in storied buildings' according to Looney's translation (Looney, 2012, p. 281). Our discussion of the issue of rural urbanisation in China and the entire policy process led us to conclude that a thorough review and analysis of the role of social mobilisation as a key socio-political and socio-economic mechanism in present-day China was urgently needed. We decided to work together on this book based on the campaign of *nongmin shanglou*.

For a long time, since the time when I was working in China, I have been mainly interested in various issues related to China's public opinion, social reactions to governmental initiatives, political dynamics, bureaucracy and elite dominance and ideology. As a young lecturer in social psychology and sociology at Beijing-based Renmin University of China, I was actively involved in a range of social psychological and sociological studies in post-Mao China. Because of my involvement, I was awarded the first and only national academic prize in sociology by China's National Commission of Education and Hong Kong-based Fok Ying Tung Foundation in 1988. It was in the mid-1980s that Professor Zhou Xiaohong and I were active researchers in the fields of sociology and social psychology in China. These academic fields and the 1980s seem to be nothing unique to the current younger generations, but as general background to this book, it must be stressed that these fields were new at the time in China after being banned for a few decades.

It was also in the 1980s that I developed research interests in social processes and the mechanisms behind various forms of social action and change. As discussed in my earlier publications, I favour the idea that 'process matters' over the thinking that 'structure matters' (Gao, 2015, p. 20), and therefore I have been interested in research looking at the ways in which social dynamics work. Because of our shared research interests, Su Yuanyuan had subsequently conducted the first part of her research project in Australia in 2015, during which we decided to not only work together on this project, but also expand the discussion to consider more levels and aspects of the whole issue to fill the gaps left behind by researchers for decades.

Jia Gao, PhD
The University of Melbourne

Acknowledgements

This co-authored book could not have been written without the help of many friends and colleagues. I owe a great debt of gratitude to those who have kindly assisted our project for years. I am very grateful to Professor Zhou Xiaohong, who contacted me in mid-1988 shortly before I was leaving China for Australia and invited me to co-author a book on social psychology, as we two then represented two active research teams in North China and South China respectively. The hard and uncertain life in my early years in Australia prevented me from co-authoring the book with him in the late 1980s, which has been one of my regrets in my professional career. I hope I have made a right decision this time. I am thankful to him for his effort to encourage Su Yuanyuan to participate in this project.

I am also very grateful to Mr Alex Pettifer, the Editorial Director at Edward Elgar Publishing, for his strong interest in the original idea for this co-authored book and his encouragement for us to write and submit the manuscript for publication. We would also like to sincerely thank all the anonymous reviewers for their helpful comments on both the book proposal and the first draft of the manuscript. Our thanks also go to Ms Aisha Bushby, Ms Rachel Downie, Mr John Hewish, Mrs Alexandra O'Connell and Ms Jessica Gamble of Edward Elgar Publishing for guiding us through the editorial process and bringing the manuscript to press.

We could not have finished this book without excellent professional help in editing the manuscript from Ms Helen Koehne, an accredited editor of Editorial Combat, and the many helpful comments and suggestions from her.

Among the many friends and colleagues who have kindly assisted us during the writing of this book, Professor Fan Ke of Nanjing University, Professor Li Lulu of Renmin University of China, Professor Lin Juren of Shandong University, Professor Xin Bo of Shandong Technology and Business University, Professor Wu Zhongzhe of Shandong University of Finance and Economics, and Professor Zhang Dengguo of Shandong Party School have all provided us with many valuable suggestions and helpful comments, which have significantly enhanced the quality of this study. We are also greatly indebted to many people in several Chinese regions who agreed to be interviewed and who offered their deep insight into a range of issues and problems that this research seeks to address. Without mentioning a long list of individual names, we would like to thank all of them, hoping that they appreciate that their deep insight and first-hand experience have made a great contribution to our new understanding of present-day China.

We would also like to acknowledge the support of both the China Scholarship Council (CSC) and the Research Grant from the Faculty of Arts, the University of Melbourne. The CSC offered generous financial support for Su Yuanyuan's research visit to Australia, and the University of Melbourne has funded both my fieldwork in China and the editing of the manuscript. These supports have made both the research project and the publication of this book possible.

A special mention goes to my wife and our son who have not only fully supported me since I had neck surgery more than ten years ago, but have also borne the burden caused by my long and never-ending writing tasks. I could not have finished all the recent research projects and the co-authoring of this book without their full support. Their continuous support and inordinate amount of patience have made this research and this book possible.

Lastly, my special thanks go to Su Yuanyuan for working with me on this book, although her new job has prevented her from contributing the three chapters that she originally planned to write. In the end, she could only manage to write two draft sections for Chapter 6. Despite such unexpected interruptions and delays, I wish to thank her for her first-hand knowledge of villages, especially those in Shandong during the rural urbanisation period of the late 2000s and early 2010s, which has supplemented my dated understanding of what has taken place at the village level due to my living in Australia. I hope she is enjoying her new job and wish her success in her future career.

Jia Gao, PhD
The University of Melbourne

1. China's current rural urbanisation and historical context

This study is positioned at the intersection of China's current rural urbanisation and the social mobilisation mechanism that has been used by the governments at different levels in China to encourage and facilitate urbanisation in China's vast rural areas. This perspective aims to seek a better understanding of social mobilisation as an important socioeconomic and socio-political mechanism and how it has been employed in present-day China.

From an historical point of view, since the early 1950s at least, rural urbanisation has been regarded as the most difficult aspect of China's modernisation. It is widely known that many Chinese people have spent decades dreaming of having 'two-story brick houses, electric light, and telephones', which are commonly known in Chinese as *loushang louxia, diandeng dianhua* (Link, 2013, p. 103; Eyferth, 2015, p. 131). These expressions emerged in the 1950s as a Chinese, but much more convincing, version of Lenin's well-known slogan about communism, which was first summarised by Lenin himself in 1920 as being 'Soviet power plus the electrification of the entire country' (Clark, 2000, p. 93; see a slightly different translation in Shanin, 1985, p. 178). However, such an advanced stage of socioeconomic development can only be achieved after decades of effort. Therefore, this study is historically positioned at a unique point in Chinese history, where its modernisation has reached a new and advanced stage that is characterised by the actual and dedicated pursuit of rural urbanisation.

Over the past decades, there have been many studies examining and theorising about various aspects of the transformations occurring not only in Chinese villages and cities, but also in China's party-state governance system and its policy-making and implementation. However, there has hardly been any real recent effort to methodically look at the intersection of rural urbanisation and social mobilisation. This chapter is the start of a new effort, but begins with background information of this book. The first section of the chapter gives more background information on China's current rural urbanisation, which is also considered a continuation of the early urbanisation effort in post-Mao China. This is followed by a section examining key theoretical issues concerning social mobilisation in China and reviewing what has previously been published in English on the topic.

This section will also clarify how Chinese research publications and the research literature on related topics – from changing central–local government relations in China, a series of taxation reforms and land finance, to rural elections – are to be used in this book. The third section is a brief outline of the organisation of the book.

CHINA'S CURRENT RURAL URBANISATION

The phrases 'China's urbanisation' and 'urbanisation in China' have been used differently in slightly different manners, depending largely on different definitions and understandings of urbanisation and which period of China's contemporary history is being considered. The term 'rural urbanisation' used in the heading above, however, might sound redundant as the basic meaning of 'urbanisation' already refers to the process of movement of people from rural to urban areas (Ley, 2010, p. 9; Fox and Goodfellow, 2016, p. 5). When first hearing the expression, many people feel that there is no any need to use the word 'rural' to modify 'urbanisation'. However, as the contemporary cliché goes, this is a typical new concept with Chinese characteristics. Examples of such special terms include 'socialism with Chinese characteristics' (Deng, 1985, p. 17), 'capitalism with Chinese characteristics' (Huang, 2008, p. 233) and 'imperialism with Chinese characteristics' (Metcalf, 2011, p. 32). The cliché aside, the notion of rural urbanisation emerged, or more precisely, was further clarified, several years ago, as the latest shared understanding and tactic that China had adopted in dealing with its rural development issue.

Because of the intricacy of urbanisation in such a populous country and the long process of reaching the current policy understanding and strategy, this section focuses on two main stages of China's urbanisation since the late 1970s, when it began its economic reforms, namely before and after the formation of the current rural urbanisation approach.

Before the current urbanisation strategy was formed, China's rural population policy in the immediate post-1978 period was largely guided by a set of ideas known as letting surplus rural labourers *litu bu lixiang* (leave the land, but not the village) and *jinchang bu jincheng* (enter the factory, but not the city) (Naughton, 1999, p. 40; Guo, 2013, p. 188; Yeh and Yang, 2013, p. 174). In the 1980s, numerous estimates were made of the number of surplus rural labourers and the numbers vary widely from as low as 60 million to as high as 156 million (Taylor and Banister, 1989, p. 2). These figures are significantly lower than the number calculated by one of the authors of this book in the 1980s, which was as high as about 390 million rural workers aged between 15 and 64 (Gao, 1987, p. 396).

Although some researchers have argued that urbanisation in post-1949 China started in the 1950s and continued in the 1960s, China's rate of urbanisation was as low as about 11 per cent in 1950 and lower than 18 per cent in 1978, which are all lower than what several OECD reports have documented (Wu, 2003, p. 90; Li and Tan, 2011, p. 107; OECD, 2015, p. 30). In fact, the latter increase can be partially accounted for by the urban population growth, because China finalised and implemented its household registration system (*hukuo zhidu*) in 1958, when its economy started running into trouble and practically stopped rural people from moving to cities. The Chinese economy collapsed in 1959, resulting in severe famines into the early 1960s (Yang, 1996; Perkins, 2013). All this clearly indicates that China was largely an agrarian society in the late 1970s when it entered the reform era, and that its leaders were very cautious about rural–urban migration as they still remembered that the rise in the urban population of less than 8 per cent in 1958 of the Great Leap Forward resulted in an increase in grain procurement by more than 23 per cent (Mao et al., 2013, p. 149; see also Lardy, 1987).

China's economic reform started in rural villages in the late 1970s through a series of policy measures to encourage rural people to work harder than before and yield more than before, for themselves and the country. However, several years after the start of reform, there was not any policy to allow them to move to cities, though the phenomenon of the so-called 'floating population' (*liudong renkou*) took place all over the country because of new political circumstances (Zhang, 1998, p. 68; Wu, 2010, p. 57). The *hukou* or household registration system was then used as a crucial institutional barrier to prevent rural people from migrating to cities and to cope with the pressure generated by irregular internal migration.

The demand for a high level of rural–urban migration increased in the early 1980s because of rapid economic development, which has since added a different, but crucial, dimension to China's rural–urban migration and urbanisation issues. Since then, there has always been a real but often hidden tension between the state control of urbanisation and the demand for labour by new industries and production lines. As migrants were spreading further, becoming a regular part of the labour supply in China, the small-town strategy as a policy solution to this emerging problem was put forward by researchers and policy analysts (Tang and Jenkins, 1990; Morgan, 1994). Among them was Fei Xiaotong, formerly spelled as Fei Hsiao-Tung, who promoted the development of township and village enterprises (TVEs) through revisiting his early study in southern Jiangsu province. He widened the scope of his original 1930s study to explore the role of township and small urban centres in China's urbanisation. His article, 'Small towns, big issues', published in 1983, especially his advice of *litu bu lixiang* (leave the land, but not the village) and *jinchang bu jincheng* (enter the factory, but not the city), were of great help to China's decision-makers as many of them simply knew how to correct Maoist mistakes through decollectivising rural production, but lacked experience in managing a rural economy, especially rural industrialisation (Gao, 2013a, p. 81).

While the small-town strategy helped China with a new approach to the problems of the surplus rural population and the lack of economic alternatives, reducing the burden from the 'floating population', it was soon also identified by more analysts as 'a unique road to urbanization' (Morgan, 1994, p. 215). Since the late 1980s and early 1990s, China has been influenced by various socioeconomic and sociopolitical forces. TVEs already employed nearly 24 per cent of the rural labour force in 1988 (Yang, 1996, p. 215; White, 1998, p. 150) and in 1994, the number of TVEs had increased to around 25 million (Cooney et al., 2013, p. 35). The demand by new factory managers and owners for stable supplies of labour has once again emerged as a more influential force than many other criticisms of rural–urban inequalities.

The increasing tension between the state control of urbanisation and the new market force gave rise to some localised urbanisation policies and schemes, such as 'blue-stamp' and 'green card' interim residence permits in some cities (Fan, 2008, p. 50). According to a policy analyst who was involved in developing rural policies, the food-coupon system attached to the *hukou* or household registration was terminated in 1993, making it easier for rural people to leave villages (Bai, 2010, p. 159). In other words, alongside the implementation of the small-town development strategy, or while intensifying the rural industrialisation, there was a parallel process of transferring some rural labourers to small towns and county-level cities. This quiet process has been called *nongzhuanfei* (to covert one's *hukou* or household registration category from agricultural to non-agricultural) (Young, 2011, p. 141; Chan, 2015, p. 28), which was in fact the real start of China's urbanisation, though many critics simply regarded these people as the 'floating population'. As an effect of the early efforts, 'a total of 286 new cities appeared in China' in the decade between 1979 and 1991, and China's urbanisation rate reached about 27 per cent in 1991, almost 10 per cent higher than it had been in 1978 (CDRF, 2013, p. 13; W. Wu, 2014, p. 88). Another vital turning point was reached in 1998 and 1999, by which time about one-third of China's total population had become urbanised, 33.4 per cent and 34.8 per cent respectively (Fang and Yu, 2016, p. 286).

China's current push for rural urbanisation has, therefore, happened in the context of further urbanisation from one-third of its population to one-half of it. However, it has been considered from different points of view. From a long-term development perspective, the current push has been regarded as a strategy to address a series of imbalances in socioeconomic development, especially urban–rural inequality, which has been overlooked in the policies of both the rural industrialisation and the local urbanisation. From a narrow economic perspective, it has also been utilised as a national strategy to sustain, if not fuel, China's high economic growth. These different views have resulted from the complexity of economic activities in China over the past two decades. While the other forms of urbanisation, as briefly outlined previously, are still going on, the strategy of rural urbanisation is partly based on the experiences of implementing the small-town rural industrialisation strategy and various local urbanisation schemes, and emphasises an integrated but *in situ* development of villages and small towns in rural areas (Garcia, 2011; p. 46; Kipnis, 2013; Zhu et al., 2013; X. Chen, 2015, p. 210).

It is over the past two decades or so that the process of forming and enacting political decisions and policies in China has also become more sophisticated, systematic and innovative than ever before. Such a complex process would become even more complicated if it took into consideration other key changes in Chinese politics, especially central–local, state–market and state–society relations and the new political power structure and process of what is nowadays frequently called the era of *boyi*. As explained in the Preface, this *boyi* era is full of political conflicts and bargaining between different social forces and groups. Because all these new changes will be discussed more fully in later chapters, this section will briefly introduce some basic ideas and facts related to the current rural urbanisation push.

More specifically, in addition to the growing influence of different industries and the market in general, there has also been an increasing demand for greater rural social and economic development, including a relaxation of the traditional control over rural–urban migration. Since the second half of the 1980s, many rural problems, or agriculture- and peasant-related issues, have been summarised by some Chinese researchers as *sannong wenti* (three rural problems), including *nongye* (agriculture), *nongcun* (rural villages) and *nongmin* (peasants) (Lu, 2008, p. 14). All these problems have become more apparent and serious than they were over the course of the 1990s and early 2000s, as many cities, big and small, have clearly been transformed and the urban standard of living has improved for a high proportion of the population. The growing urban–rural divide in the late 1990s gave rise to major debate among Chinese academic and policy researchers, which is well represented in English publications (Zhong, 2004; Murphy, 2011; Day, 2013). What has not been appropriately emphasised is that the debate generated so much pressure that the rural issue once again became the top priority of China's development strategy from the early 2000s.

In the first five or so years of the new millennium, some important national policy decisions were made to deal with the rural issues. The policy on peasant burden reduction, or on control of 'local extraction', that was contemplated by the Jiang Zemin and Zhu Rongji leadership was finally legislated under the new leadership of Hu Jintao and Wen Jiabao in 2003 (L. Li, 2012, p. 91). Unprecedented growth in these years meant increased tax revenue, which led China to make a few important decisions in 2005 to implement its new rural development strategy. The most eye-catching policy was the abolition of agricultural taxes, which became effective from 1 January 2006 (Luo and Sicular, 2013, p. 218). Another strategic decision was part of China's Eleventh Five-Year Plan (2006–2010), by far the most significant part of which was 'the stated objective of creating a more harmonious socialist countryside' (USITC, 2011, pp. 4–15). While this plan was put forward, in a general sense, to advance the economic welfare of the rural population and reduce the rural–urban disparity, it has since the beginning been defined differently by different sectoral interests. It has been simply called 'the new socialist countryside' for publicity purpose (Raman, 2012, p. 213), but various business sectors and local governments have regarded it as 'the construction drive' in rural areas (Lin, 2012, pp. 243–4).

Despite these tags, especially the label of socialist, which has made it not only less attention-grabbing than the complete abolition of agricultural taxes, but also difficult to understand its significance, the plan to build 'the new socialist countryside' is of great importance for rural development in China (Ahlers and Schubert, 2009; Schubert and Ahlers, 2011, 2012; Ahlers, 2014). This policy initiative has then been theorised by many researchers, as well as some industries, to be a new top-down push for rural urbanisation. However, as pointed out earlier, the decision-making process in China is rather complex; it is regularly influenced by various interest groups, meaning that many decisions are reversed and policies are regularly modified to echo the results of numerous negotiations. In the case of rural urbanisation, discussions have focused on how this new strategy has been financed and the central concept for understanding the debate is *tudi caizheng* (land finance), revenues from selling land (Hu, 2016, p. 124). In fact, since China started its transition to a decentralised market economy, it has experienced numerous difficulties regarding public finance (Wong, 2009, 2013). The decision to initiate and implement 'the new socialist countryside' plan has further authorised the use of land as a source of finance (Hu, 2016, p. 127).

What has happened in China since the mid-2000s is that although the abolition of agricultural taxes has been welcomed, and although this tax policy is not believed to 'have significantly affected the tax revenue of the government' (Cai, 2010, p. 172), local governments in agriculture-dependent regions have suffered the loss of local revenue, making it very difficult for them to deliver some basic services (Wong, 2007; Smith, 2015). At the same time, the *tudi caizheng* or land finance mechanism apparently became so overused that the central government decided to put more restrictions on land use in 2006, almost immediately after the new countryside strategy was put in place. One of the restrictions is the so-called *zengjian guagou* of the land use, which simply means 'linking urban and rural construction land' (Looney, 2012, p. 276), an 'idea of bounding up addition of urban land with sayings from peasant housing sites' (Han and Wei, 2015, p. 280). This restriction aims to ensure that 'the total amount of arable land within an administrative jurisdiction is not reduced' (Cai, 2010, p. 64). The new push for rural urbanisation is, therefore, not only related to the land finance practice, but also to the 'recent policy of striking a balance between farmland acquisition and reclamation' (Y. Zhao, 2013, p. 59).

All these new policies and mechanisms have indicated that the earlier tension between the population control in cities and the plan for rapid industrialisation has slowly been replaced by new demands for a better environment and resources for economic growth. However, even with the widespread dislike of the old policy of not allowing rural people to move to cities and its related *hukou* household registration system, the size of China's population has meant that control over the expansion of megacities is needed. The approach to urbanisation has been diversified to include the above-mentioned initiative of *nongmin shanglou*, a new form of localised urbanisation to let rural households live in new apartment buildings, but on the condition that they 'give up their individual housing plots' (M. Cai, 2015, p. 72). This policy has been implemented nationally since the mid-2000s, during which time China has not only been guided by many ideas put forward by researchers and policy analysts, but has also been influenced by various other local and sectoral interests and agendas. The utilisation of social mobilisation under such specific circumstances, which is defined in this volume as the transition to the post-industrial stage of Chinese modernisation, is rather different from what it was a few decades ago, and its main changes and new characteristics are the focus of this book.

HISTORICAL CONTEXT

As introduced already, this book seeks to develop an understanding of how social mobilisation is being used in China as an important socioeconomic and socio-political mechanism, in a context of competing perspectives of whether China's state capacity has declined and how meaningful mass socio-political participation can be, as often asked by China analysts and observers (Saich, 2011). As broadly defined by UNICEF, social mobilisation is a concept referring to a course of action that 'motivates a wide range of partners and allies at national and local levels to raise awareness of and demand for a particular development objective' (UNICEF, 2015, p. 1). To locate this analysis in the context of scholarly debates concerning social mobilisation in China, this section reviews the research literature, published in English in recent decades, on the utilisation of social mobilisation in China. This section is comprised of three parts. The first part is a critical review of studies focused on social mobilisation undertaken in post-revolution China. The second part looks at the research on factors and features of social mobilisation, and courses of action from other perspectives and for other purposes. The last part of this review will suggest some possible areas for further examination of the social mobilisation mechanism as it is used in China.

Focused Studies of pre-1978 Social Mobilisation

Since the 1960s, there have been many studies on various forms and major aspects of social mobilisation in China, providing this analysis with a strong theoretical foundation. The 1960s was a time of unprecedented socio-cultural change, characterised by several waves of socio-political movement and mass mobilisation in the United States, China and several European countries. Karl Deutsch is widely acknowledged as one of the first scholars to respond to the changes of the time and make social mobilisation a focus of research, by defining it as a process of social change that 'happens to substantial parts of the population in countries which are moving from traditional to modern ways of life' (Deutsch, 1961, p. 493). Though China closed its door to the West at the time, it became a subject of academic research shortly after the definition was put forward. Scholars are correct that modern Chinese history is clearly characterised by frequent nationwide social mobilisations, making many scholars believe that Chinese history, or China's development in several decades of the twentieth century, can only be analysed from the perspective of mobilisation (Schenk-Sandbergen, 1973; Bennett, 1976). This shared understanding has resulted in the wide acceptance of social mobilisation as an analytical construct. Analytically speaking, however, studies focused on social mobilisation in the 1960s and 1970s were conducted in two contexts.

The first was a broad theoretical context, in which many debates in the 1960s and 1970s centred on Deutsch's definition of social mobilisation. Chalmers Johnson studied the Chinese resistance movement during the Second Sino-Japanese War (1937–45) from the mobilisation perspective, and defined it as a term that is 'used to describe the dynamic process . . . that causes populations to form political community' (Johnson, 1962, p. 22). David Apter, a political scientist, and Amitai Etzioni, a sociologist, considered Deutsch's concept from each of their perspectives.

From his modernisation perspective, Apter (1965) believes that there are two models of modernisation: the mobilisation system and the reconciliation system. Many parts of his argument have been proven to be hypothetical, such as the point that mobilisations are likely to be short-lived and ineffective. However, he did expand his viewpoint to include more factors, such as ideology, goals and values, individuals and hierarchical power. His attention on centralised power has laid the foundation for the top-down perspective on the issue.

The new concept of social mobilisation also attracted the attention of a group of sociologists, who tried the notion in sociological studies and identified important links between the state structure and the nature of political opportunities (Nettl, 1967). Just like some other sociologists, Amitai Etzioni does not accept that social mobilisation is the same as modernisation, but believes it to be both a macro-sociological concept and a process in which a quick control of resources can be achieved. He also argues that mobilisation, as a social process, can be applied to the control of other resources, such as social, economic, political and psychological resources. Because of his structural-functionalist view, however, Etzioni (1968) seems to be more interested in the question of where the dynamism of social units comes from, and prefers the ideas that pay attention to emergent properties of collectives than those of individuals. In his conception, social mobilisations are different in their features, but no further explanations on them are given.

Among many analyses of the Deutschian theory of mobilisation, David Cameron's rational approach identified several key inadequacies (Cameron, 1974). Cameron summarises three main problems: the failure to explain the process of mobilisation; the false connection between mobilisation and modernisation; and the assumption of social determinism. His critical analysis is partly based on Samuel Huntington's argument that macro socioeconomic and socio-political changes need to be considered along with the changes in attitudes, aspirations, values and behaviours of individuals and groups (Huntington, 1968). Cameron takes the idea a step further, challenging the view that individuals are passive in mobilisation, and calling for more attention to the organisation and behavioural patterns into which individuals are inducted. Research attention has since also been given to the mobilisation process, activities of mobilising agents and the direction of mobilisation efforts.

The second context was a narrow theoretical context, in which social mobilisation was applied to explain the rise of the Chinese Community Party (CCP). Among early efforts, Chalmers Johnson applies the concept to China for the period of the Anti-Japanese War, arguing that the CCP's victory was the outcome of its ability and the process by which a people become a nation, instead of the appeals of communism. The evidence used by Johnson is that the CCP failed to gain local support during the Jiangxi Soviet period (1927–34), but achieved it when the Japanese invasion presented the peasantry with a real threat to its life (Johnson, 1962; Zhao, 2004). Franz Schurmann finds Johnson's theory problematic as it lacks the consideration of actual conditions in villages, resulting in the overlooking of the dynamics that underlay the success of the CCP in social mobilisation. Schurmann (1968) notices that the CCP did not only use many strategies to penetrate local structures, but also adapted its ideology to China's political and economic conditions of the time. Of course, David Cameron (1974) believes that these early studies overlook the role of mobilising agents in favour of social conditions, and Charles Cell maintains that it was before the Jiangxi Soviet period that 'the Communist strategy of socialist transformation through mass mobilization was forged, tested and developed' (Cell, 1977, p. 13), the argument of which is shared by other analysts in the field of contemporary China studies (Townsend, 1967, p. 45).

It is within such theoretical contexts that more China analysts have turned their attention to how mobilisation has been employed in post-1949 China and a range of new mobilisation efforts in its post-revolution transition. Although both the revolutionary and the post-revolution periods are characterised by different forms of social mobilisation (Goodman, 1994), the study of its utilisation in what is formally called the socialist transformation period, or the post-revolution phase, is constrained by the era in which researchers live. In the immediate post-revolution period, Chinese researchers were isolated from international academic discussions and non-Chinese researchers were unable to conduct research in China except via organised visits (Richman, 1969; Wheelwright and McFarlane, 1970). Consequently, many analyses are made along the 'art and prospects of mass mobilization' that the CCP learnt and used before 1949 (Townsend, 1967, p. 45), though mobilisation was 'increasingly seen as relics of an earlier and simpler era' (Harding, 1981, p. 82). All these constraints have made the analyses rather abstract, often simply emphasising top-down processes without much detail.

However, what has been proven with certainty is that there was a series of political campaigns in post-1949 China. Prior to the Cultural Revolution launched in 1966, China went through a period of frequent countrywide political campaigns, starting with the land reform and the counter-revolutionaries from the late 1940s until the 'Four Cleanups' (*Siqing*), or the Socialist Education Campaign, which was initiated in 1963 (Baum and Teiwes, 1968; Harding, 1981). In urban centres the CCP also learnt from its experiences in rural China, and mobilised the whole party and its followers to participate in campaigns one after another not only in the early years, when the CCP first took over political power, but also in the late stages (Gaulton, 1981; Whyte and Parish, 1984). Researchers have analysed all these campaigns, but the statist top-down perspective influences many analyses.

The top-down approach has been in use for decades. On the surface, social mobilisation was still considered from a perspective of mass participation in the state structure. Some efforts were made in the 1960s, including Townsend's study of 'how the workers, peasants and housewives of Communist China participate in politics' (1967, p. 2), however, too much attention has been paid to how the techniques used by the CCP are developed and how support for the regime has been created. Precisely, although the role of mass participation in the public life of post-1949 China is known, attention is narrowly focused on how to mobilise the masses for support of national objectives. Therefore, the roles and actions of lower-level establishments are not only often seen from the top-down position, but also subject to higher-level authorities (Townsend, 1967, pp. 103, 144). From the top-down perspective, also based on the study of earlier campaigns, Julia Strauss believes that the campaigns in China are always characterised by 'control from above, mobilization from below, harsh terror' (2002, p. 89). The literature on Chinese political campaigns has a gap when it comes to the dynamics and institutional process. For decades, many China analysts have simply believed that China's authoritarian system restrains mass participation in political life (Moore, 2014).

Comparative studies have helped to expand the analytical scope of the study of social mobilisation in China. Having compared the Soviet and Chinese collectivisation campaigns, Thomas Bernstein identifies several special aspects for analysing mobilisation in rural China in the 1950s. Both the Soviet Union and China were in need of breakthroughs in agriculture, but their campaigns were found to have achieved different outcomes because of 'the forces and pressures that each regime had set in motion' (Bernstein, 1967, p. 1). In addition to creating an optimistic climate, competitive pressures were also created within the party-state system, and different groups were also mobilised. The awareness of such complexities has given rise to the inclusion of more factors and subordinate processes in the analysis, such as lower-level leaderships, their experiences, training and performance, policy continuity, the interplay of local and state interests, and work teams. More importantly, the comparative viewpoint also regards mobilisation as a process. Despite the lack of details on the collectivisation, and despite the disastrous end of the campaign (Lin, 1990), our understanding of social mobilisation has been broadened as more China observers have since recognised social mobilisation in China as a complex process.

For a range of reasons, China's rural collectivisation in the 1950s has been the main topic of many scholarly efforts, while efforts have also been made to analyse some social mobilisations during the Cultural Revolution (Bernstein, 1977; Andreas, 2007). Leaving the latter aside because of its intricacy, Franz Schurmann even considers the commune organisation in rural China in the 1950s as a category of mobilisation, while revealing the link between material incentives and mobilisation (Schurmann, 1968). Barry Richman observes that like every country in postwar years, China focused its efforts on economic growth through industrialisation, which mainly 'involves the coordination of human effort and material resources' for achieving the plan (Richman, 1969, p. 21). Social mobilisation and distribution of resources are, therefore, mentioned in several studies, but its theoretic importance has not been further studied. This is partially because the CCP relied unduly on its ability to organise campaigns when the rural collectivisation started to run into trouble. Therefore, various aspects of resource mobilisation have remained unexplored or underexplored.

What happened in China from the late 1950s onwards gave rise to a narrow focus on various forms of political mobilisation. Based on the understanding that all mobilisations are politically determined, Schenk-Sandbergen identifies the role of two factors: the population base and resistance, such as clan groups, in political mobilisation (1973, p. 684). Unlike Schurmann's focus on the ideological adaption to China's local conditions, Schenk-Sandbergen (1973) emphasises the importance of ideology as a means for political mobilisation and considers class-consciousness, the CCP's 'mass-line' and people's adaptability as three ideological starting points in mobilisation. Although other scholars consider ideology just as fundamental as economic and administrative means (Hsiao, 1960; Pye, 1968), the focus on it has drawn too much attention to political and ideological aspects of social mobilisation.

Researchers have gained a fuller understanding of mobilisations in China since from the mid-1970s, shortly before and after Mao's death, but China has since also been used as an experimental ground for testing existing theories. One such effort is Charles Cell's study of dozens of campaigns from an apparently functionalist viewpoint (Cell, 1977, p. 3). Despite being imperfect, Cell's analysis has challenged popular understanding, believing that frequent and large-scale campaigns are often counterproductive (Baum, 1978). From his sociological point of view, Cell argues that campaigns seem to flow from the problems or contradictions at hand and can be divided into three types: struggle, ideological and economic. Measuring campaigns by the mobilisation level, achievements and shortcomings, Cell also argues that different kinds of social mobilisations are in fact an effective tool for promoting social change in China. A conflict perspective has also been used and tested in the Chinese context, including the relation between China's internal mobilisation and articulated hostility to foreign powers (Liao, 1976).

Since the start of China's reform in the late 1970s, researchers have turned their attention to new data accessible since the open-door policy was introduced, allowing some foreign scholars to do fieldwork in certain Chinese regions. As will be discussed in the next section, Lynn White's study of the Shanghai delta region benefits from the change, allowing it to include an innovative focus on the role of 'local leaders, social groups and individuals seizing the initiatives from the weakening grip of the state', as commented by Young (2000, p. 169). Over the same period, some other China specialists have also identified 'the consequences of unrestricted mass mobilization' (Harding, 1981, p. 233), which became apparent in the *Siqing* Campaign and worsened in the early Cultural Revolution. Such mobilisation once made China's Party leadership dysfunctional, resulting from the wholesale denunciation of lower-level bureaucrats.

China's decades-long reform since the late 1970s has also added many new topics and issues to the field of China studies. Research on China has become further diversified beyond existing viewpoints and knowledge, including the outdated and partial understanding of social mobilisation. More researchers have given attention to the issues that have emerged from China's reforms. Among the new issues, the birth-control campaign after 1979 is a reminder that mobilisation is still an active part of the post-revolution Chinese political process (White, 1990). As Tyrene White reveals in her study, the only change in using the social mobilisation mechanism is the use of new language, such as modernisation. Also emerging are in-depth analyses of the mobilisation of emotions in China (Perry, 2002; Y. Liu, 2010), filling a gap left by the overemphasis on the roles of social structure, political crisis, ideology and other factors in mass campaigns.

Despite these research efforts, which have resulted in a small body of literature and better understanding, the changes in post-1978 China have, as already noted, drawn research attention away from what we have called the focused studies of post-revolution mobilisation. However, these focused studies have revealed the importance of mobilisation both during the revolution and in the post-revolution era, and the various manners in which this mechanism has operated. Of course, these studies have paid more attention to the top-down process than to the bottom-up process and the involvement of individuals, groups and local bureaucrats in social mobilisations. Importantly, many still view various forms of mobilisation in China from the post-revolution point of view or the perspective of conflict, not as a normal part of social life, which has prevented them from having a better understanding.

Other Mobilisation-Related Studies in the Reform Period

As previously pointed out, the shifting research interests and perspectives that have taken place in China since the late 1970s and early 1980s have made studies of mobilisations highly diversified. The shift initially reflected not only the rapid changes resulting from the early rural reform of the late 1970s, but also the view believing that there was a 'decentralized, demobilized thrust of the post-Mao reforms' (White, 1990, p. 53). The thrust is believed to herald the start of China's post-revolution phase and adaptive governance, although some disagree with this assessment. Such understandings have even led some analysts to believe in the possibility of political normalisation, regularised decision-making and institutionalised rule in China, while many others have accepted the emergence of the adaptive governance that is characterised by guerrilla policy style (Heilmann and Perry, 2011, p. 7). All these perspectives have broadened the scope of research on social mobilisation, giving rise to debates on many issues related to the complex picture of China's continuing reforms. This has not only gone far beyond what was initially predicted, but also appears to be more comprehensive than a guerrilla policy style.

Because of a vast amount of literature on the new topics, this part of the review is selective by necessity, focusing on three areas: rural reforms; public policy and public administration reforms; and mass politics and media.

China's post-1978 rural reforms have been the topic of numerous studies of social mobilisation, while the one-child policy has been attracting the attention of many other researchers. The rural reforms were caused by strong grassroots pressure when China's state capacity was weakened by the Cultural Revolution (White, 1998, 1999), towards the end of which there was growing power among the peasants (Kelliher, 1992; Ash, 2001). Such strong pressure once posed a serious challenge to Maoist rural policies, but theoretically, it also gave rise to ideas that differed from the established top-down perspective. Among many studies of the changes caused by the rural reform (Goldman and MacFarquhar, 1999), Lynn White's (1998, 1999) study of the Shanghai region pays attention to the issues of when China's reform started, who initiated it and how it was carried out, from a local perspective. Though her study appears to be descriptive, it undoubtedly identifies local causes of the reform in several areas, especially many causes that were never taken into consideration in earlier debates, including the roles of local groups and interests in forming policies and actual reform programmes. Some of these factors are, in fact, an alternative way of mobilising resources and people behind a common cause. All these findings are still helpful to current discussions as they contest 'deeply engrained understandings' about the top-down nature of the Chinese state and society (Fewsmith, 2001).

While the above type of studies has broadened understanding of contemporary China, giving rise to an awareness that social processes, forces and mobilisation in China are complex, multi-dimensional and multidirectional, many analysts have still been influenced by a deterministic view of Chinese political economy and culture (Shi, 2000). Analysts are often divided, taking either a top-down or a bottom-up approach to issues, and the interactions of local and central politics are frequently overlooked, which has been one of the most unfortunate omissions in contemporary China studies. Having identified the importance of local forces, more studies have focused on a range of issues at lower levels. However, partly because of the complexity, in later reform programs, especially rural industrialisation, the issues related to social mobilisation have drawn insufficient attention compared with the efforts of economists. Even those interested in the bottom-up point of view have continued to give more attention to top-level politics and ideology than to other issues (Burns, 1988).

The complexities of politics at a grassroots level are a vital part of understanding post-1978 rural China, but many efforts are made in line with the theoretical views that are inadequately related to China's changing socio-political circumstances. This has meant that less attention is paid to how local groups and interests are involved in local economic programmes, which are vital to the restructuring of rural China, and that more attention is given to social and political forms of rural transformation. Other than rural mass protests, which will be briefly discussed later, village elections are the topic on which many studies have been conducted in the past decades (Goldman and MacFarquhar, 1999; Schubert and Ahlers, 2012). Overshadowed by such theoretical problems are rural social and demographical structures and other local factors, as well as social mobilisations in response to rural industrialisation (He, 2015). The latter has become a far more critical step in rural poverty reduction and economic growth than introducing political changes, and it has mobilised far more participants across the country than the push for democracy in rural China. Even when the CCP decided to recruit private entrepreneurs into the Party, there were few researchers devoting attention to the local responses and activities that were related to such new circumstances (Zheng, 2010). In other words, though many agree that mass mobilisation has been a key feature of Chinese political life since the Maoist era (Perry, 2002), the persistent habit of seeing China as an authoritarian regime has prevented attention being paid to new forms of social mobilisation and participation in the process of Chinese rural industrialisation.

China's recent push to urbanise rural areas, which is, as introduced earlier, called 'the new socialist countryside' campaign, has renewed research interest in social mobilisation activities since the mid-2000s (Bislev and Thøgersen, 2012; Harwood, 2014). Less attention is now being paid to the political meaning of the word 'socialist' in the name of this nationwide campaign, but more efforts have been made to study how the rural urbanisation campaign is operated and how rural regions are modernised by the initiative. Recent studies have identified several key factors that can shape the campaign, including 'the strength of bureaucratic mobilization, the weakness of rural organizations, and shifting national policy priorities' (Looney, 2015, p. 911), while some other studies have focused on the implementation and effectiveness of social mobilisations in present-day China (Perry, 2011; Ahlers, 2014). Because many other changes have occurred to China's decision-making and rural society has not been systematically studied, especially the nature of new social mobilisations, some recent studies appear to further establish that 'mobilization has remained an integral, active part of the post-revolutionary Chinese political process' (White, 1990, p. 55). The conventional narrow focus on the form, content and intensity of social mobilisation seems to have prevented analysts from forming a new explanation of the mechanism in present-day China.

The second main research area in which a range of key aspects of social mobilisation has been identified and studied relates closely to studies of public policy and administration, many of which were first conducted by economists.

China's reforms were expanded from villages to cities in the early 1980s, and the complexities of urban society made it very difficult to repeat what was learnt from rural reforms. One of the main problems was from the party-state system, a situation that has long been called *zhonggengzu* (literally 'intermediary obstacles'), which refers to different types of bureaucratic obstacles at the middle levels of China's party-state system. Officials or bureaucrats working within the system were reluctant in the mid-1980s to implement reform policies, which forced the top CCP leadership to launch administrative reform to remove some obstacles and to make the system efficient in mobilising active participations in reforms (Goldman, 1994).

Because it was impossible at the time, just a few years after Mao's disastrous Cultural Revolution, to launch a full-scale administrative or political reform, the intermediary obstruction issue of the system was dealt with in numerous ways. These small-step administrative reform measures included some changes to central–local relations to encourage lower-level bureaucracies to implement economic reform policies and the introduction of market mechanisms into economic management to deliberately bypass parts of middle-level bureaucracies (Breslin, 1996; Li, 1998). All these measures in early stages of China's urban reform greatly improved the institutional environment for implementing new reform strategies and broadened channels suitable for mobilising mass participation in different reform programmes. Local participation in rural industrialisation became possible as an effect of these changes, which reveals an interesting aspect of new social mobilisations in China.

In addition to the issue of problematic bureaucracies, attention has also been paid to the ways in which resources as a vital component of central–local relations could be better mobilised and deployed. At first sight, China's one-party rule ensures its ability to assert its power for resource mobilisation, but the concentrated political power is also found to be a problem when it comes to mobilising individuals to participate in reforms. Fiscal decentralisation has been one of the CCP's strategies since the 1980s to deal with political challenges of economic reform, especially with the central–local relations and bureaucratic obstacles. Trials on a new revenue-sharing mechanism were conducted as early as 1977 and the new mechanism was introduced nationwide in 1980 (Shirk, 1993). Though the fiscal decentralisation policy does not always work (Shue and Wong, 2007), it has been tried and modified repeatedly as both an incentive and a mechanism to encourage local participation in reform programmes, including the recent rural urbanisation scheme (Kung et al., 2013). There has been a clear transition from political mobilisation to resource mobilisation, in which the political and economic dynamics between the mobilisers and the mobilised have been transformed over time, while the position and role of bureaucratic agencies at different levels in governance have also been transformed, becoming as important as central decision-makers. Therefore, some observers believe that there has been a trend to rectify the statist tactic in China, and that pervasive localism that emerged in the late Maoist era has further evolved into a dynamic force (Whiting, 2000).

Some political economists have also considered the issue of social mobilisation based on various policy changes, and attention has been devoted to China's state capacity and the sustainability of its growth. Economic reforms in China have always been subject to the fluctuations of economic cycles, producing numerous ups and downs over the past few decades. However, the state's ability to 'mobilize all sorts of society's resources, to unite all forces in society', as well as to form a consensus and to maintain the solidarity of the nation, has been regarded as an essential mechanism for driving modernisation (Wang and Hu, 2001, p. 3). Though some observers believe that there is an erosion of 'the ruling regime's ability to mobilise political support' (Pei, 2008, p. 168), the CCP is still believed to have the 'organizational capacity to launch Mao-style political campaign' (Zeng, 2013, p. 126). Of course, there are few analysts who still believe that recent campaigns in China are characterised by the Maoist style, but social mobilisation has been found to be an effective means of implementing new policy initiatives and driving the economy out of a downturn, through mobilising human and material resources at a societal scale. Recently, the state capacity viewpoint has given rise to a perspective of dynamic interaction, which emphasises that new policy initiatives are not based on a one-sided national strategy, but decided 'by day-to-day interactions between state agents of various levels and different social groups in multiple arenas' (Zeng, 2013, p. 24).

The third key area in which the social mobilisation mechanism has been actively studied is relatively new, which is its utilisation in mass politics and mass media.

China's ongoing reforms since the late 1970s and early 1980s have resulted in several rounds of administrative decentralisation and many new forms of mass politics, such as rural resistance and urban labour protests. Some student protests, especially the one in 1989, have attracted the interest of China analysts (D. Zhao, 1998). Recently, social mobilisation has been seen in efforts to encourage 'people to take action and prepare themselves for the future' (Chapin, 2014, p. 519). At the same time, the dynamics of various social movements as a category of mobilisation have also changed significantly, and the participants, if not the facilitators, are no longer those left behind by China's rapid economic growth, but members of the so-called new middle class (Wasserstrom, 2009). Many popular protests, including those by middle-class groups, are still political, but previously common approaches of politicising protests are no longer widely used, as protests are now found to be set off by specific events, rather than ideology (Bruun, 2013). All these non-institutional mobilisations or social activism are now considered to be part of new social mobilisations in China, but they often take the form of popular discontent and protests, bottom-up modes of mobilisation (Cai, 2010). Therefore, the trend of divergence in studying them as a phenomenon, and as a social mechanism, not only remains, but has also reached the extent that many correlated issues need to be reconsidered theoretically.

Different from the above-mentioned forms of social mobilisation, mass-protest mobilisations have been so widespread or routinised that they are now considered a crucial sign of the emergence of new models of state–society relations or new categories of authoritarianism (X. Chen, 2012). These new models or forms seem to suggest that a mass perspective, a different type of bottom-up perspective, of Chinese socio-political life has been further developed and adopted as a way of looking at present-day Chinese society and politics. However, analysts have different views about how to explain, or theorise, the bottom-up mass mobilisations, and some still see them from the conflict perspective, tending to separate challengers or protests from not only state- or elite-led mobilisations, but, more importantly, also from other normal socio-political activities. Although the dynamics of contention perspective have been introduced to the discussion (O'Brien, 2008; Liu, 2015), interactions between the state and other challenging agencies are still considered disconnected by some, and the paradigms of high democratisation and activism or popular riot are so dominant that they seem to have slowed the process of forming a more sophisticated, understanding of social mobilisation and movement. To explain why individuals can be easily mobilised to participate in mass protests when the state encounters problems in mobilising the nation behind its goals, the concept of the 'microfoundations' of the macro-phenomena is introduced to emphasise the importance of both the micro–macro link and the new elite–mass relations (Zha, 2015, pp. 1–2).

Despite many theoretical distractions, the studies of mass protests since the 1990s have formed some shared understandings. While more researchers now accept that the routinisation of protests as the repetition of such social mobilisations has not destabilised China's political system and process as predicted, other researchers agree that protests and other forms of activism as a disruptive force are becoming a vital form of political participation (Cai, 2010). Such viewpoints imply that social mobilisation has not only become part of normal political life in China, but has also been expressed in different ways. With more analysts accepting social mobilisations as part of everyday Chinese life, many have turned their research attention to different forms of activism and mobilisation, especially those that mainstream the elite still refuse to accept. However, politics in China is now highly polarised, and political elites still do not recognise certain forms of activism and mobilisation as a way of socio-political participation. This remains a big challenge to China's post-industrial phase of development. At the same time, some studies of rural activism are guided by urban-biased concepts or imported theories, and some inherent factors, such as clan networks, are overlooked (Shih, 1995; Ma, 2006).

Fortunately, modern China has never stagnated for lack of change and diversity. In the past decades, while more local and global factors have been closely intertwined to cause changes, new communication technologies, including new media, as a type of disruptive force have also played a crucial role in political participation and mass activism. The Chinese media started its partial commercialisation in the 1980s, and it has continued while being controlled by the party-state. The role of the media in mobilising socio-political participation from both top-down and bottom-up directions has been disrupted and accelerated by the internet and various other new communication and media technologies. Because of the changes, dichotomies of 'freedom versus control', 'democracy versus authoritarianism', 'regime versus resistance', and 'coevolution' of the new media environment and civil society, are all believed to be no longer sufficient to explain what has taken place in China (deLisle et al., 2016, p. 3). While the new media environments, including media liberalisation, eventually created more chances for mass activism and mobilisation, researchers are still unable to identify a new holistic or integrated approach, rather they create other dichotomies based on the theoretical separation of society and state. What looks promising now, however, is that various viewpoints have been put forward to analyse the Chinese state, such as responsive authoritarianism (Reilly, 2012; Heurlin, 2016) and the nature of mass protests, such as the notion of political contestation (Fewsmith, 2001; Xia, 2008). What is needed now is to consider various forms of social activism and mobilisation as a normal part of socio-political life in post-industrial China.

Towards a Holistic-Dynamic Approach

The previous two sections have reviewed the existing literature on social mobilisation in China, focusing on various issues crucial to the understanding of social mobilisation as a key socioeconomic and socio-political mechanism in China. Since its introduction, the concept of social mobilisation has been applied beyond what Deutsch originally considered as an overall process of moving from traditional to modern ways of life, and it has since been used to study not only various campaigns, but also various China-related issues. As indicated, the latter efforts were made in two different stages, and have prepared the ground for further inquiry into social mobilisation in post-industrial China. Based on this review, there is an obvious need to update our understanding of the social mobilisation mechanism in present-day China, especially its use at the current post-industrial stage of Chinese development. There is also a need to consider this mechanism not only from a holistic point of view of taking more factors of the whole reality into account, but also from a dynamic perspective to treat it as active interactions of multiple institutional and individual forces and agencies.

As mentioned at the start of this chapter, this review aims to clarify how Chinese research publications are used in this book before a new analytical perspective is further discussed. A reason for this is that there has been a large volume of research publications, mostly articles in journals, published in China in the past 15 or so years. These publications have not only covered what has been explored by research publications in English, but also include the many emerging issues and topics that Chinese analysts have identified from their direct involvement in everyday life. While the former fact has not been fully explained to non-Chinese readers, which means many of them still believe that Western ideas are strange to Chinese minds, the latter has offered far more research outputs in the field than other researchers could produce. Since the Chinese publications have had a much smaller readership, they will be used as documentary or textual sources along with other secondary sources, such as policy documents, policy analyses and media coverage of related issues.

Theoretically, these Chinese publications are helpful in examining social mobilisation in present-day China in at least two different ways. First, they tend to relate their analyses of social mobilisation to many other issues, ranging from changing central–local relations in China, a series of taxation reforms and land finance, to rural elections. Second, such broad perspectives have already revealed a new understanding of the nature of present-day Chinese politics, according to which China's domestic politics, political structure and power relationships have been transformed considerably, and have entered what Chinese analysts have often called the era of *boyi*, 'strategic game playing' (Lee and Zhang, 2013, p. 1486). This current era is no longer guided or dominated by any rigid ideology or political doctrine, as some analysts have wrongly assumed. Instead, it is clearly characterised by a post-Deng, if not post-revolution, political order that has brought almost all social classes and sectors of Chinese society into the national political equation, turning China into a country that is full of political tensions and negotiations among different social forces and groups (Liang, 2014, p. 119; Tang, 2014, p. 124). It is under such circumstances that China started its current round of rural urbanisation and has since implemented it in many regions.

The use of the social mobilisation mechanism in China's new *boyi* era, therefore, is one of the main research questions of this book. It is also worth pointing out that the concept of social mobilisation, as it is used in this book, is based on a few earlier definitions, including those by Deutsch (1961) and UNICEF (2015), but the concept is used here to specifically refer to the large-scale advocacy of a series of actions proposed by high-level, decision-making institutions, and supported by other stakeholders, to achieve a long-term strategic goal of national, subnational or regional socioeconomic development. Since social mobilisation is a complex process, this book is based on what has been defined as a holistic-dynamic approach to focus on the following points.

First, social mobilisation as a crucial mechanism is not only still in use in China, but is also playing a more pivotal role in organising and directing China's social, economic and political life than before, especially because of China's high level of economic activity and socio-political participation by the public. As mentioned, there has been a debate on whether social mobilisation still plays a role in China now, and there are analyses that dispute the idea that post-revolution regimes 'lose capacity and desire to use mobilizational means' and emphasise that 'mobilization remained an essential instrument' in present-day China (White, 1990, pp. 54–5). However, some analysts have challenged the latter part of the argument, because there is a lack of in-depth studies to support the explanation.

While the confusion over the mobilisation mechanism is a result of numerous changes in China, especially those connected to party-state bureaucracies, governance and social control practices, the emergence and diversification of many studies of the issue have blurred our understanding. Since the late 1970s, there have been numerous efforts made by Chinese reformers to identify new mechanisms to replace or supplement old governance practices. Since the responsibility system was tried in rural China, it has been widely regarded as a practical and efficient way of connecting national interests with individual benefits. The complexity of urban reforms, however, has resulted in the lack of focused attention on the use of the social mobilisation mechanism, and the fragmented understanding of all these issues by some analysts has been reduced to the dilution of political power and social mobilisation in China. Therefore, what requires research attention is not only how this mechanism has evolved into what it is now, but also how it has lately been used and its nature and new characteristics. The first step of such new research efforts is to identify and analyse both the existence and importance of the mechanism in this rapidly changing society.

Second, the key issue in forming a new understanding of the social mobilisation mechanism in China is not only to go beyond the current understanding of both top-down and bottom-up processes, but also to examine and define the basis on which social mobilisation functions and is used, as well as its political and economic nature. In the 1960s, Chalmers Johnson defined social mobilisation in China as a dynamic process, a definition that has since been shared by many analysts. However, the meaning of 'dynamic' has not yet been fully unfolded. Some analysts have paid attention to its temporal dimension, while others have emphasised the role of different forces or actors in the process. Lately, because of the rapid and far-reaching changes, it has now become even more difficult than before to clearly tell what forces and motivations are involved in any mobilisation process. Without such understanding, mobilisation in this rapidly changing country is no longer a known process, and now there is hardly anyone who can explain how each part of the system is mobilised and its role in the process. What has happened since the end of the Cultural Revolution in the late 1970s is a far more complex process than earlier studies revealed. Social mobilisations are found to involve not only sharing ideas and aspirations, employing institutional resources and symbolic powers, but also distributing and channelling material resources and benefits, in which bargaining for the interests of the mobilisers and the mobilised, and negotiations and even protests, have taken place at all levels.

As mentioned, the new rural household responsibility system was expanded to other sectors in Chinese cities, and one of the many new practices in non-agricultural sectors has been called the performance-based assessment system. Having been directed by the pragmatism of Deng Xiaoping, the new system fitted China's need to reform its economy at the time. However, it has further weakened the ideology-based rule, and social mobilisations have since displayed a clear trend, moving towards a new politics based on shared needs, and material interests and benefits. While some analysts are still using the outdated top-down approach, more have realised that grassroots groups, lower-level officials and citizens have played a crucial role in initiating and driving various forms of social mobilisation. These new forms can be defined as the bottom-up process, but social mobilisation is no longer operating along the top-down and bottom-up dichotomy. In fact, even the interactive approach is no longer reliable for explaining how the two processes have interacted. All these should be further explored, especially the new nature of common interest-based social mobilisations.

Third, the process of developing new explanations about the use of mobilisation in China has been particularly challenged by the issue of how to define many forms of mass popular protests and activism. This has been a difficult issue because such protests in China are normally directed against government policies and institutions. That is, they are frequently considered from the conflict perspective. Similar actions in some other countries are seen as part of normal social life, but those taking place in China are regarded as not only conflicts, but also as abnormal ones that cannot be resolved simply. Such a theoretical orientation has, of course, been challenged by the relatively stable development that China has achieved so far, but various theories based on such orientations remain influential, preventing researchers from seeing socioeconomic and socio-political life in present-day China as normal. There is ample evidence indicating that conflicts have accompanied China's transition to an industrial society, and that parties on both sides of a conflict should be considered as participants in societal-level negotiations. Evidence from a few less-politicised fields also suggests that there has been a general trend called *minjin guotui*, showing that private sectors have been advancing while the state has been retreating (Lardy, 2014, pp. 89–93). The trend is not limited to economic activities, but has also spread to other areas. Social mobilisation has, to some extent, played a role of compensating the managerial decentralisation through allowing grassroots groups and citizens to seek what they require. However, these emerging relationships between the state and society, especially numerous forms of social mobilisation, can only be clearly understood by looking beyond the paradigm of irresolvable conflict.

Finally, the holistic-dynamic approach employed in this book will be of great help in addressing a special age-old problem in studying social mobilisation: the overemphasis on authoritarianism. It was since the work of Deutsch that political scientists' involvement in the study has led to more attention being paid to authoritarian regimes and the top-down process. This review has revealed that researchers have seen and analysed new and complex forms of social mobilisation in China from viewpoints of different disciplines. Such interdisciplinary efforts have made it clear that the mobilisation mechanism has not only been applied in non-political contexts, but has also often been involved in multi-step, multi-directional and multi-faceted processes or interactions. Because dogmatic beliefs are often influential, many previous studies have separated out not only certain categories of social mobilisation from the others, but they have also separated research in one discipline from research in other fields, making it difficult to reach a fuller and clearer understanding of how social mobilisation is utilised in present-day China, and therefore resulting in the academic tendency to 'know more and more about less and less' (Shambaugh, 2013, pp. ix–x). The holistic-dynamic approach suggested by this literature review emphasises that analysts should go beyond disciplinary and political boundaries, and take into consideration more factors or issues than those already known to make qualified analyses of social mobilisation in contemporary China.

Methodologically, this book is primarily based on the data collected through the joint efforts of the two authors. As noted in the Preface, co-author Yuanyuan Su spent a few months in Shandong province, which is one of China's eastern provinces in north China, southeast of Beijing, and she did her fieldwork in the region in 2012–13 after being accepted as a PhD candidate in sociology at the School of Social and Behavioural Sciences, Nanjing University. By employing the research skills that she learnt as a BA and MA student from the same school, she conducted a series of interviews, both structured and unstructured, with village residents and leaders, as well as officials from a few local government offices.

Observations were also made in a village-turned-town in a central region of the province, where local households at the time were all in the process of deciding whether *shanglou*, to move elsewhere or to accept the offer to move into new apartment buildings. A wide range of regulatory documents and historical archives about the policy and the region was also collected.

Co-author Jia Gao also interviewed many people, mainly officials and bureaucrats, policy analysts, academic researchers, business operators and owners in a few cities in Shandong and Beijing. Such face-to-face meetings are helpful for understanding local activities in executing this new countryside strategy and local responses to the campaign, but the focus is largely on the roles of each stakeholder in the process. Similar interviews were also conducted in Australia, where many hundreds of new migrants come from China's Shandong province. Many of them have witnessed the changes and activities in association with the new socialist countryside campaign in their home regions. Jia Gao also did numerous rounds of online search for more publicly available information, especially openly published documents, from the websites of concerned authorities and institutions. The online search identified many government documents and media coverage of the campaign in many regions in China, including some in Shandong, revealing a clear picture of how the new countryside campaign is organised.

ORGANISATION OF THE BOOK

What has been introduced up to this point is the general background, both historical and theoretical, to this analysis. This book is about the use of social mobilisation in China in a new era that is largely characterised by both the new political reality, which is widely called the era of political *boyi*, and the post-industrial stage of Chinese socioeconomic development. To systematically and credibly explain and theorise how the social mobilisation mechanism has been deployed recently in China, and how the mechanism has evolved into its current form and state, this book has six discussion chapters detailing and examining the main findings, plus a concluding chapter.

Chapter 2 builds on background information provided in this first chapter and considers the evolving role of China's central decision-makers in launching new policy initiatives. Many issues at this level of Chinese politics and governance have been considered by researchers, giving rise to various ideas, such as 'the retreating of totalitarianism' (Frenkiel, 2015, p. 123), 'the decline in the Chinese state's political capacity' (Misra, 2016, p. 149), and even the optimistic consideration of the CCP as a transformed 'organizational emperor' (Zheng, 2010, p. 16). However, there are not many studies dedicated to the consideration of the central decision-makers' recent role in developing and implementing a major policy initiative, in the context of which the dynamics of the process can be fully unfolded. To illustrate the whole process, both historically and spatially, Chapter 2 begins with a section that analyses the new political reality of post-Mao China. The second section looks at the reformist responses to the political reality, especially various multifaceted transformations of China's centralised, authoritarian political power, which have been going on since the early 1980s. The third section turns attention back to the central question of this book, which is why the mobilisation mechanism is still seen as the core of state capacity in China while it has been decentralising power. The fourth and last section details the circumstances under which the current rural urbanisation strategy is initiated as the CCP's legitimacy-seeking efforts in China's transition to a post-industrial economy.

Chapter 3 focuses on the politics of social mobilisation at the provincial level, the example of which is based on China's eastern province of Shandong. The role of Chinese provinces in the country's socioeconomic development has drawn the attention of many researchers and because of the general recognition of the increasing importance of the party-state systems at the provincial level, some even believe that there has been a development of 'local state corporatism' (Oi, 1992, p. 99) or an apparent 'emergence of local state corporatism' (Goodman, 2015, p. 4). After several rounds and forms of decentralisation, it now seems impossible to understand China without adequate knowledge of provinces (Bo, 2015). Because of the vertical complexity of China's party-state systems and the sizes of provincial population and economy, the analysis of current uses of social mobilisation in China also requires more attention to be shown to the province level than previous studies have done. This chapter examines how social mobilisation is implemented, especially how it is eventually translated into political power, action and, therefore, a new form of local politics in Shandong. The first section briefly introduces some background information about Shandong province, especially its past involvement and role in the formation of various rural polices in China. The second section looks at the routine efforts by provincial bureaucracies to implement the new rural strategy, with special attention devoted to their role as shaped by their position, which is not only vertically positioned between the central government and lower-tier governments, but also horizontally positioned among different parallel government agencies. The third section focusses on the creative implementation, as well as decision-making, by provincial bureaucracies, which have generated the various types of dynamics that have been powerfully directing and driving the implementation of the strategy in the province.

Chapter 4 looks at a newly emerging dimension of the use of the social mobilisation mechanism in China in recent years, which is the function of the market, or market forces, in social mobilisation. The market as an important driver of socioeconomic progress has gradually emerged in China since the 1990s because of China's ongoing reforms in the economy and public administration, if not politics. Nowadays, market forces are playing an increasingly important role in governing economic activities and shaping socio-political conditions of present-day China. However, this is an area of research that has rarely been studied along with the function of formal party-state bureaucracies or beyond political-economic debates of market liberalisation. The discussion in this chapter is a preliminary attempt to include this main aspect in the discussion of social mobilisation in contemporary China. This chapter starts with a review of China's market liberalisation that has taken place since the early years of its reform. This historical background section is followed by two discussion sections. The first discusses the role of market forces in driving the new rural building scheme in Shandong at provincial and prefectural levels. The second section looks in detail at how local companies had acted as the mobilisers at county and township levels in Laiwu.

Chapter 5 examines the function of the prefectural level of China's middle bureaucracy in social mobilisation. Theoretically, many earlier studies have focused attention on two obvious ends of the mobilisation process, which are the central leadership and the grassroots reactions. What has not been adequately examined is the role of bureaucracies at both the prefectural level and the county level, which may perhaps be defined as China's middle bureaucracy. This chapter pays attention to the prefectural level of the bureaucracy. Because this is still an under-researched area, this chapter will start with an analysis of how the *zhonggengzu* (intermediary obstacles) issue has been debated and handled from the viewpoint of central–local relations. This is followed by three sections looking specifically at how social mobilisation for the new rural plan has been undertaken in Laiwu, the smallest prefectural-level city in Shandong. The first section is an introduction of Laiwu and the second section is the discussion of how the tasks of mobilising local participation in the new plan are prioritised by Laiwu's leadership and bureaucracies. The third section looks at the project-driven approach that Laiwu has adopted to implement its prioritised projects, with the aim of showing how the rural construction scheme is being put into operation and how the land finance (*tudi caizheng*) is used at the prefectural level.

Chapter 6 deals with the awkward roles of the county and township governments in the rural urbanisation campaign. There are some studies of what has been happening at the county or the township levels from the policy implementation perspective, but few studies have considered these in the context of implementing a national strategic policy. Consequently, the roles of these two lowest levels of bureaucracy have hardly been studied in a broader context or in a systematic manner. The roles of the county and township governments were found to be awkward when this analysis placed them in the context of both the entire bureaucratic system and the whole process of policy implementation. Their awkward roles are in fact a pointer to a unique feature of social mobilisation in contemporary China, which is the frequent change in its bureaucratic management and the goal-oriented performance tied to the specific objectives of different reform programmes. This chapter will start with an explanation of why the governments at these two levels have become awkward in the new rural urbanisation campaign. Despite the awkwardness of their roles, the governments at these two levels still have their roles to play in executing the new rural strategy, which is the focus of the second and third discussion sections of this chapter.

Chapter 7 extends the discussion to grassroots reactions to the new rural urbanisation scheme, with an aim to show the entire process of social mobilisation in contemporary China. As indicated in the heading of this chapter, this discussion considers various forms of reactions or protests from a participatory perspective to offer a new explanation of the nature of grassroots discontent, resistance and protests in China in recent years. The latter has been a popular subject among researchers, China specialists and journalists for a few decades, which has even resulted in an impression that China may collapse at any moment because of widespread protests. What these analysts and commentators have overlooked is the close correlation between social reactions and government initiatives, and the individual interests and motives behind social actions, as well as strategic games played out for achieving their goals. This chapter challenges the inadequately explained nature of grassroots reactions to the new rural construction and details how some forms of social reactions have been used to influence the decision-making process and obtain material benefit. This chapter has three sections. The first introduces some basic information about the villages on which our analysis is based. The second and third sections examine two main aspects of the grassroots reactions to the implementation of the new countryside scheme in Laiwu.

Chapter 8 is the conclusion of this book, where we look at the two important remaining issues of this project. First, this chapter further summarises the main theoretical points that can be derived from this study. The chapter aims to offer theoretical insights into how the social mobilisation mechanism in China could be better considered. Second, this chapter also puts forward some suggestions for future research directions on this topic.

Social mobilisation is not only a very important mechanism in socioeconomic and -political life and a key aspect of state capacity, but it offers a unique perspective to understand a social system and process. Based on the experience gained conducting this study, this concluding chapter offers advice for further research on the topic.

2. The evolving role of central decision-makers in launching policy initiatives

For several decades, the Chinese central leadership has attracted more research attention from academic researchers and policy analysts than any other aspect of present-day Chinese society and life. Such highly focused excessive attention has come from a variety of perspectives, some of which are highly, both negatively and positively, opinionated and ideological. Therefore, readers are often confronted with analyses that turn out to be even more confusing and uncertain than before. As noted in Chapter 1, many new explanations about political power and governance at this level have been put forward by analysts. For example, some analysts have recently observed that there has been a visible and steady 'decline in the Chinese state's political capacity' thanks to 'the devolution of authority' (Misra, 2016, p. 149), while other researchers have witnessed the emergence of 'conditional democracy' because of 'the retreating of totalitarianism' (Frenkiel, 2015, p. 123). Some years ago, at a policy-making level, the Organisation for Economic Co-operation and Development (OECD) assessed China's current policy-making system as follows:

> While Western observers may perceive the Chinese policy system as monolithic, the policy-making system has nevertheless changed in recent decades. The most prominent change is the progressive involvement of a whole set of new players in the policy process. They include individuals, organisations and informal groups, a development which has led over time to more democracy in government decision-making processes. (OECD, 2008, p. 431)

Although the above explanations are new and more credible than what China experts would have provided a few decades ago, some of them are still clearly influenced by ideas of the past and traditional interpretative approaches. Much of the findings of earlier research is still unable to answer whether, and to what extent, China is a totalitarian state or its political system is an open system. In fact, the above explanations are different from each other, which shows how diverse the field of China studies still is, and how researchers and analysts have differently interpreted the same set of facts. As indicated in the introductory chapter, the use of social mobilisation in China today is neither a top-down nor a bottom-up process, while it is also no longer ideologically driven. Current Chinese politics, including what happens at the central level, is played out through negotiation and bargaining among competing interest groups to maximise their shares of material benefits and political influence. Social mobilisation has of late been used in China in the changing political environment.

This chapter is divided into four sections to explain how China's central decision-makers have slowly transformed their role in changing political circumstances in post-1978 China, through which new ways of using social mobilisation will be discussed. It begins with an analysis of the changing political structure in China since entering the post-Mao era and reformist responses to the new realities. The second section details the multi-faceted transformations of China's centralised, authoritarian political power, which have been going on since the late 1970s. The third section focuses on the central question of this book, which is why the mobilisation mechanism is still considered the core of state capacity in China while it has been decentralising power. The fourth and last section looks at the circumstances under which the new countryside, or new rural urbanisation, strategy is developed and implemented as one of the CCP's major legitimacy-seeking efforts in China's transition to a post-industrial economy.

THE NEW POLITICAL REALITY OF POST-MAO CHINA

There are several different sets of discourses analysing what took place in Chinese politics after the death of Mao in the autumn of 1976. Three perspectives appear to be the most relevant to this study. The first perspective is from a modern, if not foreign, political viewpoint, paying attention to a range of political ideas that have been introduced to China from Western countries since the late Qing Dynasty. Such new and introduced ideas or concepts include democracy, freedom, rights and different forms of ideology (Goldman, 1981, 1994, 2005; Pye, 1981, 1990; Rankin, 1986; Moody, 1988, 1994; Cherrington, 1991, 1997a, 1997b; He, 1997; He and Guo, 2000; Gu, 2000; Sausmikat, 2003). It is rather understandable if such viewpoints from observers living in lands physically far away from China and cultures that are very different from Chinese, a deeper and fuller understanding of which may also be gravely affected by the level of language skills. In fact, this part of history and understanding have been more often twisted by Chinese, both activists and thinkers, who have been searching for new ideas for dealing with the problems that China has experienced since the mid-nineteenth century (Yan, 1992; Kelliher, 1993; Y. Guo, 2004; S. Guo, 2012).[1] For more than a century, a large proportion of educated Chinese – both better-educated and less-educated; both China-trained and overseas-trained – have been trapped, if not imprisoned, in a mentality that reflects neither the traditional Chinese political culture nor the current reality in China. A leading American China specialist, Arthur Doak Barnett, warned new researchers as early as the mid-1950s to be cautious of the 'limited value' and 'dubious reliability' of the reports from people of Chinese origin who 'misconstrue situations' in China (Barnett, 1964, pp. 60–61).

What has been overshadowed by this modern viewpoint is a Chinese historical perspective. Many published analyses of post-Mao China are rather like what Zhang Xudong once wrote about many discourses of the image of China, which 'overwhelm our appetite for contradictory descriptions and frustrate our established analytical and conceptual framework' (Zhang, 2008, p. 25). In more accurate words, many of the published analyses of post-Mao China have no connection with China's past and have been conducted with almost no reference to domestic political circumstances within the CCP and Chinese society, but only relate to a set of concepts and theories familiar to people in specific academic fields and those who are involved in activities that are guided by imported ideas. One of the regrettable misunderstandings of post-1978 Chinese politics, which has also been promoted by a small group of China experts, is the over-emphasis of the role of Wei Jingsheng, who was even called 'the father of Chinese democracy', in advocating democracy as 'the fifth modernization' (Nathan, 1985; p. 22; Kornberg and Faust, 2005, p. 43). China has frequently been considered through Western lenses and is represented in many publications, in both European languages and Chinese, as a late-developed country in northwest Europe.

The second historical viewpoint focuses on China's own past political events, culture and transitions and their present-day relevance. From this perspective, the death of Mao in 1976 is regarded as the end of the rule of Chinese communist revolutionary heroes and strongmen, and the beginning of China's new post-revolution period. Many researchers were aware that China was then suffering from 'reduced legitimacy and weakened dominance over society' (Teiwes, 2000, p. 159), but few of them ever considered the situation in a historical context of dynastic changes. A productive, also active, Chinese historian at the Chinese Academy of Social Sciences (CASS) wrote the following comment on his Weibo-blog from the historical perspective:

The death of Mao signified the end of the heroic era, and China has since gradually become a normal society. Chinese politics has also evolved into a normal form of politics. there is still the real possibility that another authoritarian leader, like Mao Zedong, would emerge in China, but a rational China would stop any such superhuman from emerging. (Ma, 2014, n.p.)

Based on China's long dynastic cycle, the authority of the ruling class and its elites would commonly be weakened after the first-generation rulers of each dynasty or the 'post-dynastic rulers' in the words of Barmé (2008, p. 6). No matter whether the succeeding generations of rulers of each dynasty should be called *youzhu* (young or infant ruler), *ruozhu* (weak ruler) or even mournfully *houzhu* (last ruler) (Hucker, 1975; Fu, 1996; Haar, 1998; Wagner, 1998), it has for some dynasties been common knowledge that a core feature of the post-heroic era is the weakened authority, both individually and institutionally. Without any intention to one-sidedly analyse modern China within its long dynastic cycle, its history and political traditions are the central dimensions that must be taken into consideration in order to understand this most populous and ancient country in the world (Loewe, 2005; Kinkley, 2015).[2] This particular point makes sense considering that, as noted in Chapter 1, approximately 82 per cent of the Chinese population in the late 1970s were peasants, who were influenced by old feudal ideologies (Breslin, 2014), and that the CCP's first-generation leaders were all born in the late Qing Dynasty (1644–1911).

Despite this historical and political-cultural background, the post-Mao CCP leadership picked up the hint as early as 1978 from the popular enthusiasm for the concept of *sihua*, or *sige xiandaihua* (four modernisations – agriculture, industry, science and technology, and national defence) put forward by the then premier Zhou Enlai a year before his death in January 1976,[3] and turned the concept into its new official discourses of reform, which have since been used to 'provide a unifying language for unified nation actions' (Xu, 2000, p. 19). This is the third main category of discourse, which is largely characterised by two well-known concepts: *gaige* (reform) and *kaifang* (opening-up) to the outside world. In the late 1970s and early 1980s, these new ideas or concepts were vigorously promoted by the CCP leadership of Deng's generation to regenerate and sustain its ruling legitimacy, on which its authority may be built (Hsü, 1990; Chen, 1999; Blecher, 2003).

The CCP's new official reform discourses are based on one critical assessment of China's economic situation in the late 1970s, which was judged as *binlin bengkui*, or *bengkui de bianyuan*, 'moving towards the edge of structural collapse' (Lin, 1997, p. 45). This judgment is hardly mentioned in English publications, which partly explains why Wei Jingsheng's fifth modernisation, political democracy, has drawn more attention from Western countries than other pressing economic issues facing China at the time. Also misinterpreted is Deng's solution to the issue, *boluan fanzheng*, which was initially considered to be a slogan to criticise Mao's Cultural Revolution, but has lately been translated as 'to restore order from chaos and return things to normal' (Wu, 2005, p. 107). In fact, Deng himself made it clear that *boluan fanzheng* was to return to the 'correct line' or political strategy that was developed and agreed upon at the CCP's Eighth National Congress in 1956, which was to focus attention on economic development (Gong, 2002, p. 425).

The new political slogans, as well as development-focused policies and actions, that China quickly adopted in the early years of the post-heroic era were obviously not sufficient to solve all the problems facing the country and its rapidly growing population. The CCP under Deng Xiaoping's leadership had no choice but to turn attention to the restructuring of the party-state or political power, which was aimed at rebuilding its authority. Such a political effort was, for a short period, called the administrative reform (Deng, 1985; Goldman, 1994; Cheek, 2016). The restructuring of political power opened a space for various debates, including the push for democracy from liberal-minded young people, such as Wei Jingsheng. Several rounds of debates took place, centred on whether political reform, or democratisation, needed to be prioritised over economic reforms and whether Western influences were a danger to China.

The debates of the late 1970s and 1980s took place shortly after the Cultural Revolution, when what was disliked most by a large majority of Chinese people was the 'empty talk' of isms and ideologies after almost three decades of Mao's leadership (Hsü, 1990, p. 47). The new leaders still remembered past failures and decided to focus their attention on economic reforms. Among their many efforts to deal with new challenges, they made accurate judgments on two critical issues.

First, they effectively rejected both the push for prioritising numerous non-urgent socio-political changes including democratisation, and the notion of Western influences as an immediate threat to China. The best example of such effort is Deng Xiaoping's speech in 1980 on the reform of the party-state leadership system (Goldman, 1994; Sun, 1995). The first author of this book was involved in the debate in the 1980s and once argued that China's *fengjian canyu* (feudal legacy) posed a more vital threat to the course of Chinese modernisation than Western culture and practices, the influence of which was visible and superficial (Gao, 1987).

Second, although China has a long political tradition of *xuefan* (to remove or strip the governing power from local military or civilian governors), the post-Mao leadership decided to use a different strategy.[4] As a leading American China analyst observed, Deng in the above-mentioned famous speech 'criticized not only the feudal legacy but also the party's prevailing overconcentration of power' (Goldman, 1994, p. 64). There are many ancient tales and old sayings in Chinese about how risky it might be to inadequately decentralise governing powers, as dramatised in a Chinese story of *beijiu shi bingquan* (depriving generals of military power by offering them a drink) (Ho, 1992, p. 117).[5] The painful lessons from the Maoist period and Deng Xiaoping's 'pragmatic, and "whatever works" kind of ideology' in the words of Cohen (cited in Twohey, 1999, p. 97) meant that the new leaders ignored the risk of decentralisation. Deng's original aim of criticising the over-concentration of power was aimed at Maoist mistakes and separating the CCP from the government system, which has been seen to be 'too idealistic and not feasible' (Zheng and Weng, 2016, p. 36), but his idea was soon expanded by his heirs-apparent and used to deal with central–local relations.

From the social mobilisation viewpoint, the separation of the CCP and the state was indeed unworkable in the 1980s, but China's central–local relations have greatly benefitted from the decentralisation policy. Before the mid-1980s, many new reform policies and initiatives were delayed, shelved or watered down, if not totally blocked, by officials of the massive party-state machinery. As introduced in Chapter 1, such intermediary obstacles have been called *zhonggengzu*, and posed more serious challenges to new reform strategies than the demands made by liberal-minded intellectuals and pro-democracy activists. One well-known example of such an obstacle was the resistance of the local leadership of Yantai in Shandong province to the introduction of the household production responsibility system in the early 1980s, the example of which is relevant to this book as it reveals more background information about Shandong and its political past. As shown in Figure 2.1, Yantai is not a place of *shangao huangdiyuan* (the mountains are high and the emperor is faraway), but its leadership became almost the only local leadership in the country to reluctantly implement the new responsibility system (M. Wang, 2006; G. Wang, 2011; Xu, 2013). This forced the central decision-makers to pay attention to their relations with local party-state systems in order to be able to rely on their support.

It is worth pointing out that there were numerous other changes in the early years of post-Mao China, and the above changes occurred at the same time as the CCP was making other efforts, such as adjusting the political relations between the elite and the masses, especially with intellectuals (Lum, 2000), restoring 'inner democracy in the Party' (Dutt, 1981, p. 84) and reforming industrial enterprises (Chen, 1999).

Source: Drawn by the authors of this book.

Figure 2.1   Location of Yantai, Shandong province

However, the changing central–local relations are not only 'one of the most profound results of China's decade-long reform process' (Hao and Lin, 1994, p. 1), but are also a very important perspective to take when analysing the utilisation of the social mobilisation mechanism in China. Despite its importance, the decentralisation and associated deregulation cannot be regarded as a 'voluntary action' as assumed by some observers (Shih, 1995, p. 36). In fact, it resulted from various pressures from different stakeholder groups and the tensions caused by many overwhelmingly divisive regional and sectional differences. The CCP's secretary-general at the time, Hu Yaobang, was the main advocate for the decentralisation, but 'his efforts radically to decentralize economic decision-making' in part contributed to his removal from the post in the late 1980s (Baum, 1994, p. 152).

CONTINUOUS EFFORTS IN RESTRUCTURING CENTRAL–LOCAL RELATIONS

As the most direct or relevant background for understanding the social mobilisation mechanism in present-day China, the decentralisation of central government authorities to regional governments is believed by some analysts to have been attempted a few times before the early 1980s (Zhao, 1994). This explanation refers to what was once called *liangxia* (two occasions of decentralisation) and *liangshang* (two occasions of centralisation) that had taken place from the early 1950s to the early 1970s (World Bank, 1995), but all these pre-reform centralisations and decentralisations were largely part of the political experiments that the new People's Republic of China (PRC) had tried in the early years after its foundation in 1949 in order to form and strengthen new party-state or governmental systems. As a functional political or policy measure, it was only after the early years of the post-1978 rural reform that the CCP leaders once again realised the importance of utilising the decentralisation measure to mobilise the entire party-state system to implement reform policies. Since the early 1980s, the CCP leadership has kept using this important measure and making various changes to its use to maintain the momentum of reform.

When the theoretical preparation for restructuring central–local relations was first conducted in the official communist discourse, it was deliberately free from unfamiliar concepts, both foreign and traditional feudal. Specifically, it stated that part of the CCP's post-1978 aim was to restore *minzhu jizhongzhi* (democratic centralism), while the famous but rather philosophical debate on 'seeking truth from facts' was going on during the late 1970s and early 1980s (Hua, 1995; Yu, 2010). Borrowed from the Lenin-led Russian communist party, the democratic centralism is regarded as 'a model of organizational structure and decision-making', and in theory it 'allows for substantial debate on policy issues before formal decisions are taken' (Sullivan, 2012, p. 80). It has a set of rules designed to ensure its members' participations in decision-making and implement the final decision when it is reached. In practice, this set of organisational rules has been developed to cope with the reality facing the CCP and its government. As indicated by Figure 2.2, China has an enormous administrative system nationwide, which at present has five levels, but it is in fact more intricate if also viewed horizontally. Apart from the 'vertical/functional' lines of authority, there are also 'horizontal/ territorial lines' of authority (Lieberthal and Oksenberg, 1988, p. 151; Lieberthal, 1995, p. 169).

China's huge administrative system creates enormous obstacles to the implementation of its national strategies and policies, the situation of

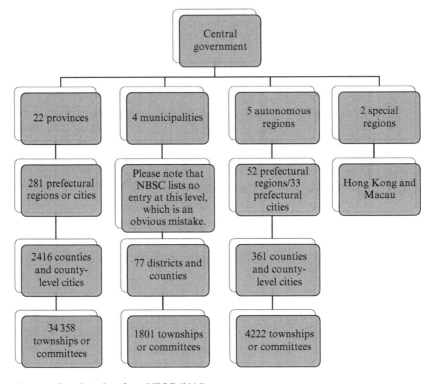

Source: Based on data from NBSC (2016).

Figure 2.2   China's governmental structure, 2015

which was particularly bad when the country was in a state of radical transition from Maoist to reform politics. The demand for reform since the early 1980s has resulted in numerous continuing efforts to make changes to the structure and operation of the party-state system, both vertically and horizontally. There are numerous ways to consider and explain the changes made over the past few decades, including using a large collection of historical anecdotes. For example, the leadership of the CCP's Yantai prefectural committee was restructured in the early 1980s as a direct result of their reluctance to implement the household responsibility system in the region (Wang, 2006). For the same reason, almost two dozen county leaders in the Yantai region were also replaced within a short period, the decision swiftly made by reformist central leaders by using their organisational and political power. Among these possible perspectives, however, two crucial efforts in restructuring central–local relations have drawn particular scholarly attention: administrative or governmental reforms and fiscal system reforms or fiscal decentralisations.

What has been confusing about China's efforts in improving its central–local relations is that the efforts have often been understood differently by researchers from different disciplines (Yang, 2002; Zheng, 2007), overlooking the original approach to this crucial issue, which is what Deng Xiaoping frequently said *liangshou zhua* or *liangshou yiqi zhua* (to grasp or seize with two hands) (Huang, 2000; Brady, 2008). This is what has been widely called Deng's 'two hands' approach, which has influenced the formation of two types of strategy. On the one hand, the CCP's reformists decided as recently as the early 1980s to eliminate *zhonggengzu*, intermediary obstacles existing in its party-state system. On the other hand, whoever supports reforms must be rewarded, and an improved financial system of *fenzao chifan* (eating in separate kitchens) was also introduced in the early 1980s to mobilise local enthusiasm (*diaodong defang jijixing*) for contributing to both rural and urban reforms (Shirk, 1993; Hao and Lin, 1994).

Because of the holistic-dynamic approach that this book has used, which is characterised by taking more aspects and factors into account and considering them as part of interactive processes, this discussion looks at both types of political effort made by reformist leaders of the CCP to reform central–local relations. Some less-prominent secondary efforts and activities, such as those aimed at reforming the CCP itself and transforming government functions, will be analysed in a related paragraph of this section.

To make the party-state system efficient or to remove intermediary obstacles as much as possible, China has undertaken seven governmental institutional, or organisational, reforms (*jigou tiaozheng*, or *jigou gaige*) since 1982, the latest of which was in 2013. Among these seven reforms, five of them were done before 2006 when the new countryside plan was introduced. Before the first institutional reform in 1982, the party-state system had gone through a *zhengdun* process (rectification or organising) (Huang 2000; Dillon, 2015). During the rectification, the Dengist 'two hands' approach was already deployed. Its punitive measure was the purge of *sanzhongren* (three categories of people), specifically rebels, factional partisans and 'beat-smash-burn' elements from the ten years of the Cultural Revolution (Liu and Link, 2006, p. 206), while at the same time promoting the new constructive measure of appointing new leaders, which is called *ganbu sihua* or 'cadre four modernisation' (to be revolutionary, young, educated and professional) (Zhong, 2004; Guo, 2012).[6] Since it was impossible at the time to completely remove a large group of Maoists, the first effort to institutionally and structurally deal with the problem was made in 1982. As detailed in Table 2.1, the same effort has been made every five years, with the latest one in 2013.

Table 2.1   Reductions in the number of State Council agencies

Year	Ministries incl. the General Office	Directly affiliated agencies	Executive agencies	Commissions and bureaus	Total
1981	52	43	5	0	100
1982	44	15	2	11	72
1988	42	19	7	15	83
1993	41	13	5	15	74
1998	30	17	6	18	71
2003	29	19	4	10	62
2008	28	15	4	15	62

Source: Based on Li and Mao (2010).

All these institutional reforms have lately been frequently criticised by the Chinese media and academic analysts for being nothing more than spin, because none of the restructurings avoid the vicious cycle of starting with a reform and ending with a swollen bureaucracy (Weng, 2013). Such criticism has overlooked the fact that the governmental restructuring has not only been institutionalised as a regular part of the ongoing institutional reform (Li and Mao, 2010), but has also deeply transformed China's central–local relations from a centrally dominated authoritarian regime to a mixed central–local political structure, establishing a new interactive relationship between the central government and local governments (Zhong, 2009). Of course, the latter does not simply result from a few rounds of institutional reform, but also from numerous other changes, including financial reforms, which will be discussed next.

The focus on economic development since the late 1970s, and the subsequent efforts to cultivate a market economy, once raised the question of how the planning system could be made more flexible and effective and how the scope of mandatory planning (*zhilingxing jihua*) could be reduced (Hsu, 1991). Such discussions, especially a range of shared ideas such as the idea of guidance planning (*zhidaoxing jihua*), soon made their impact on other parts of the party-state system. While direct challenges to China's existing system have never been allowed, numerous reformist ideas have been initiated from *tizhinei* (within the system) and tried, including proposals for transforming the function of government (*zhengfu zhineng zhuanbian*) (Jeffreys and Sigley, 2009). Ideas for realising this transformation, have, since the mid-1990s, been behind most of the institutional reforms listed in Table 2.1, and have also been guiding many other efforts to ameliorate central–local relations. This core idea that aims to maintain economic momentum and provide better policy options, especially the attractive concept of *fenquan* (division of powers or decentralisation), has made the decision-making more open and accessible than before. Therefore, the idea of transforming the role of government has also made *minzhu juece* (democratic decision-making) possible. In the second half of the 1990s, the new practice of *minzhu juece*, along with other measures of democratic management and supervision *(minzhu guanli* and *minzhu jiandu*) were already introduced nationwide at all levels of government, including the township level (Schubert and Ahlers, 2012).

Once the ideas of division of power and responsibility were in place, the CCP's *zhizheng nengli* (its governance capacity) became a real issue for transforming the party-state system. The vital issue of governance capacity is how to maintain and improve the capacity of mobilising not only the entire party-state system, but also the support of at least a majority of the masses. Despite the serious challenges generated by restructuring central–local relations, Deng Xiaoping's idea of *fazhan caishi ying daoli* (economic development is the only hard truth or the ultimate justification [for the CCP's ruling legitimacy]) has been guiding central decision-makers to continue the restructuring, and also to expand it to include the decentralisation of financial control, a bigger incentive for lower-level governments.

The second main clue to understanding what China has been doing since the late 1970s to restructure its central–local relations is its fiscal system reforms or decentralisations (Wong, 2007; Hsu, 2017). It is the rewarding or constructive aspect of the restructuring in terms of Deng Xiaoping's 'two hands' approach. Dengist leaders were fully aware as early as 1978 of the importance of 'two enthusiasms' for both the local and the central governments (Liu, 2008), and the constraints of its old fiscal control policy of *tongshou tongzhi* (unified revenues and unified expenditure, or collecting revenues and spending them uniformly). To mobilise support for various reform programs, a new political thinking was put forward to overcome the mentality of *youyao ma pao, youyao ma buchicao* (making a horse work without feeding it). The very first step of the post-1978 financial reform was taken in 1979, allowing the state-owned enterprises to keep part of their profits. This first step has been summarised as *fenquan rangli* (splitting powers and giving up some profits). As listed in Table 2.2, China has since undertaken fiscal reforms in four key areas: fiscal allocations between central and local levels, and between governments and enterprises, taxations and infrastructure investments (Guo and Yang, 2008).

Table 2.2 summarises the main financial reform efforts before the new rural urbanisation scheme started in the mid-2000s, but what it is unable to reveal is that the 1994 *fenshuizhi* (tax-sharing) reform resulted in a decline in local government revenues; almost 60 per cent of the total revenue was

Table 2.2   China's main post-1978 financial reform efforts

Year	Chinese term	New fiscal policy introduced
1978	*Tongshou tongzhi*	Uniform collection of revenues and uniform expenditures
1979	*Fenquan rangli*	'Splitting powers and giving up some profits', allowing state enterprises to keep some profits
1980	*Caizheng baogan (fenzao chifan)*	The fiscal responsibility (or contracting) system, also known as 'eating in separate kitchens'
1983	*Li gai shui*	Substituting taxes for profits
1985	*Fenji baogan*	The multi-level responsibility system (based on classifying revenues and expenditures)
1988	*Dabaogan*	'A complete package', allowing provinces to retain all locally collected revenues after paying a base figure (with a percentage increase each year)
1989	*Lishui fenliu*	The separation of taxes and profits (into different streams), or the tax plus profit system
1994	*Fenshuizhi*	The tax-sharing system, allowing local government to share tax revenues with the central government
1998	*Gonggong caizheng gaige*	The public finance reform, aimed at forming a new public finance system
2000	*Yusuan gaige*	The budgetary reform to regulate governmental behaviours
2004	*Difang caizheng gaige*	The local budgetary reform

Sources: Based on Li (1998), Lin (2002), Dabla-Norris (2005), Wong (2007), Gao (2009), Jia (2011) and Hsu (2017).

controlled by the central government. Because of this, the 1994 reform is regarded by some as a setback in terms of decentralisation, or it is at least a re-centralisation effort (Zhou, 2006; Wong, 2000). Despite being without a clear word to name it, the real issue behind the debate that started after the 1994 fiscal reform is about the utilisation of the social mobilisation mechanism and the capacity to use it. From a reformist perspective, the mobilisation of *liangge jijixing* ('two enthusiasms', for central and local bureaucracies) should always be considered. However, from the perspective of state capacity, inadequate decentralisation resulting from a string of fiscal reforms had seriously weakened the capacity of the central party-state system to mobilise and regulate economic development (Wang, 1997; Zhou, 2006). The first post-1978 major alteration to the method of using the social mobilisation mechanism took place at this time.

China was a very different place in the early 1990s. It was not only deeply shocked by the political turmoil of 1989, but was also led by a group of educated professionals, who possessed almost no revolutionary political capital except being promoted through the party-state system. What was different from the final years of the Maoist era, however, were the new political power structure and the new norms governing central–local relations. The old hierarchical top-down political process and dominant role of the central government were changed and partly replaced by a newly formed bargaining relationship, if not quite a negotiating one. Such new relations are now widely called 'game-playing' between the central and local governments (Xu and Cui, 2011, p. 547). Because of such change, Lou Jiwei, former director of research of the National Commission for Restructuring the Economic System and the former Minister for Finance (2013–16), once wrote the following on why the re-centralisation was needed after the 1994 fiscal reform:

> The [central] government must retain control over macroeconomic regulation in order to create conditions for fair competition and further decentralise a wide range of economic activities. However, in the current [pre-1994 reform] system, fiscal revenues are far too decentralized, which neither helps local governments nor promotes autonomous enterprises. (Lou, 1997, p. xvi)

These changes in both thinking and approach took place directly after Deng Xiaoping's inspection tour to southern China (*Nanxun*) in early 1992 (Wong, 2014). Deng's talks during the tour eventually removed ideological barriers to more pragmatic approaches to reform, especially his remarks on planning and market, which are no longer regarded as 'marks of either socialism or capitalism', but simply 'two methods and forms of deploying resources' (cited in Wong, 2014, p. 48). Thus, just like Deng Xiaoping's 'black cat white cat' theory, decentralisation or centralisation no longer matters ideologically or politically, if it drives economic growth. While such changes have made the decision-making in China rather pragmatic and flexible, what the Chinese have since frequently called *shiquan* (localised tasks and responsibilities) has also been decentralised to local governments, especially many new social services, while sustaining local economic growth.

Unlike the negative comments made by some China analysts, local governments and officials have in fact welcomed this part of *zhengfu zhineng zhuanbian* (transformation of the role of government) because more *shiquan* (localised tasks and responsibilities) provides them with hands-on opportunities for gaining benefits, both fairly, such as creating and improving personal career paths, and otherwise, such as creating jobs for those in inner circles or even extracting other material or financial benefits. While China-based scholars reveal that 'more responsibilities mean more power and more budgets' and 'carry certain types of personal benefits' for local officials (Ma, 2013, p. 19), many other China analysts find that this new reality has generated the request for 'increasing extra-budgetary funds' (Fewsmith, 2013, p. 74). The latter was a specific and crucial step taken in the late 1990s in the formation of what has since been called 'a new game with new rules' (Zheng, 2004, p. 105). Specifically, the central power or authority has, on the surface, been retreating, despite the above-mentioned effort to re-centralise the power by mobilising various resources for new reform programmes, but at the same time, there has also been an effort to rebuild new central–local relations. The strategic idea behind such effort is the understanding of the need for *liangge jijixing* ('two enthusiasms' for the central and local governments), which was stressed by Jiang Zemin in 1995 as a formal recognition of the interests and powers of the central and local governments (L. Feng, 2011).

A major nationwide, social mobilisation plan after the 1994 financial reform was the housing marketisation reform, which was also called the housing monetarisation reform to reflect the meaning of the original phrase, *zhufang huobihua gaige*. This change has been considered 'a watershed and a big thrust in China's long housing reform process' and the termination of public housing provision in all Chinese cities (Zhu and Lee, 2007, p. 228). From the perspectives of both state capacity and social mobilisation, however, this reform was a very serious test of not only China's post-1978 political structure and new central–local relations, but also of its governing capacity, including the capacity to mobilise supports and resources to implement new policies after the 1994 fiscal reform. This major change took place when local governments were in very desperate need of new revenues to make up for lost tax revenue after the 1994 fiscal reform, and more importantly, this reform has also resulted in the rapid emergence and utilisation of *tudi caizheng* (land finance) to extract revenue locally from transferring, or selling, land-use rights for urban expansion (Zhou, 2015). Despite many critical analyses of these reform measures, which even prompted the sudden emergence of the 'new leftist' in China (Liu, 2001, p. 51), these changes have not only further improved China's central–local relations, but have also altered its utilisation of social mobilisation, making it no longer simply an ideology-oriented approach, or an authority-driven hierarchical mode of top-down decision-making.

MOBILISATION AS THE CORE OF STATE CAPACITY

In the years since the 1994 fiscal reform, Wang Shaoguang and Hu Angang have been widely considered 'the most vocal advocates' for re-centralisation in China from the position of the Chinese new left (Liu, 2004, p. 164). They not only believe that many post-1978 fiscal reforms had adverse impacts on the capacity of the Chinese state, but also argue for a direct link between the social mobilisation mechanism and state capacity. In their well-known book on China's state capacity, they start their critical analysis with the following:

> The process of modernizing a country requires the mobilization of the human and material resources of the entire society. It is also a process of the continuous strengthening of the state's capacity. In order to respond to the demands of modernization, to mobilize all sorts of society's resources . . . it is urgently required that there be a stronger and more authoritative central government. (Wang and Hu, 2001, p. 1)

The last sentence of the above passage has been controversial over the past two decades. What Wang and Hu did not clearly consider in their analysis is China's recent past experiences in dealing with the delicate balance between centralisation and decentralisation, which is typically expressed as *yizhua jiusi, yifang jiuluan* (centralisation leads to rigidity, decentralisation leads to chaos) (Lu, 1996, p. 10). China was troubled frequently by such a vicious cycle in the pre-1978 years (Lanteigne, 2015), which is why all post-Mao Chinese leaders have stressed the importance of 'two enthusiasms' for the central and local governments and their role in driving economic reform. Despite the over-reaction to negative outcomes of pre-1994 reforms, especially to decentralisations, Wang and Hu have correctly established a connection between social mobilisation and state capacity, which has helped researchers in China realise that social mobilisation is the core of state capacity.

In fact, the decentralisation of various localised tasks and responsibilities, and the development of extra-budgetary financing as new governing mechanisms, are a clear reflection of the fundamental changes in the foundation, structure and process of China's post-1978 state leadership system and decision-making. They can also be considered part of what some young Chinese scholars have recently defined as 'collaborative governance' (Jing, 2015, p. 1). The latter is a product of a long search that China has undertaken since the death of Mao in 1976, especially since the CCP formed its political strategy to reform itself and strengthen its governing capacity. Shortly after being appointed as the top leader after the 1989 turmoil, Jiang Zemin started stressing the importance of modernising the

CCP from a revolutionary party to a ruling party and the urgent need to strengthen its capacity to lead. This strategic thinking further evolved throughout the 1990s into Jiang's 'three represents' theory, which has radically changed the ideological basis for the CCP's political legitimacy. The state capacity theory is, in effect, a theoretical response from the new left to what has, since the early 1990s, been called *zhizheng nengli jianshe* (improvements and strengthening of governing capacity) in the CCP's official discourse (Zhang, 2001; Li, 2015).

The CCP's efforts to improve and strengthen its capacity to govern have attracted much scholarly attention, but two features of the efforts, which should also be considered as part of the capacity, have not been adequately analysed. First, despite various campaigns against Western influence, such as those against spiritual pollution, liberalisation and Westernisation, since the late 1970s China has made a very systematic effort to not only learn scientific and technological knowledges from developed Western nations, but to study their experiences in managing a complex socioeconomic system. One such example is what was called *congshure* (book series craze) in the 1980s (Chen and Jin, 1997, p. 179; Chen, 2001, p. 78). China's state-controlled publishers in the 1980s translated and published a far larger number of management and economics-related books and journal papers from English into Chinese than many university students in developed nations could read in their university years. This relatively minor aspect of China's opening-up to the West may well explain why certain practices in China have appeared more capitalist than Western countries. The research attention paid to some established topics, such as campaigns against Western influence, has prevented some researchers from forming a clear understanding of the change.

Second, to cope with the increasing demands and complexities of many reform programmes, China has established, or transformed in many cases, a massive and complex system of think tanks. It is true that China had a reputation for preventing the public from taking part in the processes of political and administrative decision-making (McGann and Johnson, 2005), but the old practices have slowly been altered and replaced as a direct result of economic reforms. There are some studies of such types of Chinese research teams or institutes and their activities, but their roles are often either mystified or politicised, or studied from outdated perspectives, such as in the roles of propaganda devices or brainwashing institutions. A typical example of such misreading is the role of the CCP's Party School system, which is simply considered in terms of its function of cadre training. Only recently have researchers started analysing its role in governance-capacity building, and as a think tank of policy analysis, consultation, training and research (Ahlers, 2014; Lee, 2015).

Based on such research capacities and activities, China has slowly developed its new understanding and practices in utilising the social mobilisation mechanism in more advanced stages of economic reforms. In addition to the 'de-ideologicalization of Chinese political system' (Fewsmith, 2010, p. 156), the following part of this section will summarise other key elements of the improvements, some of which need to be considered in the context of China's transformation from Maoist socialist revolution to the current post-industrial stage. Also important is that this summary needs to be read alongside what has been discussed already.

First, new central–local relations have been trialled, developed and accepted as the new political structure and norm, laying the institutional foundation for using the social mobilisation mechanism. Although this point was discussed earlier, it is so important and relevant to the core issue of this book that further discussion is required. Unlike various ideological preparations that the CCP made after the Mao era, ranging from *zhenli biaozhun dabianlun* (the great debate on the criterion of truth) in the late 1970s and early 1980s to the new idea of *sange daibiao* (the three represents) in the early 2000s (Barmé, 1999; Wang, 2003; Zheng, 2010), which have helped to de-ideologicalise or de-radicalise China (Chun, 2013), the various changes to central–local relations are directly applicable to governance activities in practice. As an analytical paradigm, such operational and institutional changes are defined in several different ways. Apart from the previously mentioned theory of collaborative governance (Jing, 2015), such alterations are also considered to be the 'regionally decentralized authoritarian regime' (Xu, 2011, p. 1078). In practice, apart from the local enthusiasm created by reformed central–local relations, the latter has also deeply altered the decision-making process and behaviour of governments, making the CCP's mass line more institutionalised. The decisions made based on the mass line practice, which is expressed as *cong qunzhong zhong lai, dao qunzhong zhong qu* (cycles from the masses and to the masses), are usually welcomed by local governments (Hsiao and Cheek, 1995; Bray, 2005; Hu, 2014). That is, the new relations have laid the basis for not only gaining support from local institutions, but also mobilising them for executing new polices.

Second, China's fiscal reforms have also transformed the nature of social mobilisation, making it no longer just a political process. Some analysts consider fiscal reforms as either decentralising or a re-centralising, but from the state capacity view, they are mixed with both, aiming at improving governance capacity and efficiency to cope with new challenges, one of which is shown in Figure 2.3.

Figure 2.3 shows one of the fundamental changes that has occurred in China in recent decades. As an effect of the strong push for rapid economic

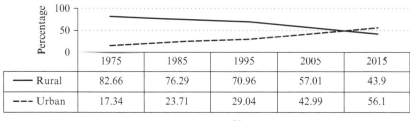

	1975	1985	1995	2005	2015
—— Rural	82.66	76.29	70.96	57.01	43.9
--- Urban	17.34	23.71	29.04	42.99	56.1

Year

Source: Based on data from NBSC (2016).

Figure 2.3   Urban–rural distribution of population in China, 1975–2015

development, China's massive population has been shifting continuously and markedly from rural areas to urban centres. This significant and constant change has generated numerous new demands for government services and many new issues for decision-makers to deal with, which have driven China to modernise its governance in terms of both structure and function. Since the late 1970s, each CCP leadership has devised its own approach to the fiscal system as an essential part of new central–local relations. All the approaches appear to be fiscal, but they all serve the purpose of dividing powers and functions, allocating tasks and responsibilities, and increasing managerial convenience and efficiency (Shirk, 1993; Chen, 2004). Leaving aside the new opportunity provided to lower-level governments by *tudi caizheng* (land finance), which will be detailed next, the creation and combination of *shiquan* (localised tasks and responsibilities) and local fiscal autonomy, especially the expansion of extra-budgetary and off-budgetary funds, have not only diversified the financial system and its role, but have also established a close link between new initiatives and financial support. Social mobilisation aimed at implementing new policy initiatives can now be supported financially or by material resources. Although it is minor, but still unethical, it is worth noting that a high level of local fiscal autonomy is often accompanied by various forms of corruption, which is considered by some researchers to be the *runhuayou* (lubricating oil) of China's rapid economic growth (He, 1998; Li, 2001a).

Third, China's massive but repeatedly reformed bureaucracy has been the backbone of the Chinese authorities at both the national and local levels, and has therefore been a guarantee of the use of the social mobilisation mechanism (Aglietta and Bai, 2013), although the party-state bureaucracy is regularly troubled by *zhonggengzu* (intermediary obstacles) when trying to implement new policies. Two bureaucracy-related points must be explored here to understand the importance of bureaucracy in governance practice and the manners of managing them. Since the early 1980s, bureaucratic teams have been reformed by *ganbu gangwei zerenzhi* (the cadre job responsibility system) (Faure, 2006; White, 2006). This new feature of the cadre system shows what reformists have learnt from new, if not Western, management ideas and practices. The system also includes some performance goals and measures, especially the performance appraisal practice. All these new practices have also been incorporated into their use of the social mobilisation mechanism.

Fourth, the performance-based, cadre promotion system that has been adopted and further developed by the CCP in recent decades has also played a very important role in social mobilisation. If there is any central power or authority that has not been decentralised since the Mao period, or even longer because of China's authoritarian tradition, it is the control of 'personnel matters of subnational governments' (Xu, 2011, p. 1086). It is true that China's cadre system has been reformed based on its democratic centralism, and also by modern management ideas and practices, which have made the system highly institutionalised (Li, 2001b), but the CCP's top leadership has hardly relaxed its control over appointing, supervising, transferring and demoting leaders of the party-state system at central, provincial and prefectural-municipal levels. Such direct and stringent control over lower-level leadership positions has long been considered by analysts to be 'the major instrument used to make regional officials comply with the central government's policy' (Xu, 2011, p. 1087).

Regardless of whether new leadership management practices, such as the cadre job responsibility system, should be regarded as a political tournament (Han, 2014; He, 2014) or a set of GDP-oriented demonstrations of sectoral and local leadership (A. Wu, 2014; Yu, 2015), the performance-based cadre promotion system, *ganbu renqizhi* (cadre tenure system) and the use of key performance indicators (KPIs) are practical measures for mobilising sectoral and local leaders and bureaucrats, through which new policies can be implemented and accomplished. Of course, such new practices have adverse consequences, resulting in an overheated economy, including runaway urbanisation in many regions, because many local leaders are driven by the 'cadre assessment system', needing to achieve more to meet performance targets (Zhou, 2015, p. 156). In terms of the use of social mobilisation, however, the CCP's dependence on such systems and practices since the early 1980s has already transformed it from having 'ideological legitimacy' ('a state's right to rule is justified by a grand vision based on a future promise') into relying on 'performance legitimacy' (the right to govern is justified by the economic prosperity and security of the nation) (Zhao, 2001, p. 22).

Finally, just like the outdated top-down directive process, the deployment of traditional propaganda and mass media campaigns, including mass persuasion and education that the CCP was famed for before the reform period, has clearly become less frequent and intense (Wang, 1996, 2008; Y. Zhao, 1998). There are many reasons for such change, some obvious and some not easily observable. Apart from the political, cultural and social changes in people's acceptance of traditional propaganda and mass media campaigns, which has developed into widespread dislike and distrust resulting from the misuse of them during the Mao era, two of the above-mentioned changes seem to have a more direct effect than other factors on the mode in which new policies and programs are presented and promoted. The first change is the emergence of numerous financially well-resourced social mobilisations, which has undeniably lessened the difficulty of promoting new policies and initiatives among local governments. The second change that has partly replaced old-style propaganda and mass media campaigns is the changes in decision-making processes, which have been reformed as a positive effect of the post-Mao emphasis on democratic centralism, and even on 'democracy and the legal system' (Wang and Madson, 2013, p. 290). Specifically, new policy initiatives are often developed through repeated negotiations between the central and local governments, which therefore have not only included many incentives for local governments in many new initiatives, but have also made it possible to not rely on traditional promotion methods that are disliked by many people.

As mentioned, the complexity and totality of the recently improved approach to social mobilisation in China need to be considered together with a range of issues that have emerged during China's current rapid transition to an industrial economy. China, as a late industrialised economy, has in recent decades enjoyed more economic development opportunities than developed economies, defined as a 'late-development advantage' (Hu, 2009, p. 40; Lin, 2014, p. 48). That is, China has for a long time been able to identify some of its less-developed areas, compared with developed economies, and find new *zengzhangdian* (economic growth areas) (Qiu, 2009; Nyiri, 2010) because it still enjoys *fazhan kongjian* (spaces for economic expansion) (Ahlers, 2014; Brown, 2015). Since the mid-2000s, amid its rapidly shrinking list of economic expansion opportunities, China has once again turned its attention back to rural social and economic development.

THE THREE RURAL ISSUES AND THE NEW RURAL URBANISATION STRATEGY

As introduced in Chapter 1, China's latest rural development strategy, officially known as the construction of new socialist countryside, was first introduced in two important documents in the second half of 2005, when the CCP had finally finished its first post-Mao, trouble-free leadership transition from Jiang Zemin (1989–2004) to Hu Jintao (2002–12). At first sight, this rural development strategy was part of China's Eleventh Five-Year Plan for the period 2006–10 and its Twelfth Five-Year Plan for 2011–15, but it has also been a preferred national strategy to solve the so-called three rural problems that have always troubled the CCP regime since the founding of the PRC in 1949. The exceptional importance of rural socioeconomic and socio-political issues in China has been substantiated by two historical transitions prior to the 2000s. The Mao-led CCP succeeded in the late 1940s in gaining the power to rule through the Maoist peasant revolution, and the Dengist reforms of the late 1970s and 1980s also began in rural villages through focusing on addressing the difficulties in the lives of hundreds of millions of peasants. China in the early 2000s entered another new era in terms of national leadership and economic development. Among many urgent tasks, the Hu Jintao leadership that emerged from the CCP's Sixteenth National Congress held in November 2002 identified rural China, overlooked by the previous leadership, as a top priority in China's new development programmes, at least in its two Five-Year Plans.

China's current rural problems are often simply called *sannong wenti* (three rural problems), comprising *nongye* (agriculture), *nongcun* (rural villages) and *nongmin* (peasants) (Lu, 2008; Day, 2013). There are several contributors, both individual and institutional, to the formation and popularisation of the concept of *sannong wenti*. In addition, the rural issues have long been the theme of what the Chinese often call 'No. 1 Central Document', referring to the very first document issued by the CCP's Central Committee and China's State Council every year, which is regarded as a policy guideline for key tasks for the year (Qi et al., 2013). A simple calculation reveals that five of such No. 1 documents were issued between 1982 and 1986, and 14 of them have been issued since 2004, including year 2017 (C. Wang, 2016; Wang and Liu, 2016; Dong, 2017). Despite the neglect of rural issues by the Jiang Zemin leadership, which was caused by the turmoil of the late 1980s and its attempts to reform state-owned enterprises, Jiang's successors identified the rural issues as the key area for strategic plans and actions (Lai, 2016).

The new countryside strategy is a result of a range of historical and economic trends in post-Mao China, but consideration should also be given to the party-state leadership at the time it developed and implemented the new countryside strategy. As mentioned above, the strategy emerged when Hu Jintao took over the CCP leadership from Jiang Zemin, and Wen Jiabao succeeded Zhu Rongji as Premier to run the State Council. Because the new leaders adjusted economic policies shortly after the leadership transition, the new policies were widely praised as *Hu–Wen xinzheng* (Hu–Wen new political thinking and approaches). The Chinese phrase *xinzheng* has been used for many centuries in different contexts, but it always refers to important changes favoured by a large proportion of the population. There are many research publications in both Chinese and English on the pro-people, or pro-poor, aspect of the Hu–Wen leadership, praising them for devoting 'more attention to the needs of the lower social classes' (Zheng, 2006, p. 256). This point of view seems to have also been stirred up by the family backgrounds of both Hu and Wen, who are ordinary non-communist and non-revolutionary families. While personalities and other personal features can sometimes matter more than the institutions they lead, this point of view discounts the importance of socioeconomic and socio-political development as a driving force in policy change and development.

The identification and selection of rural issues as the top priority in China's domestic economic development strategy are ultimately based on the logic of economic development. Besides the changes in urban–rural population distribution as illustrated in Figure 2.3, revealing that more people are moving out of villages, the income disparity between rural and urban residents in China has grown so much that since the 2000s the country has become 'one of the most unequal societies in the world' (Gul and Lu, 2011, p. 102). As shown in Figure 2.4, the rural–urban income disparity has actually been growing since the mid-1980s, but it had become so large by the early 2000s that political leaders need to take decisive action.

Such serious inequalities have worsened since China entered an advanced stage of industrialisation, which enabled the party-state leadership to pay more attention to the agricultural and rural development problems, and also to invest in various rural development projects, including the abolition of all agricultural taxes announced by Premier Wen Jiabao in early 2005. Of course, the increased attention on rural problems and various investments made by the central government are depicted in the traditional left-wing discourse as an active initiative by the CCP to generously help peasants in times of economic hardship. Many Chinese researchers, including policy analysts, however, do not reflect these changes from a political moral perspective, or in terms of being active or passive. More analyses have been undertaken from a rational choice standpoint or a political-economic point of view. Specifically, the new strategic focus on rural problems and development is not simply a result of the increasingly

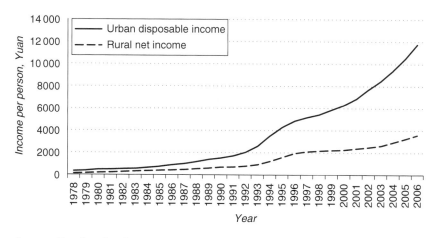

Source: Based on data from NBSC (2016).

Figure 2.4   China's rural–urban income gap, 1978–2006

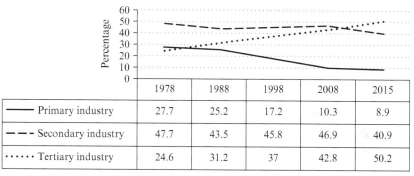

	1978	1988	1998	2008	2015
—— Primary industry	27.7	25.2	17.2	10.3	8.9
– – – Secondary industry	47.7	43.5	45.8	46.9	40.9
· · · · · · Tertiary industry	24.6	31.2	37	42.8	50.2

Year

Source: Based on data from NBSC (2016).

Figure 2.5   China's GDP across three sectors, 1978–2015

widening income gap between rural and urban residents, but because of numerous macroeconomic and macro-political changes in China.

The most important context in which China's *sannong wenti* (three rural problems) have been addressed is the particular stage of Chinese economic development. As briefly noted in the Preface, China was near the post-industrial stage of economic expansion in 2005 when the new strategy was developed. As shown in Figure 2.5, which needs to be read alongside

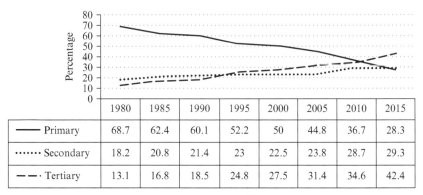

	1980	1985	1990	1995	2000	2005	2010	2015
—— Primary	68.7	62.4	60.1	52.2	50	44.8	36.7	28.3
······· Secondary	18.2	20.8	21.4	23	22.5	23.8	28.7	29.3
— —· Tertiary	13.1	16.8	18.5	24.8	27.5	31.4	34.6	42.4

Year

Source: Based on data from NBSC (2016).

Figure 2.6   Percentages of employment across three sectors, 1980–2015

Figures 2.3 and 2.4, China's transition to a post-industrial economy was completed a few years ago, as the service (tertiary) sector accounted for more than 50 per cent of its GDP (NBSC, 2016), a few percentage points higher than the GDP contribution from the construction and manufacturing (secondary) sectors. At the same time, China's agricultural sector (the primary sector) has become less important in its economic weight.

Structural changes in occupation, and therefore in employment, have been another essential dimension of the coming of a post-industrial society (Bell, 1976; Ross, 1991). Because of the general transformation revealed in Figure 2.5, a rapidly growing service sector in China has also resulted in a gradual increase in employment in service industries. Figure 2.6 confirms the occupational change, while also showing that the tertiary sector is now the single largest source of employment in the country. Although such change is commonly believed to be correlated to upward occupational mobility, it also indirectly shows the economic pressure on the lives of hundreds of millions of peasants in terms of jobs and income.

Under all these circumstances, the central party-state leadership must make adjustments to its development strategy. Despite the positive comments in the media, many critical Chinese analysts and researchers believe that the formation of the new rural strategy is still predominantly driven by China's new political mentality, if not party-political doctrine or ideology, which is focused on GDP and the related cadre evaluation system (Wu, 2014; Yu, 2015). In the minds of Chinese people, this has applied to all leadership levels, including the central leadership, since Deng Xiaoping's southern inspection tour in 1992 when he warned that 'whoever doesn't reform will have to step down' (Bao, 2015, n.p.). Being hungry for higher GDP growth turned the attention of central and local leaders to rural issues, which since the early 2000s has been employed, in the words of some critical Chinese, as *jiuming daocao* (the last straw to clutch at) to maintain economic momentum.

More than ten years have passed since the rural development issue was prioritised in China's Eleventh Five-Year Plan. This decade-long process has proven to be the new *zengzhangdian* (economic growth areas), not as useless as *jiuming daocao* in keeping the economy afloat. From the three rural problems to the new countryside strategy, the Hu Jintao leadership succeeded in obtaining high levels of commitment and performance among local bureaucrats. The core strategic thinking behind the new countryside plan continues to be upheld and is still used by the Xi Jinping leadership. Table 2.3 shows evidence of the persistence of this strategic focus in the 14 successive No. 1 Documents issued by the CCP's Central Committee and the State Council since 2004. It is evident that the rural economic development has not only been part of China's long-term strategy, but has also always been regarded as 'the problems to be solved urgently' (Qi et al., 2013, p. 230).

Each central document is supplemented with some additional documents in the form of guidelines, amendments or procedures, from either the CCP's institutions or the government system, which could also take place before the decision is made or, more often, afterwards. Because of such practices, this book will use this type of documentary evidence in two ways. Some initial policy measures introduced in the early years of the campaign in 2004 and 2005 will be detailed in this section. All the other measures and supplementary changes and instructions that the central decision-makers have issued since 2006 to regulate the rural urbanisation drive will be introduced as appropriate for discussion in later chapters.

As listed in Table 2.3, the new socialist countryside strategy, or the new rural urbanisation drive as far as this book is concerned, became official in 2006, and some publications have considered the issue from this point in time (Ahlers and Schubert, 2009; Looney, 2015). Policy analysts and researchers in China, however, often begin their analyses with the State Council's document No. 28, issued in October 2004. As part of the preparation for introducing the new rural development plan that was then still under internal discussion and consultation, the 2004 document entitled 'Decisions on deepening reforms and strengthening land management' (Lin, 2009, p. 318) stressed the urgency of putting real effort into the control of the land use in rural areas 'in very strict language' (Trappel, 2016, p. 62). This document appears to be a usual central government directive

Table 2.3   Key strategic ideas of 'No. 1 Document' from 2004

Year	The title of 'No. 1 Document'
2004	Policy suggestions for boosting peasant incomes
2005	Policy suggestions for further strengthening rural work and improving the overall production capacity of agriculture
2006	Policy suggestions for promoting the construction of a socialist new countryside
2007	Policy suggestions for actively developing modern agriculture and firmly advancing the construction of the socialist new countryside
2008	Policy suggestions for earnestly strengthening the agricultural infrastructural construction and further advancing the agricultural development and the increase of peasant incomes
2009	Policy suggestions for advancing a stable agricultural development and the sustainable increase of peasant incomes
2010	Policy suggestions for expanding the strength of coordinated urban and rural development and further consolidating the foundation of agricultural development
2011	Resolution on speedy development of water conservation
2012	Policy suggestions for speedily advancing agricultural scientific innovation and continuously strengthening the supply capacity of agricultural produces
2013	Policy suggestions for accelerating agricultural modernisation and further strengthening rural development vitality
2014	Policy suggestions for comprehensively deepening rural reforms and accelerating agricultural modernisation
2015	Policy suggestions for expanding the strength of reform and innovation and accelerating agricultural modernisation
2016	Policy suggestions for implementing new development ideas, and accelerating agricultural modernisation, and achieving the goal of building a comprehensive well-off society
2017	Policy suggestions for advancing agricultural supply-side structural reforms and accelerating the cultivation of new driving forces for the development of agriculture and rural areas

Source: Based on data from China's Ministry of Agriculture (http://www.moa.gov.cn/ztzl/yhwj2017/).

to cool down the overheated housing and construction market, but more significantly, it has since placed a very rigid restriction on land use, and therefore on the widely used land finance. Specifically, this document introduced a new approach to land use, which has been known confusingly as *zengjian guagou*, the literal meaning of which is 'bundling up addition with reduction' (Ye and Qin, 2015, p. 261; Han and Wei, 2015, p. 276). As an abbreviated phrase for the state policy of 'interlocking the regulation of urban and rural construction land', the real meaning of *zengjian guagou* is about 'allow[ing] for urban expansion only if at least the same area of rural construction land is being recultivated' to prevent further decreases of the total area of farmland (Meyer-Clement, 2016, p. 121).

The State Council's circular, No. 28 of 2004, was a crucial step in developing the policy framework for the new rural strategy, but it also raised two sets of serious dilemmas: the local governments' dependence on land finance and the *zengjian guagou* policy; and 'the green light to take rural construction land for urban development' as discussed by Kristen Looney (2012, p. 276) and the repeatedly revised regulations on the land requisition for construction and land-use conversion, which will be discussed next. That is, the rural urbanisation scheme had already been steered into a rather narrow course between Charybdis and Scylla even before being formally launched at the Fifth Plenum of the CCP's Sixteenth Central Committee in late October 2005.

Because of the complexity and scale of the new rural development strategy, as well as the sophistication of its implementation, the social mobilisation mechanism needed to ensure that this multi-purpose strategy was properly implemented, or at least is not badly compromised. In the words of one Beijing-based policy specialist, the role of the CCP's central leadership and its government in leading the country had changed after a few rounds of decentralisation, plus their wish to maintain local enthusiasm for better GDP figures, and all they could do was draw red lines, affirming what they wanted to do and what red lines provinces were not permitted to cross (X. Chen, 2013). In 2004 and 2005, all the preparatory efforts made to introduce the new countryside plan focused on solving the previously mentioned two dilemmas created by two new red lines.

The first dilemma, which is also the first reason to utilise the social mobilisation mechanism, has been mainly caused by the new land-use restrictions on *tudi caizheng* (land finance) that has been used by local governments to extract a rather large proportion of their revenues from the sale of land-use rights since the 1994 fiscal reform. In addition to what was briefly noted earlier in this chapter, the 1994 fiscal reform is also generally called the tax-sharing reform, which has divided taxes into three types: central taxes, shared taxes and local taxes (Chan et al., 2008; A. Chen, 2015). The last one includes about a dozen taxes, especially the taxes on the uses of arable land and urban land, all of which are paid to local governments. Such tax revenues are important for local governments to function and fund other local projects. The notion of *tudi caizheng* has since entered China's policy discourse, and this way of increasing revenues for local purposes has become a huge incentive for local governments.

Though the State Council's 2004 circular has in fact made the land transfer and sale more legitimate, the strict rule of 'linking the contraction of rural construction land with the expansion of urban construction land' (M. Cai, 2015, p. 73) has added new rigid restrictions that local government must follow while raising revenues from selling and transferring land-use rights. This *zengjian guagou* policy was new then, and in the words of Zhou Qiren, a well-known policy analyst in China, this policy focus on the rural land transfer and sale was then in the process of being elevated from a political slogan to a policy target first, then further upgraded to a law, and in 2004, it was finally elevated to be one of China's few *guoce* (a fundamental state policy) (Zhou, 2013). Under such circumstances, the party-state bureaucracies need to be mobilised to not only implement the new strategy, but also steer it smoothly between the red lines.

The second dilemma that has also required the utilisation of social mobilisation was created by another new policy, called *zhaijidi zhihuan* ('the exchange of rural housing-land use rights for urban commodity housing') (Sato et al., 2013, p. 96). This new policy rule is part of the repeatedly revised regulations on land requisition for construction and land-use conversion, but it has been a big challenge for many rural residents who want to upgrade their living conditions. This is not only because many could not afford it in the 2000s, or did not want to spend too much of their hard-earned savings on relocating themselves into modern apartment buildings, but also because many rural families are reluctantly giving up their housing-land use rights. This has been a difficult task. There have been outcries, nationally and internationally, about the living conditions of Chinese peasants in the early 2000s, but insufficient analysis has been conducted to understand how the rural housing-land rights have slowed down the process of moving to better housing conditions. Unlike urban household registration holders, each rural household in China is allocated a piece of land for building their house, and because of the increasingly tight control over land use, the housing lands or housing sites (*zhaijidi*) have become part of the rural development strategy. Local governments are now allowed to convert rural construction land for urban construction use, and the easy way of achieving it is to 'make occupied rural construction land available for ownership conversion' (M. Cai, 2015, p. 74). Thus, rural households must be persuaded and convinced to give up their housing-land rights. But before such social mobilisation reaches out to villages, especially rural households and some village-based groups, local governments at provincial, municipal (previously called prefectural) and county levels need to be mobilised to promote this new policy measure actively, creatively and honestly, promoting it as an opportunity for rural residents to improve their housing conditions quickly and economically.

Since 2005 when this rural strategy was endorsed at the Fifth Plenum of the CCP's Sixteenth Central Committee as part of the Eleventh Five-Year Plan (2006–10), local governments have been playing a more significant role than the central leadership in executing the new rural strategy and contributing to the solutions of this specific but difficult rural problem.

NOTES

1. To have a better understanding of this part of Chinese history, readers can read more about the *Yangwu Yundong* (the Westernisation Movement) (1861–95) of the late Qing (Huters, 2005; Scott, 2008) and the *Wusi Yundong* (the May Fourth Movement) in 1919 (Schwarcz, 1986; Eastman, 1991; Lee, 1991). The latter was characterised by 'the attack on sentimental attachment to tradition with slogans like "Welcome Mr. Science and Mr. Democracy" and "Down with the rotten band of Confucian shopkeepers"' (Schwarcz, 1986, p. 125), and since then young Chinese intellectuals, including many first-generation members of the CCP, have been heavily influenced by imported foreign ideas.
2. Michael Loewe once argued, 'it has been convenient and customary to consider the history of China in terms of dynastic changes and chronological divisions . . . As political frameworks can rarely, if ever, exist without a philosophical basis, it would be improper to disregard dynastic changes entirely when considering religious or intellectual history' (Loewe, 2005, pp. 2–3). For more information about this perspective, readers are referred to the following books: Terrill (2003) and Zarrow (2012).
3. The death of Zhou Enlai in January 1976 and the popular support for the 'four-modernisations' that Zhou put forward in his last government report in 1975 triggered off a mass occupation of Tiananmen Square in the week leading up to the traditional Qingming Festival (also known as Tomb-Sweeping Day or Pure Brightness Festival) in early April 1976 (Watson, 1994; Baum, 1994). This Tiananmen incident laid the foundation for Deng Xiaoping's return to power and China's adoption of reform policies. Because of the latter, this Tiananmen event played a more direct role in changing the course of Chinese politics than another Tiananmen protest in June 1989. Interested readers can read more about it in Goodman (1994) and Baum (1994).
4. There is no sufficient explanation in English publications of *xuefan*, or *xue fan*, as a traditional Chinese political culture and practice. Qizhi Zhang once simply described it as 'the policy of weakening kingdoms (Xue Fan) pioneered by Emperor Wen of Han and Emperor Jing of Han' (Zhang, 2015, p. 166). What is also important in traditional Chinese political culture are *junxianzhi* (a unified and centralised political system with local administrative prefectures and counties) and *fengjianzhi* (a system of giving land in exchange for loyalty, which is nowadays commonly called feudalism) (Hao and Lin, 1994, p. 1). For more general background information about it, readers are referred to the following books: Waldron (1993), Mote (2003), Filipiak (2015) and Lorge (2015).
5. There are many mentions of *beijiu shi bingquan* in English publications. Jianying Zha offered the following explanation:

    > [It] is an allusion to the most famous banquet in Chinese history: Zhao Kuangyin, the first emperor of the Song Dynasty, grew uneasy with the powerful top generals who had helped him to win many bloody battles on the way to his throne, so he invited them to a banquet, where he stripped them of their military powers over a cup of liquor. (Zha, 1995, p. 167)

    Interested readers can read more in Ho (1992) and Lorge (2015).
6. The elimination of *sanzhongren* (three kinds of people) that the post-1978 CCP leadership wanted to do is not only 'hardly recorded' (Gao, 2016, p. 155), but is also

under-researched and poorly understood by many China specialists. Dittmer correctly notes that 'Deng did not press for a sweeping purge of radicals from the middle and lower bureaucracy' at the time because of the worry of splitting the CCP (Dittmer, 1987, p. 231). This is now believed by numerous Chinese commentators to be the main reason for the Mao Zedong fever that has frequently taken place in China for many years, and to be a hidden problem for China's near future. Interested readers can read more about it in Friedman (1995) and Zhao (2004).

3. The politics of social mobilisation at the provincial level

This chapter turns attention to how provincial CCP organisations and government offices are mobilised to promote and implement the new rural urbanisation strategy and how they have subsequently mobilised socio-political, institutional and financial resources inside and outside the system to support the implementation of the national strategy. As mentioned in Chapters 1 and 2, the empirical analyses of this book are based on a variety of experiences of Shandong, an eastern province in northern China, and its geographic location is shown in Figure 2.1 in Chapter 2. The provincial bureaucracy is part of the local governance system in a general sense, but it often plays a more crucial function in governance than the central leadership and bureaucracy. This is partly because the population size and land area, as well as the scale of local economy, are very large in some provinces; many are larger than some leading industrialised countries (Bo, 2015). For this reason, the role of provinces in China's socioeconomic development has now become an active area of research, which has led to the emergence of some inspiring perspectives, such as local state corporatism (Oi, 1992; Goodman, 2015), de facto federalism (Zheng, 2007) and subnational perspectives (Rithmire, 2014). As also noted in Chapter 1, due to the complexities of China's party-state systems and the sizes of provincial populations and economies, this analysis of the current use of the social mobilisation mechanism in China needs to include a consideration of what would happen at the province level.

Because of the special importance of the provincial bureaucracies, this chapter will analyse their roles in nationwide social mobilisation and their way of conducting it at the intersection of two vital functions that the provincial bureaucracies usually play in China's massive and complicated party-state systems: policy implementation and policy innovation. These are the two basic perspectives, and the main clues guiding the study of the complex politics of social mobilisation at the provincial level. This is because on the one hand, they must play the principal function and implement the policies decided by the central leadership, and on the other hand, policy innovation at this level can not only help demonstrate their capacity for governing and future leadership, but also identify the best way to satisfy local needs and interests. Therefore, this chapter will focus on how social mobilisation is organised, especially how the new policy is eventually translated into political power, action and a form of new local politics in the province. The first section introduces some background information about Shandong and its past involvement in the formation of national rural polices. The second section examines the routine efforts by provincial bureaucracies to implement the new countryside plan, with attention given to how their roles are shaped by their position within the entire bureaucratic system. The third and final section of this chapter looks at the creative policy implementation and local decision-making by provincial bureaucracies, which have created various types of dynamics to direct and drive the implementation of the new rural strategy in Shandong.

THE PROVINCE OF SHANDONG

Shandong province is located on the east coast of the north China plain and around the estuary of the Yellow River. Known casually as Shandong, which means 'east of mountains', referring to the Taihangshan range in northern China, the province is China's second most populous province, with around 98.5 million people at the end of 2015, roughly 10 million less than the total population of Guangdong, formerly known as Kwangtung or Canton (NBSC, 2016). A group of China analysts have repeatedly warned that when examining regional issues in China, special care and attention need to be given to the size of land area, population size and other factors that may affect local economic development strategy and politics. In the case of Shandong, its land area is relatively small by Chinese standards, about 157 100 square kilometres, which is also smaller than France, Germany and Britain. The total population of Shandong, however, is approximately 18 million larger than that of Germany and about 30 per cent larger than that of France and the UK.

Shandong is well known for its ancient history and its considerable economic weight in contemporary China. Historically and culturally, Shandong is the birthplace of Confucius (551–479 BC) and some other key contributors to the formation of Confucianism as China's most influential indigenous philosophical tradition, including Mencius (372–289 BC).[1] Lao-Tzu (604–484 BC), the legendary founder of Taoism (or Daoism) as the second indigenous belief system in China, was also believed to be born in the province of Shandong. At the time when Confucianism and Taoism were formed, there was an emergence of a different school of philosophical thought, which is Mohism or Moism, and its originator, Mo-tzu (470–391 BC), was also born in Shandong. It is not often now that Shandong can claim to be the cradle of Chinese civilisation, but it is the proud birthplace of the most influential Chinese philosophical thinkers and traditions. That is why Shandong often proudly labels its local culture as Qi-Lu Culture (also spelt as Qilu Culture), named after the ancient State of Qi (1122–211 BC) in the vast northern region of present-day Shandong, and the State of Lu (1100–771 BC) in the south of present-day Shandong (Li, 2013; Zhang, 2015). Although the State of Qi was bigger and stronger than the State of Lu, the latter is used as the abbreviated name of Shandong, as Confucius and Mencius were both born in the State of Lu. The single character 'Lu' is therefore used everywhere in Shandong, on car registration plates and in many company names.

In the contemporary era, Shandong has been a critical province for China's economic expansion in terms of both agriculture and industry. As shown in Figure 3.1, Shandong has been ranked as one of the top three provinces in China in terms of GDP.

For almost two decades, Shandong has been statistically graded as the most productive agricultural province in China. It has also been modernised to be the largest food-manufacturing province, accounting for about 17 per cent of China's total processed food production in 2015, and food exports, which reached as much as 25 per cent of China's total food exports in 2015 (Guo, 2002; Sun, 2016). As one of China's traditional agriculture regions, Shandong is famous for not only growing wheat, corn, sweet potato, soybeans, millet, rice and sorghum, but also cotton, peanuts, leaf tobacco, apples and pears, among other produce. Such a big population and huge agricultural outputs have, for a long time, carried political implications for Shandong's leaders and officials working at both the provincial and sub-provincial levels.

As documented in the long, serialised article 'Mao Zedong and Shandong', written by a retired senior official from the provincial bureaucracy, Shandong came to the attention of central leaders soon after the founding of the PRC, especially after the late 1950s when the Chinese economy started running into grave trouble (Gao, 2011). Mao Zedong inspected Shandong many times during the 1950s and 1960s, which set a new tradition for the party-state leadership of selecting experienced local leaders from Shandong for the central leadership or its organisations, and identifying in Shandong successful examples of implementing new policies, trialling new programmes and creating local initiatives. The central leadership has long been using various Shandong practices to guide agricultural activities nationwide. Although Mao Zedong decided in 1964 to vigorously promote two economic models based on the experiences of two other regions he had never visited, which were reflected in his famous slogan: 'In agriculture, learn from Dazhai! In industry, learn

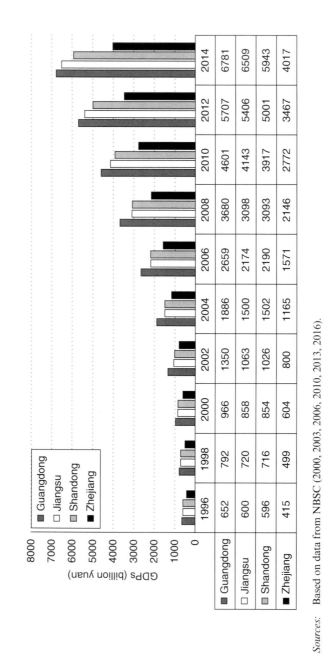

	1996	1998	2000	2002	2004	2006	2008	2010	2012	2014
■ Guangdong	652	792	966	1350	1886	2659	3680	4601	5707	6781
□ Jiangsu	600	720	858	1063	1500	2174	3098	4143	5406	6509
▨ Shandong	596	716	854	1026	1502	2190	3093	3917	5001	5943
■ Zhejiang	415	499	604	800	1165	1571	2146	2772	3467	4017

Sources: Based on data from NBSC (2000, 2003, 2006, 2010, 2013, 2016).

Figure 3.1 Shandong's GDP compared to other rich provinces, 1996–2014

from Daqing' (Cheng, 1982, p. 103),[2] Mao had paid much more attention to rural Shandong than to other regions. For this reason, the province has often been used a *shidian* (trial or experimental) field for China's new rural policies or related programmes (Gao, 2011). It was in Shandong that Mao Zedong formed and proposed his clear idea of the People's Commune in 1958 as a new way to organise rural production (J. Liu, 2010).[3]

Shandong was set neither by Mao as a model for managing rural society and economy as Dazhai was, nor by Deng Xiaoping as a reformist model to introduce the household production responsibility system to replace the Maoist People's Commune in the late 1970s as both Anhui and Sichuan provinces were,[4] and the local Yantai leadership was reluctant in the early 1980s to establish the Dengist household production responsibility system in the Yantai region. Yet many Shandong officials have been promoted since the 1990s to the central party-state leadership to take care of agricultural economy and many other reform schemes (B. Chen, 2012). This phenomenon is not only because of the economic weight of Shandong's agriculture in the whole country, but more importantly because of the rich experiences that many Shandong officials acquired from the province. In fact, the current rural urbanisation strategy was tested first before it was officially implemented nationwide, and Shandong was once again chosen as a *shidian* (pilot) province to try the new scheme. That is, Shandong's good records in managing agriculture and related sectors have brought more opportunities to the province.

In addition to its productive agricultural sector, Shandong has also developed a sizable industry since the 1960s. As shown in Table 3.1, Shandong's industrial gross output value in 1949 was only slightly less than half of its agricultural gross output value. The change seems to have taken place in the early 1960s, when its industry generated more than agriculture, forestry, livestock and fisheries. Its industrial sector had developed over the ten-year period of the Cultural Revolution (1966–76), because in 1970, its gross output value was already slightly more than double that from the agricultural sector. Since the late 1980s and early 1990s, Shandong's economy has become an industrial one, although its agriculture is still of strategic importance to the national economy.

The figures shown in the second half of Table 3.1 are rather useful for explaining a peculiar phenomenon that has yet to be systematically studied, which is that unlike in other regions, among Shandong people there appears to be an absence of disapproval and condemnation of Maoist practices from the 1950s to the mid-1970s. In other words, just like the above-mentioned response of the Yantai leadership to the rural reform policy in the late 1970s, Dengist policies are, in general, not enthusiastically hailed by a large ratio of Shandong people. Because of reasonable agricultural yields in

Table 3.1   Shandong's gross industrial and agricultural output (billion yuan), 1949–2015

Year*	Agriculture#	Industry
1949	2.007	0.915
1955	4.497	3.010
1962	3.832	4.570
1965	5.049	7.138
1970	6.678	14 122
1975	9.343	18 978
1980	16 091	34 032
1985	33 542	68 278
1990	64 575	220 085
1995	167 816	890 660
2000	229 435	1 250 953
2005	374 181	3 538 743
2010	665 094	8 385 140
2015	954 963	14 596 420

Notes:
* Pre-1970 figures are not listed in five-year intervals.
# Agriculture includes forestry, livestock and fisheries.

Source: Based on data from SPBS (2016).

many regions of Shandong, there are even many people who have almost no memory of famines suffered in China in the 1960s. In fact, one of China's most militant current critics of post-Mao reforms, Zhang Hongliang, is originally from Shandong, and his understanding of pre-reform China is partly influenced by Shandong's relatively better economic conditions than other provinces (Su and Link, 2013; Anderlini, 2016). Such economic conditions have shaped Shandong's socio-political culture, resulting in a general leaning towards left-wing and Maoist ideas.

Figure 3.2 is based on the data in Table 3.1, with the intent of offering a clearer picture of Shandong's continuous industrial expansion while it has maintained its productive agriculture. To show the correlations between the two sectors clearly, Figure 3.2 is logarithmically scaled.

Shandong's industry has, for a long time, been ranked as China's third largest, after Jiangsu and Guangdong as shown in Figure 3.1. The latest data from the NBSC has, however, shown that Shandong is more competitive than before. This improvement can be assessed from three perspectives or using three sets of figures. First, in terms of the total number of enterprises, there were 383 148 in China in 2015. However, about 11 per

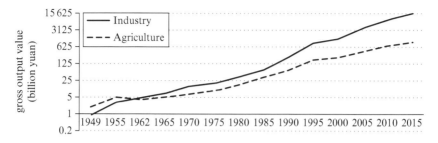

Source: Based on data from SPBS (2016).

Figure 3.2 Shandong's gross industrial and agricultural output values, 1949–2015

cent of them were in Shandong (41 485 precisely), after Jiangsu (48 488) and Guangdong (42 113). Second, in terms of the total industrial assets, China had industrial assets worth RMB 102 339.80 billion in 2015, and in the same year Shandong had total assets worth RMB 10 134.40 billion, which is smaller than Jiangsu (10 706.20), but much larger than Guangdong (9541.10). Third, China's total national industrial profits have fallen for two successive years from its peak of RMB 6 837.90 billion in 2013 to RMB 6618.70 billion in 2015, but Shandong's input to the profits in 2015 was worth RMB 886 billion, less than Jiangsu (969 billion), but more than Guangdong (772 billion) (NBSC, 2016). That is, Shandong contributed more than 13 per cent of the national total industrial profits in 2015, positioning it as the second most productive industrial province in China. In fact, as recently as March 2017, Chinese premier, Li Keqiang, praised Shandong for creating more than one million new jobs in its cities and towns in 2016, approximately equivalent to 10 per cent of the national total, while at the same time achieving a GDP growth rate of 7.6 per cent, almost 1 per cent higher than the national growth rate (6.7 per cent) (*Xinhua News*, 2017a).

Shandong's industry is well diversified after a few decades of development, producing a very wide range of goods ranging from Tsingtao beer, Changyu wine, white goods and consumer electronics (such as Haier and Hisense), to coal and petroleum, and heavy machinery. Table 3.2 shows the expansion of Shandong's industry, especially gross output vales of light and heavy industries.

As revealed in Table 3.2, Shandong's light industry was much larger than its heavy industry before the 1960s, when Tsingtao beer and textile products were very famous. The discovery of oil reserves (the Shengli

Table 3.2 *Gross output values of Shandong's light and heavy industries (million yuan), 1949–2015*

Year	Industry in total	Light industry	Heavy industry
1949	915	825	90
1955	3010	2536	474
1962	4570	3122	1448
1965	7138	4821	2317
1970	14122	8188	5934
1975	18978	9665	9313
1980	34032	18381	15651
1985	68278	37041	31287
1990	220085	111876	108209
1995	890660	440384	450276
2000	1150953	596470	654483
2005	3538743	1312413	2226330
2010	8385140	2716178	5668961
2015	14596420	4677590	9918830

Note: Pre-1970 figures are not listed in five-year intervals.

Source: Based on data from SPBS (2016).

Oilfield) in the early 1960s and the subsequent production in the mid-1960s turned Shandong into not only an industrial province (see also Table 3.1), but also into a heavy industrial one. As China's second largest oilfield, the Shengli Oilfield supplied about 20 per cent of the country's total oil production (Chung, 1997) for many years. A Shandong provincial government paper has also revealed that there are 136 large enterprises in Shandong, accounting for almost 50 per cent of its total gross output value (SEITC, 2010). Such enterprises are called *longtou* (dragon head) enterprises in Chinese (Brown et al., 2005; Schneider, 2017) and they are important to the province's economy. Their role in social mobilisation will be discussed in Chapter 4.

To manage and support its massive and productive agricultural and industrial economies, by Chinese standards, Shandong has also staffed the huge party-state apparatus as detailed below in Table 3.3. The first two bigger urban centres listed in Table 3.3 are the so-called *fushengji* (literally, deputy-provincial or sub-provincial level) cities, and they are hierarchically different from all the other 15 municipal centres, which are equivalent to what was previously called the prefectural region. As the home city of numerous productive enterprises, Qingdao (Tsingtao, or even Ch'ing-tao,

Table 3.3   Lower-level governments under Shandong, 2015

Prefectural-municipal governments	Population (million)	No. of county-level governments	No. of township-level governments
Ji'nan*	7.1	7 districts and 3 counties	143
Qingdao*	9.1	6 districts and 4 cities#	145
Binzhou	3.9	2 districts and 5 counties	91
Dezhou	5.7	2 districts, 2 cities and 7 counties	134
Dongying	2.1	3 districts and 2 counties	40
Heze	8.5	2 districts and 7 counties	168
Jining	8.3	2 districts, 2 cities and 7 counties	156
Laiwu	1.4	2 districts	20
Liaocheng	6.0	1 district, 1 city and 6 counties	135
Linyi	10.3	3 districts and 9 counties	156
Rizhao	2.9	2 districts and 2 counties	55
Tai'an	5.6	2 districts, 2 cities and 2 counties	88
Weifang	9.3	4 districts, 6 cities and 2 counties	118
Weihai	2.8	2 districts and 2 cities	71
Yantai	7.0	4 districts, 7 cities and 1 county	154
Zaozhuang	3.9	5 districts and 1 city	64
Zibo	4.6	5 districts and 3 counties	88

Notes:
* The city is at *fushengji* (deputy-provincial level, or sub-provincial level).
# Cities are at the county-level.

Source: Based on data from SPBS (2016).

as it was once spelled), was given a special fiscal status in 1987 as a *jihua danlie* (separate planning) city. While it sounds like a privilege for these important cities to be free from 'the province's patronage and power', in fact it was to put some high-yield cities under the control of the central government, so they would act against the 'financial clout and autonomy at the local levels' (Solinger, 2015, p. 211).

Politics does not simply take place between the central leadership and provincial-level governments. Sub-provincial governments at all levels detailed in Table 3.3 are another major source of political tension, which should be considered more complex, difficult and widespread than inter-governmental politics. By the end of 2015, Shandong had 17 prefectural-municipal governments, under which there were 137 county-level governments, including many urban district governments, and 1826 township-level governments as also listed in Table 3.3 (SPBS, 2016). In simple and functional terms, such multi-level governments are meant to be an institutional strength because they are key, valuable instruments in social and economic development, and crucial resources for any social mobilisation effort. However, various local interests, different methods of realising different goals and diverse socio-political sentiments have not only become sources of tension among individuals, groups and organisations, but also permanent features of local politics in present-day China. Internal tensions could be intensified or complicated by a range of contributing factors, but three of them are very basic to a better understanding of the use of the social mobilisation mechanism.

First, as various early studies found, tensions are regularly caused by two parallel party and state structures. Although some reform efforts have been made in the post-Mao years to prevent these structures from affecting reform programmes, this dual-structure arrangement has evolved little since their inception. This is partly because that in the context of Chinese politics, this dual-structure arrangement is believed to play a crucial balancing role.

Second, local governments and officials are found to be increasingly dependent on local economic activities for incomes and a range of rewards, including career promotion and tenure (Li and Cheng, 2012; Fewsmith, 2013). For this reason, local politics now often takes place in the name of the local economy or the welfare of local people. New practices and rules, both official and informal, have been formed based on such local reasons and new dynamics. As pointed out in earlier chapters, Chinese politics is no longer based on ideology, but on political bargaining and negotiation among competing interest groups seeking their shares of benefits and power. One might argue that 'routine Chinese politics is exclusively a matter of relations among carders and officials' (Pye, 1968, p. 198) or that it is essentially the art of control (Lam, 2015). It would also make sense if regarding Chinese politics as a way of transferring benefits (Pei, 2016) or as a series of power–benefit exchanges (Y. Cai, 2015). However, it could be misleading to consider local governments in China narrowly from only an ideological viewpoint. This was common before the mid-1980s, and it is still used by numerous media outlets that are politicised, lazy and resource-poor, which may prevent readers from forming a better understanding of China's economy and politics.

Third, the tensions among sub-provincial governmental units and their bureaucrats are often created and intensified when they are confronted with unexpected changes and tasks. The new countryside drive in the mid-2000s was one such a challenge for sub-provincial bureaucracies.

PROVINCIAL BUREAUCRATIC ROUTINES

Thanks to its economic weight, as well as its experience and political orientation, Shandong was chosen to be one of five pilot provinces to trial the new socialist countryside scheme, especially the new land-use policy of *zengjian guagou* (linking the reduction of rural construction land with the increase of urban construction land). The central leadership shifted its policy focus towards rural issues, as indicated in 2004's 'No. 1 Central Document' listed in Table 2.3. A few months after the central document, the State Council issued its circular, No. 28 document, 'Decision on deepening reform and strengthening the land administration' (OECD, 2005, p. 70). In 2005, China's Ministry of Land and Resources issued its No. 207 directives, 'Suggestions on regulating the pilot projects of linking the increase of urban construction land with the reduction of rural construction land' (Ye and LeGates, 2013, p. 384). This second document clearly states that Shandong was among a few provinces that had earlier applied for the opportunity to be a pilot site for the new scheme. In fact, Shandong provincial leadership acted before the Ministry of Land and Resources, and issued its 2004, No. 116 directives only a few weeks after the State Council's No. 28 circular (World Bank, 2006). It was because of such a positive response that Shandong was officially named by the Ministry of Land and Resources in 2006 to be the pilot site. This section looks at what the provincial government has done to mobilise its bureaucratic teams to implement the new scheme since the initial stage, focusing on routine practices and efforts made by provincial bureaucracies.

There are obvious changes to the way in which the social mobilisation mechanism has been used in post-1978 China. Chinese researchers introduced the social mobilisation concept into China in the early 2000s, and many of them reached a shared understanding that ideology and revolutionary politics, such as class struggles, are no longer the driving forces of social mobilisation. Many of them also believe that campaign-style governance is no longer dominant, and social mobilisations in China are now driven by many forces (E. Chen, 2015; Wen, 2017). The hierarchical top-down process and outdated campaign-style governance have, therefore, also been transformed and updated. One of the changes is the routinisation and standardisation of institutional communication and organisational procedures in terms of conveying information and guiding lower-level governments.

In studying the role of the provincial government in promoting the new countryside scheme, seven routine methods have been identified: communicating documents; holding work conferences; media promotion; training key leaders; arranging personnel; arranging resources; and gathering feedback.

Communicating Documents

Communicating documents, directives and the like from higher levels of the party-state system (*wenjian chuanda*) is an important practice in Chinese political life and bureaucratic operations. The practice was discussed by non-Chinese scholars before the phrase became a noun, when it was expressed as *chuanda wenjian* (document reading or study sessions) (Liang and Shapiro, 1984). Now the term is used to refer to conveying, studying and discussing key documents of the party-state system.[5] To meet the basic requirement for each lower-level leadership to respond to their superiors, numerous meetings have been held to inform and explain the new rural plan. There are so many meetings that no local official can accurately recall how many meetings, big and small, they have had to discuss the documents and meeting minutes regarding the new policy. One of the most serious policy changes caused by the scheme is *zengjian guagou* (the restrictions on the use of construction land). For implementing this important policy alone, a string of so-called central work conferences held by the central leadership have discussed the land-use issue over the past ten or so years. Table 3.4 lists some of the central conferences that have contributed to the construction land-use policy according to media reports and analysis by policy analysts. According to local officials and researchers in Shandong, each central conference is normally followed by a few dozen meetings at sub-national levels to pass on key messages.

Though there are different understandings of the transfer or trading of surplus land quotes in China, which remain to be explored, Table 3.4 evidently reveals a rather rapid and pressurised process for central and provincial decision-makers to continue perfecting the policy design of the new rural scheme. In addition to countless meetings to convey key policy changes made at higher levels, lower-level governments usually also issue their own circulars or other forms of documents to spread information in writing. For example, apart from the 2004 No. 116 directives, Shandong also issued its No. 168 notice in 2005 to relay the information from the aforementioned No. 207 directives from the central Ministry of Land and Resources. In 2006, Shandong issued another provincial document, No. 111, to respond to other changes to the land-use policy. Communication of documents as a method of mobilisation is found to have been done via meetings and in writing, at the very least.

Holding Work Conferences

Holding work conferences for local leaders and section representatives, even including researchers, at the provincial and sub-provincial levels has

Table 3.4   *Central rural work conferences and the rural land-use policy,*
            2004–15

Year	New points added to the land-use policy
2004	Priorities the rural issue, and *zengjian guaguo* was first mentioned
2005	Emphasise no change to the rural land policy, and more strict control on land-use change
2006	Decision on a nationwide pilot project on *zengjian guagou*
2007	More strict policy on the rural land use, and the 'red-line' of 1.8 billion *mu* of arable land is introduced*
2008	Further regulation of pilot projects and reduction of the scale of land acquisitions
2009	Allow additional 19 provinces to trial the *zengjian guagou*
2010	Detailed regulations on rural land management, but introduce the policy to transfer land contract rights
2011	Urge local governments to rectify excessive land acquisitions and return land profits to peasants
2012	Identify challenges to the rural issues and new initiatives for rural growth, including new land sources
2013	Introduce the *zengjian guagou* assessment system while expanding it to 29 provinces and re-emphasising the 'red-line' of arable land
2014	Allow orderly transfers of surplus land quotas gained from *zengjian guaguo* while prohibiting the de-agriculturalisation of rural areas
2015	Introduce *zengjian guaguo* quotas and strengthen the transfer of surplus land quotas

Note: * One Chinese *mu* equals 667 square metres and 1.8 billion *mu* equals more than 124 million hectares (OECD, 2015).

Source: Based on media reports and Ma (2013), Zhou (2013), Tan (2014), Y. Cai (2015) and Cai (2016).

been another key method to further mobilise and regularise local and sectoral actions. This type of meetings is different from those aimed at reading and conveying new central party-state policy papers and circulars. It is in some way comparable to the previously mentioned central work conferences, but held at provincial and sub-provincial levels. Modern China is a kingdom of *wenshan huihai* (mountains of directives and the oceans of meetings), but conferences to discuss how to deal with specific issues have been one of the most frequently used mobilisation mechanisms. Table 3.4 lists 12 central work conferences on the land-use (*zengjian guagou*) issue, all of which, according to Shandong media reports, are routinely followed by several meetings of the CCP's provincial standing committee. At such meetings, the provincial leadership chooses when and how to hold a provincial work conference.

An analysis of local media coverage of the new countryside policy shows that in the first three years, from 2004 to 2006, of executing the new rural scheme, Shandong had to hold three to four provincial work conferences, including teleconferences, after each central conference. The complexity of the scheme and local interests are the main reasons behind multiple provincial work conferences. A local official believes that the plan has created a difficult situation for local bureaucracies: policies are difficult to understand, but they must be implemented, and each sub-provincial region or bureau cries out for resources. Almost all local bureaucrats have found that the strategy was initially introduced in an unnecessarily complicated fashion. For example, while this new rural scheme was widely regarded as an opportunity to expand land finance of local governments – from the simple rural construction land-use policy to the supervision of land quota trading markets – Chen Xiwen, China's top rural policy adviser, warned that the new countryside plan could not be simply understood as the construction of villages, but as a strategy to introduce five major mechanisms into rural China:

> The key to the building of socialist new villages is to institute five key mechanisms: to form a long-effect investment mechanism of 'industry nurtures agriculture and cities support rural areas'; to set up a working mechanism of joining the efforts of branches of the party-state system and coordinating the promotion of rural socio-economic comprehensive development; to introduce an incentive mechanism to guide peasants to carry forward [the spirit of] self-reliance and arduous struggle with the support of national policy, and to build a happy homestead through their own hard work; to establish a participation mechanism to enable the involvement of the whole society in the construction of new countryside; and to progressively develop a socio-economic management system for both urban and rural areas. (X. Chen, 2006, n.p.)

Media Promotion

Added to both the complication of interpreting the new plan and the promotion of the scheme is the role of the media, which is characterised by intense scrutiny and the spreading of critical policy ideas outside the party-state system. Just like the CCP's control over media and communication at the national level, where the central leadership primarily relies on Xinhua News Agency, the *People's Daily*, CCTV (China Central Television) and CNR (China National Radio), Shandong has three primary media institutions and outlets for promoting the CCP's key ideas and new strategies, and publicising what the provincial leadership has been doing. These provincial media institutions include the *Dazhong Daily*, Shandong TV and

Shandong People's Radio, and all of them are under the direct leadership of the CCP's provincial committee's Department of Propaganda. Even if the media in China now are partly influenced, if not controlled, by market forces (Zhao, 1998), spreading political information for the party-state system and, therefore, promoting new policy agendas, are still vital to the media's role. In Shandong, there are more than 130 newspapers – big and small, daily and otherwise – in circulation, according to the listings on the websites of two Shandong media advertising agencies (*admaimai* and *kanliewang*). More than 30 of them are the institutional mouthpieces of the local CCP committees at provincial and municipal levels. The *Dazhong Daily* (*Dazhong Ribao*) is a typical example in terms of the role of the local media in mobilising support for the new countryside strategy.

As the most authoritative newspaper in Shandong, the *Dazhong Daily* has frequently used multiple pages each day, and for multiple days, to report on each provincial work conference on the construction of new countryside. Its coverage on this topic has included many events taking place at sub-provincial levels, or being held by some provincial bureaus, offices and semi-official associations to show broad support across the province for the new policy, such as reports on meetings by commerce associations or science groups. Social media has shown various negative responses to the new plan, which will be discussed in the section on gathering feedback, but official local newspapers, as well as their websites and local television and radio stations, have been playing a crucial role in drawing the attention of the public to the new scheme and mobilising public enthusiasm for it. For this reason, a massive media infrastructure is still a crucial condition for social mobilisation.

Training Key Leaders

Leadership training has been an important practice in China, but the training for the new countryside policy has been aimed at producing more 'highly qualified frontline commanders' according to an article in *People's Daily* (Dong, 2007, n.p.). The article reported the CCP's Central Party School and the State Council's Chinese Academy of Governance had jointly run 50 training programmes in 2006 and trained more than 5400 county-level *diyi bashou* ('first hands' or number-one bosses), the highest leaders of the CCP's county committees and the county governments. This was clearly an unusual arrangement since these two central training institutions usually do not train cadres below the prefectural or municipal level. Also unusual was that it was conducted while several training programmes for provincial leaders were also being run. Based on some Shandong websites, deputy leaders at county and district levels were trained one group after another, soon after the central training programmes. These local training sessions were conducted by either Shandong Party School or Shandong Academy of Governance, which, like the central training schools, are under the control of the provincial CCP committee and the government respectively.

The leadership training at different levels is a sophisticated form of social mobilisation, which appears to only target bureaucrats, but in fact aims to refine the policy itself. For example, the above *People's Daily* report summarises two main functions of the leadership training programmes, which include joint 'brainstorming' sessions and 'practical training' experiences (Dong, 2007, n.p.). The collective brainstorming sessions are found to be particularly helpful not only to policy-makers, who can then identify various problems in the policy, but also to local cadres, who are better prepared for implementing the new strategy through learning about the experiences, both positive and negative, of other provinces and regions.

Arranging Personnel

Personnel allocations for new and key national initiatives are always taken seriously in China, and the new countryside policy is no exception. As a province applying to trial the initiative, Shandong established what is called the new countryside building *lingdao xiaozu* (literally 'leading small group', referring to a working party or group, or a leadership group). Such leadership groups were originally seen to be 'informal bodies' with 'the curtain obscuring aspects' to their function (Miller, 2008, p. 1), but now they are understood to be a form of 'integrative mechanisms' to deal with emerging issues or the problems beyond the horizontal and vertical divisions of government (Schlager, 2013, p. 20). Shandong's working group for the new countryside scheme was upgraded after the province was officially chosen to trial the new scheme. Since then, in 2006 and 2007, governments at municipal and county, or district, levels have set up their own *lingdao xiaozu*, the details of which will be discussed in later chapters. These are personnel and management resources to sustain an essential level of mobilisation for accomplishing the new national plan. For this reason, one of the highest provincial leaders, the CCP secretary or the governor, becomes the chair of the group, and deputies in charge of rural issues, or agriculture in general, are assigned to manage the daily operation of the working group. Interestingly, because of the nature of this new rural strategy, the representatives of the provincial Bureau of Land and Resources in the group have been playing a more influential role in the decision-making than they were previously.

Arranging Resources

Arranging other essential resources besides personnel, especially financial resources, is critical for mobilising support for the new policy. It must be admitted that because of China's changing central–local relations, various finance-related issues have now become more passionately pursued, and fiercely contested, than political and ideological issues. Many local bureaucrats now believe that a lack of financial backing means they are unable to perform adequately, or to establish their *zhengji* (demonstrable political career or governmental achievement). While reforming the local budget system (see Table 2.2 and the discussion section on pp. 41–43) and allowing the wide use of *tudi caizheng* (land finance) as discussed in the fourth section of Chapter 2, the state has introduced almost 130 categories of rural-supporting funds (*zhinong zijin*) since the early 2000s to deal with many specific rural issues, such as compulsory education, health care and *dibao* (the minimum livelihood guarantee system) (Yue et al., 2009; Gao, 2017). Such special funds are aimed at mobilising and guiding local governments to achieve the central leadership's goals for China's vast rural areas.

Shandong has paid much greater and more special attention than it did to the mobilisation of financial resources since it formally became the pilot province to trial the new rural scheme. The previously mentioned provincial document No. 111 of 2006 outlined how the new rural plan would be funded. It has, since then, acted in at least two critical ways, another innovative use of the 'two hands' approach. On the one hand, the province dutifully redistributed the special central funds to the projects that should be supported. For example, the central fund for renovating degraded and unsafe rural houses (*weifang gaizao*) has been a huge investment, and it appears to have been fully re-allocated to sub-provincial governments. Among the central and provincial documents reviewed by the authors, more than a half of them contain some details about how to fund each part of the new plan. To implement the rule of *zhuankuan zhuanyong* (specified funds for specific uses), in 2010 Shandong signed an agreement with central ministries of Finance, and Land and Resources for securing RMB 2.4 billion to invest in the project of *tudi zonghe zhengzhi* (land comprehensive enhancement) (Lü, 2010). From this specific fund, totalling up to RMB 10 billion because of match-up funds from the province, the sub-municipal region of Laiwu, on which part of this research is based, received RMB 150 million from 2010 to 2012 for the land enhancement project.

On the other hand, as will be further discussed in the next section and Chapters 5 and 6, Shandong made smart use of its newly gained autonomy, especially the national reform initiative to create an innovative financial management system, to find its own ways to fund some projects. According to a few government-appointed researchers, Shandong has attempted, several times, to tactically re-categorise some central funds according to its own strategical priorities. As mentioned, there were almost 130 types of rural-supporting funds from the central ministries, so that at one stage, a few municipal governments managed about 200 funding categories (Yue et al., 2009). Offering so many funding categories evidently reduced the impact of each type of funding, while increasing the cost of managing these funds. This is a form of *zhonggengzu* (intermediary obstacles) of the party-state system, and affects mobilising efforts. After a couple of years of implementing the policy, Shandong decided to manage all rural funds using an approach, called *tongchou guanli* (coordinated management). Under this approach, rural funds have been combined into six or seven categories based on regional conditions, maximising their impact on mobilising low-level bureaucracies and rural residents to support the new rural plan (Yue et al., 2009).

Gathering Feedback

Gathering feedback has been emphasised by the provincial leadership and it has been used to strength the mobilisation process. According to a Shandong-based policy researcher, no one has total confidence in the new policy design, its implementation process, and the public acceptance of the policy, although the policy formation was based on consultations and discussions with many institutions and individuals. To guarantee the success of mobilisation, a variety of methods have been utilised to collect feedback. These methods can be divided into active and passive approaches, according to the same researcher. The active methods include meetings and training, publicly sponsored research and surveys, and journalist reporting. Also included are inspections by senior provincial officials and supervision tours by experts. According to a report from a provincial bureau, each governmental division also has a team of inspectors, who are not only regularly inspecting each region, but also holding regular meetings to analyse findings (Duan, 2012). Of course, the government can also passively sense public reactions and receive feedback from a variety of protests, or through other channels, such as *xinfang* (written petitions), *shangfang* (in-person or visit petitions) or, increasingly, even court cases. Such passive ways of receiving feedback will be further discussed in Chapter 7.

CREATIVE IMPLEMENTATIONS AND NEW POLITICAL DYNAMICS

Bureaucratic routines were not always able to inspire the best possible responses of provincial and sub-provincial bureaucrats to the strategically significant new national project. In the early 2000s, many provincial leaders were already aware that the old-style approaches, such as relying on the CCP's internal disciplines or promoting its lofty mission and ultimate objectives, were no longer working efficiently, neither were small material incentives. What they also realised was the need to put in place mechanisms for ensuring that actions were taken by bureaucrats under their leadership, and that duties were performed as efficiently as possible. For this reason, more strategic and proactive measures than those utilised in the past were explored. In China's official discourse, these are part of the *ganbu zhidu* (cadre system), or administrative, reforms. Among academics, this process is as simple as introducing the rural responsibility system into both the urban setting and the management of cadres and bureaucratic systems, the latter of which is responsible for introducing performance management into public sector institutions. In Shandong, several new measures have been attempted, along with a range of bureaucratic routines, when implementing the new rural plan. Some of these approaches were rather creative and political, exerting pressure on officials to take the new countryside scheme seriously.

As noted briefly in Chapter 2, the understanding of how to manage China's huge number of bureaucrats after the Maoist years was still as basic as finding a way to avoid 'making horses work without feeding them' (*youyao ma pao, youyao ma buchicao*). Up to the mid-2000s, it became even more difficult to manage bureaucratic teams, and a popular joke likens the problem to the impossible task of letting pigs climb trees, a version of which is as follows:

> How to let pigs climb trees? There are four solutions: *Solution 1*: promoting a visionary blueprint, telling pigs how wonderful their future will be and that they can be as capable as clever monkeys. *Solution 2*: evaluating performance, warning that they will be on the dinner table if not climbing up a tree. *Solution 3*: adopting responsibility systems, assigning each task to a different pig with time requirements, and the schedule to butcher some. *Solution 4*: creating their own approach, cutting down trees and letting pigs have photos with falling trees. (Ling, 2012, n.p.; *Yibaitt, WeChat*, 2015, n.p.)

The above is based on what a deputy-editor of China's popular *Caixin Weekly* published in 2012 and WeChat's 2015 list of the most popular passages (*yibaitt*),[6] but what they did not include in these versions are the witty remarks in the second half of the joke, which go like this: the central leadership often chooses to use the first solution; the provincial leadership prefers to try the second solution; the prefectural-municipal government opts to employ the third solution; and lower-level bureaucrats are found to often act in the manner described by the fourth solution. To handle the issue caused by shirking bureaucrats, or bureaucratic inaction in general, the provincial government often must act in a creative way, generating sufficient internal pressure to drive or induce more bureaucrats to act. This process operates parallel to the above-mentioned bureaucratic routine approaches, but efforts on this front are characterised by the calculated allocation of opportunities and resources, especially those critical for building a career profile, or even for transferring some benefits. Though the latter sounds immoral and abnormal, it is hoped that these measures can disrupt bureaucratic procedures, rectify bureaucratic inactions and generate a high level of internal pressure on bureaucrats.

Fortunately, in the mid-2000s when the new rural policy was ready for implementation, Shandong not only needed more growth initiatives, but also had possibilities to develop further. That is, despite the significance of Shandong's agriculture and industry as sketched in the first section of this chapter, a peculiar phenomenon has become visible, which is its current population distribution as shown in Figure 3.3.

A simple comparison of Figure 3.3 with China's national urbanisation rate listed in Figure 2.2 reveals that there are fewer people living in urban centres in Shandong. As shown in Figure 2.2, China's national urbanisation rate was 56.1 per cent in 2015, but Shandong in 2014 achieved only 44

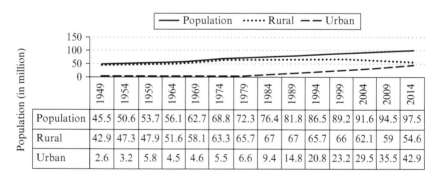

	1949	1954	1959	1964	1969	1974	1979	1984	1989	1994	1999	2004	2009	2014
Population	45.5	50.6	53.7	56.1	62.7	68.8	72.3	76.4	81.8	86.5	89.2	91.6	94.5	97.5
Rural	42.9	47.3	47.9	51.6	58.1	63.3	65.7	67	67	65.7	66	62.1	59	54.6
Urban	2.6	3.2	5.8	4.5	4.6	5.5	6.6	9.4	14.8	20.8	23.2	29.5	35.5	42.9

Note: * The numbers of rural and urban residents are based on the place of household registration, not where they live and work.

Source: Based on data from SPBS (2001, 2016).

*Figure 3.3   Population of Shandong and rural–urban distribution**

per cent (42.9 million urban residents out of a total population of about 97.5 million as listed in Figure 3.3), and only 47.8 per cent in 2015. When the new countryside scheme was ready to be implemented nationally in 2004, the national urbanisation rate was 41.8 per cent (NBSC, 2016), but Shandong was at about 33 per cent (SPBS, 2016). This is so different from what was discussed in the first section. As mentioned, Shandong is often 10 percentage points higher than the national averages in terms of several key indicators, including the number of enterprises, industrial assets and profits, but its level of urbanisation is surprisingly almost 10 per cent lower than the national level.

There are at least two frequently used explanations for Shandong's lower-than-average level of urbanisation. First, many local people believe that this is because of Shandong's agriculture and rural industrialisation, which are more developed than many other provinces or regions. This explanation is not only shared by almost all the people interviewed by the authors in Shandong, but is also consistent with the facts that have been analysed earlier in this chapter. Specifically, Shandong's lower-than-national average level of urbanisation is believed to have resulted from its relatively active and diversified agricultural economy and rural industry. Second, many Shandong people believe themselves to be cultur-ally traditional, and reluctant to leave their home town. A careful reading of provincial statistical data reveals that the SPBS (Shandong Provincial Bureau of Statistics) appears to have fully realised the complexity of rural–urban population distribution and it has, since 1985, been using two related categories to guide its population survey. These categories include the surveyed figures and the numbers of household registrations. The first category is based on China's regular national census that is conducted every ten years, and another small national survey called the National One-Percent Population Sample Survey.[7] These surveys produce data about where people live and work. The second type is based on where people's household registrations are. These two sets of figures show that there are no big differences between them over years, suggesting that Shandong's rural population is less mobile than some less-developed provinces. A researcher in Shandong regards this as a reflection of the spiritual aspect of the *Qi-Lu* or Shandong culture.

Regardless of which explanation is more accurate, the lower-than-average level of urbanisation in Shandong is seen by many local officials and entrepreneurs as a good opportunity, indicating that the province has great development potential, especially in terms of urbanisation or *nongmin shanglou* (letting rural households move into new apartment buildings). The social mobilisation mechanism has been used in Shandong under these socioeconomic conditions and in such a political environment. According to the Shandong-based observers who have pointed out the local paradox of being a well-off province with a lower level of urbanisation, Shandong has also tried a few more sophisticated and creative approaches than the usual routine procedures to implement the new rural scheme. There are five such measures that have not only been utilised by the provincial leadership, but have also been found to be rather provocative to its bureaucrats. These measures are a round of: province-wide planning; province-wide evaluations and classifications of rural areas; identifying and selecting pilot areas; introducing *tongchou guanli* (coordinated management) of financial resources; and making use of market forces in the process.

Province-Wide Planning

A round of province-wide planning was started soon after the province was chosen to be a pilot site for the new countryside scheme. Guided by its long-used and accustomed principle of *guihua xianxing* (planning goes first) (Wang et al., 2011, p. 229), terms of reference of the planning were also proposed by the province leadership, which were summarised in an internal report to the central Ministry of Finance as being 'a higher-starting-point, higher-standard, and based on a longer-term [vision]' (Ding, 2006, n.p.). In the eyes of some Shandong-based specialists, such planning processes have never been just for planning itself, but, importantly, for driving the implementation of new policy central initiatives. As a criticism of the process in Shandong, a few specialists wrote the following about the function of the government in using the process to mobilise officials at provincial and sub-provincial levels.

> The planning in our country has long been handled from a supply point of view, and this round of new rural planning has also been dominated by the government. Although experts, the public, and enterprises should be playing their parts in the planning process, and taking their initiatives to strengthen the certainty of planning outcomes and the sustainability of the execution, the greatness of the government's willpower has surpassed the influence of other parties on the process. (Wang et al., 2011, p. 230)

The early planning phase started as early as 2006 and continued until 2010. Despite the criticisms, this process did indeed further activate the implementation of the new rural strategy beyond meetings and discussions among officials. It has not only been a long process to guide lower-level bureaucracies through, but also included a range of divisive and provocative policy initiatives, as will be detailed next, to let each region and government branch give every attention to the new scheme. The process was also used to draw a boundary, or the red line as noted in Chapter 2, between the rural land use and the new construction scheme. On the surface, this sounds like throwing cold water on the fire, eliminating enthusiasm for the rural building, especially the control measures set out in the provincial document No. 111 of 2006, but it is believed by some observers that the process was also meant to tell local officials how to make tactical, if not beneficial, use of their transferable land, while ensuring that the land-use policy of *zengjian guagou* was justly executed in the province (Yi et al., 2011). For this reason, some even regard this aspect of the planning as the mobilisation for further use of land finance (*tudi caizheng*).

Province-Wide Evaluations and Classifications of Rural Areas

A special part of the province-wide planning process was the evaluation and classification of each region, district and county within the province based on the principle of 'treating differently, guiding by categories' (*qubie duidai, fenlei zhidao*), which was first laid down by the provincial leadership before the planning was started (Ding, 2006, n.p.). As clearly indicated by this principle, the task of assessing and grading each area's conditions and potential for the new countryside scheme was an openly discriminatory exercise, generating a tense political atmosphere provincewide. In the report submitted to the central Ministry of Finance, the grading system used in Shandong was praised as being innovative, especially for the following approach.

> [Shandong] has divided 135 rural counties into three categories, and among them, 30 economically strong counties and 15 urban districts are defined as Category One, 30 less-developed counties are categorised as Category Three, and all other 60 counties are classified as Category Two. Based on these new categorisations, different objectives, work tasks and focuses, practical steps, and policy measures have all been formulated accordingly and drawn up clearly. Each county has also repeated the above procedure to, actively and steadily, drive the execution of the new countryside construction plan further. (Ding, 2006, n.p.)

This grading practice or system, which was also summarised as 'three construction stepladders' in the same report (Ding, 2006, n.p.), clearly shows that some counties and districts were assessed more favourably than others. Though socioeconomic differences among counties and districts are known to exist, local leaders and bureaucrats were still profoundly disturbed by the practice and the prioritisation of development projects. According to the above report, the development timeline for each type of county had been set. Category One had to complete the new rural building scheme by 2015, Category Two by 2020 and Category Three by 2025.

Since the current Chinese cadre system is largely performance-based, this complex grading system has significant socioeconomic and socio-political implications for local leaders and many officials in terms of their career advancement and the socioeconomic expansion of their region. From the standpoint of ambitious local officials, those classifications clearly imply different levels of special attention and real funding, or other forms of financial backing, from their superiors at either provincial or prefectural levels. Both the attention and the funding are critical to their performance, since less of these would unquestionably result in less achievement and less chance for career advancement. Even from the viewpoint of inactive officials, different ratings are not fair to many low-priority counties or districts, especially in terms of unfairly distributing funds, giving them fewer financial resources to use.

Identifying and Selecting Pilot Areas

What is more provocative or disturbing to some local leaders and officials than the measures discussed so far is the selection of pilot sites in the province and the subsequent identification and recommendation of four models for guiding the execution of the rural urbanisation plan in other counties or districts. This tactic has two steps, starting with the identification and selection of 35 pilot sites in Shandong's 17 municipal regions, and concluding with four models for the province-wide implementation. These two steps are related, which is the reason that they are discussed here together, but the authors' field visits have found that sub-provincial bureaucrats are further stirred, if not disturbed, twice. In the eyes of local researchers, this is a form of creative politics, moving bureaucrats in the directions that the provincial leadership wants to go. From the view of officials, however, whichever county, or district, is chosen to be a pilot site would mean to be shortlisted for funding and many other benefits, including career advancement. Like the reactions to other mobilisation tactics, internal tension and competition among local leaders and their bureaucratic teams, and different regions, increased.

As an outcome of the 35 pilot projects, four different models were clearly identified and have since been promoted within the province. To fully understand this mobilisation mechanism, these early models of Shandong could be described as follows.

1. The 'multi-village-community' model based on the pilot case of the city of Xintai is characterised by keeping original villages, but amalgamating them administratively into one bigger community, with a central town providing community services.

2. The 'combined-village-community' model is based on the experiences of the county of Junan, and its main feature is breaking up the original administration and arrangement of villages, amalgamating a few neighbouring villages into a big central village.
3. The 'one village–one community' model based on the pilot case of the city of Jiaonan is characterised by making no change to the current village arrangement, but building a community centre for each *jianzhi-cun* (administrative village).
4. The Zouping-based 'enterprise-style community' model means that an enterprise invests in residential housing for local rural residents who would like to give up their small piece of *zhaijidi* (rural housing land or allotment) in exchange for free or very low-cost new housing (Wang et al., 2011).

The field visits conducted by the authors discovered that after the provincial recognition of the above models, another round of political rivalries was soon initiated by some sub-provincial leaders. In other words, though there is politics in the formation of those models, politics is a creative activity, and the officially confirmed models were unable to stop other politically skilled sub-provincial leaderships from making new efforts to promote their own experiences in the rural development. It is possible because, just like the provincial leadership, sub-provincial leaderships also control, and thus can utilise, a range of media platforms, such as radio and television stations, newspapers and magazines, as well as many websites and social media platforms. The head of the Institute of Economic Studies at the Shandong Academy of Social Sciences, a top provincial think tank, argued as early as December 2006 that 'more effective models must be allowed' (Zhang, 2006, n.p.). There are also other options for some shrewd local leaders and bureaucrats to make use of national media or personal contacts to promote their own regional experience and their own leadership skills. Because of such efforts, Shandong has, since the above-mentioned early models, created a range of other models, such as the Shuoguang model for organising financial loans (Li, 2008) and the Laixi model for village economic development (Wu and Wu, 2006). All these types of efforts and local political rivalries will be further detailed and analysed in the following chapters, especially Chapter 5.

Among the five non-routine measures that the province has used to mobilise sub-provincial bureaucracies to pay attention to the new rural strategy, two of them reflect what has lately taken place in Chinese politics and deserve special attention. These two special non-routine measures have been driving the implementation of the strategy both internally and externally.

Introducing Coordinated Management of Financial Resources

Internally, the provincial leadership has utilised its authority to *tongchou guanli* (coordinate the management) of financial resources while allowing the wide use of *tudi caizheng* (land finance). This approach was discussed in detail as part of the explanation of the sixth routine mobilisation approach in the previous section, but it also needs to be considered in conjunction with the actions revealed in this section. As a finance-driven approach, it has been criticised for giving some officials the chance to abuse the system. While this charge is valid and serious, the measure itself is also considered by some observers in Shandong as a complementary element of the process of planning and cultivating new local models for mobilising the entire province. In the words of an analyst, it is one of the two crucial aspects of the political effort, in which they selected 35 pilot sites from 137 counties, while at the same time combining about 130 funds into fewer categories in line with the provincial strategy. It was because of this part of the measure that the planning, especially the selection of pilot sites, once had financial implications, which made it useful and advantageous to influence sub-provincial leaders and officials. As mentioned, social mobilisation in China now is no longer a simple top-down implementation process, but must be negotiated with various divisions of bureaucratic and non-bureaucratic systems. In the case of the Shandong, it is said to be very difficult to let sub-provincial bureaucrats really follow the instructions without such a political manoeuvre.

　　Abstractly speaking, several Chinese analysts believe there is what they call the 'freeway phenomenon' in present-day China, by which the central authority can only set a clear limit for the maximum speed, but not for the minimum speed. This is because of the central leadership's understanding of the importance of economic growth to China, and the role of local governments or local *jijixing* (enthusiasm) in sustaining the growth. Local governments are, therefore, given the financial autonomy to maintain a high economic growth rate regardless of how the various central funds are used. Also permitted is the use of what is called the market mechanism.

Making Use of Market Forces

The notion of market mechanism emerged in China in the 1980s. By the mid-2000s, when attention turned to the rural development issue, the Chinese economy was already highly marketised, and various market forces had not only become a reality, but could also be utilised for driving new economic expansions. This is also true in the case of Shandong and the new rural scheme. Chapter 4 looks at the role of some market forces in social mobilisation, but it also needs to be considered when analysing the actions taken by the province. There are numerous theories being set forth to explain the role of market forces in Chinese life, ranging from condemnations of corrupt Chinese officials and evil capitalists to glorification of new institutional innovations. The reality, however, is that the provincial leadership must fulfil its primary role, executing what has been decided at the central level, but the process is increasingly hampered by a range of difficulties. Bureaucrats are often lazy and uncooperative, while the provincial leadership often runs out of ideas for how to make use of their bureaucratic teams, due to the increasing complexity of economic activities, let alone that some local officials often set short timelines for achieving their own KPIs or set higher GDP growth targets. Because of these reasons and more, the market mechanism has become a *jiuming daocao* (the last straw to clutch at), as explained in the last section of Chapter 2, in securing the successful implementation of new initiatives. A few Shandong bureaucrats argue that there are two parallel systems, or power structures, working together at provincial and sub-provincial levels: the party-state system and the market, and that when the bureaucracy does not function, or if the provincial leadership is worried about the prospect of effective execution, it is natural for them to seek to use external mechanisms.

Admittedly, it is not easy to collect related information from either official sources or enterprises involved in some government-initiated projects, especially as China in recent years has been conducting an anti-corruption campaign. However, as noted in Chapter 2, since the 'three represents' theory was put forward by Jiang Zemin in the early 2000s, the importance of the market in China has been accepted, and now the Chinese economy is highly marketised and privatised. As a result, new state–market relations have emerged as being as vital as central–local relations, but such relations are a trouble zone, and are often linked by *liyi shusong* (transferring benefits or interests). This intricate issue has been complicated by the role of former and current state-owned enterprises. In whatever way, the market mechanism is used in Shandong's implementation of the countryside policy, and the functional aspect of the state–market relations deserves more attention than before. In a recent commentary on Shandong culture, a critic has pointed out that Shandong culture is always full of paradox (*beilun*) in the sense that it is mixed with different cultural norms and forces (Ye, 2017). State–market relations are a paradox, one that is used in Shandong while giving it some troubles.

NOTES

1. It should not be too difficult to find more information about these important contributors to the formation of Confucianism. The first author's former university classmate, Professor Xinzhong Yao, once drew up a very useful chronological table of Confucianism throughout history. For more information about the table, readers are referred to Yao (2000, pp. xiv–xviii). Interested readers can also see Rainey (2010) and Gardner (2014).
2. Dazhai (formerly also romanised as Tachai or Ta-chai) is a mountainous village in the middle-eastern region of Shanxi province. When China was suffering from agricultural difficulties in the early 1960s, Dazhai became famous because of its persistence in the Maoist People's Commune system and collective farming practices in much harsher conditions than rural Shandong. For more information about Dazhai and the so-called Dazhai experience, see Tsou et al. (1982) and Teiwes and Sun (2016). Daqing (formerly romanised as Taching) is a city that was built in the early 1960s after vast oil reserves were discovered in the west of Heilongjiang, a northeastern province in China, neighbouring with Russia. The Daqing oilfield once contributed significantly to China's goal of energy self-sufficiency, and because of its political importance, Mao called on all industrial sectors in 1964 to learn from Daqing. For more information about Daqing and the Daqing model, see Li (2014) and Taylor (2014).
3. The People's Commune was one of the CCP's three grand strategies developed in 1958, which was also called *Sanmian Hongqi* in Chinese, Three Red Banners, or Three Red Flags, referring to the Great Leap Forward, the People's Commune and the General Line of Socialist Construction. For more information about this period and the three grand strategies of the late 1950s and early 1960s, see Teiwes and Sun (1999) and Shapiro (2001).
4. Both Anhui province and Sichuan province played important roles in utilising and helping to shape the household production responsibility system in the late 1970s. For this reason, Zhao Ziyang, the then first secretary of the CCP Sichuan provincial committee, and Wan Li, the then first secretary of the CCP Anhui provincial committee, were both promoted to the central leadership in 1980, shortly after Deng Xiaoping regained the political leadership. These political changes were neatly summed up in a popular punning rhyme of the time: *Yaochiliang, Zhao Ziyang, yaochimi, zhao Wan Li* (If you want to eat grain, call Ziyang; if you can to eat rice, call Wan Li). Interested readers can refer to, for example, Shirk (1993), Bramall (2009) and Teiwes and Sun (2016).
5. According to the 'Regulations on the use of official documents in party and state work', which was jointly issued by the CCP's General Office of the Central Committee and the State Council in 2012, there are 15 types of party-state documents: resolutions, decisions, orders, announcements, public notices, gazettes, opinions, circulars, communiques, official reports, instruction requests, officials replies, motions, official letters and minutes. This long list and the definition of each type can be found at http://www.gov.cn/zwgk/2013-02/22/content_2337704.htm.
6. WeChat is called *weixin* in Chinese, literally means micro-message. It is a Chinese social media application developed by Tencent. WeChat started as an instant messaging application just like WhatsApp and Facebook, but it can also be used for group chat, voice chat, video chat and so on. It is China's most popular smartphone application, currently with about one billion active users worldwide.
7. China has conducted its National Population Census six times, in 1953, 1964, 1982, 1990, 2000 and 2010. Since the end of the Maoist period, China has decided to conduct the National Population Census every ten years, and in the fifth year between two national censuses China also conducted its National One-Percent Population Sample Survey, in 1987, 1995, 2005 and 2015. In addition to the censuses and surveys conducted by the National Bureau of Statistics of China, there are also other types of national population data gathered by other central government departments, such as the 1986 urban migrant survey and the 1988 two-per-thousand fertility survey. Interested readers are referred to Scharping (2003) and Greenhalgh and Winckler (2005).

4. The emerging powers of the 'invisible hand'

It is important to start this chapter by explaining why we would like to place this discussion of the 'invisible hand' right after the analysis of the role of the provincial bureaucracy in Chapter 3. This seems more than necessary, considering that some of what will be discussed in this chapter is taking place at, or even under, the prefectural-municipal level, which is the focus of Chapter 5. It has become evident from the beginning of our research that market forces, famously called the 'invisible hand', have been playing their powerful role not only in implementing the new countryside strategy but also in mobilising support for it. As will be explained next, the role of market forces has become obvious at the provincial level, and readers should therefore be reminded of the extent to which market forces have been expanding and becoming dominant in China's political-economic life. In the case of the countryside scheme market forces have become capable not only of influencing decision-making processes at the provincial level but also of being involved in building projects as part of their daily business operations. Through this arrangement of chapters, we would like to emphasise the increasing importance of market forces in China in general and, more specifically, in social mobilisation.

The 'invisible hand' has been cultivated in China since the 1980s because of China's ongoing economic and public-administration reforms, and it now plays an important role in economic and socio-political life. This is an under-studied area of research, especially as it has rarely been considered along with the function of formal party-state bureaucracies, or beyond hypothetical political-economic or even ideological debates in relation to market liberalisation. In other words, the vital role of market forces in the general economy is being recognised by more researchers, but the influence of those forces on the implementation of new policies, especially on related social mobilisation, is still in need of exploration. This is the second reason this under-studied feature needs to be discussed here before we examine what has taken place at the prefectural-municipal level. The discussion in this chapter is a preliminary attempt to include this main aspect in the discussion of social mobilisation in contemporary China. Therefore, this chapter will start with a brief review of China's market liberalisation since the early years of post-Mao reform. The discussion will then focus on the role and characteristics of local market forces in driving the new rural project in Shandong at provincial and prefectural level. The third and last section will look at how various commercial companies have acted as mobilisers in Laiwu.

MARKET LIBERALISATION IN CHINA

By the mid-1970s, shortly before the death of Mao Zedong in 1976, China had become a notorious country that was strictly controlled by a set of ideological beliefs and principles defined by theorists of the CCP as Marxism, Leninism and Mao Zedong thought. In those years, ruling CCP leftists forced more people to believe that adequate food, clothing and housing were not as important as upholding Marxism, Leninism and Mao Zedong thought. At the grassroots level, such a call for sacrifice in the name of ideological principle lost its momentum and appeal after the death of Mao, especially following the arrest of the 'Gang of Four', an ultra-leftist group of ideologues led by Mao's last wife.[1] All the radical and foreign isms introduced by different political groups or forces since the early twentieth century, including both Nationalists and Communists, were no longer as convincing as Deng Xiaoping's pragmatic thinking and approach. The latter carried almost no ideological baggage at that time and it was characteristically expressed in an old Chinese peasant saying: 'It doesn't matter if it is a white cat or a black cat, as long as it catches mice'. This has become known as Deng Xiaoping's 'cat theory', which was welcomed by ordinary Chinese people and has also been seen approvingly as 'a modern version of pragmatic rationalism' (Ju, 1996, p. 44).[2]

Having shifted from fundamental Marxist and Leninist teaching to the Dengist pragmatic 'cat theory', China staged a sudden and radical transformation, which could well be summed up by another old Chinese proverb: 'Poverty gives rise to a desire for a change' (*qiong ze sibian*). Rural China quickly abandoned the collective-farming system, and the household-production-responsibility system was introduced. However, there were still many CCP members and others in urban China whose social status, privileges and whole life were so deeply interconnected with the former beliefs that they were unable even to clearly understand them but simply followed them and took them as their identity. One such belief or ideological symbol was socialism contrary to capitalism. Associated with this ideological divide were notions of a planned economy and the free market. Table 4.1 shows how careful and persistent reformist leaders and theorists were in introducing the market-competition mechanism

Table 4.1   *Introduction of market forces into the Chinese economy, 1978–2004*

Year	The acceptance of the market concept by party-state decision-makers
1978	'The planned economy with consideration of Marx's law of value', and 'introducing some market mechanisms into the economy' were widely discussed
1981	'Planning as a principal part, and market as a supplementary part' was proposed at the 6th Plenum of the 11th CCP Congress and adopted at the 4th Session of the 5th People's Congress in November 1981
1982	The 'planned economy as the mainstay and market adjustments as supplementary' was put forward at the 12th CCP Congress in September 1982
1984	'Socialist planned commodity economy' was defined at the 3rd Plenum of the 12th CCP Congress in October 1984
1987	'The state regulates the market, and the latter regulates enterprises' was detailed at the 13th CCP Congress in October 1987
1988	'Deepening enterprise reform' and 'the separation of government functions from enterprises' was emphasised at the 3rd Plenum of the 13th CCP Congress in September 1988
1989	'Effective combination of both the planned economy and the market regulation' was put forward at the 5th Plenum of the 13th CCP Congress in November 1989
1992	'Socialist market economy with Chinese characteristics' was defined at the 14th CCP Congress in October 1992
1993	'Letting the market play a fundamental role in resource allocation' and 'establishing modern new enterprise mechanisms' were key policy changes at the 3rd Plenum of the 14th CCP Congress in November 1993
1997	'Developing multiple forms of ownership including private, cooperative and other forms' was introduced at the 15th CCP Congress in September 1997
1999	An amendment to the Constitution was made at the 2nd Session of the 9th People's Congress in March 1999, recognising 'multiple forms of ownership', putting private enterprise on an equal footing with the state sector
2001	Jiang Zemin's 'three represents theory' was formulated, and recognised the importance of the private sector in the economy
2002	'Two necessities' – the equal importance of both public and private sectors – was recognised at the 16th CCP Congress in November 2002
2003	'The diversification of the ownership structure' and 'the relaxation of market entry restrictions allowing private capital to invest in more sectors' was the new policy of the 3rd Plenum of the 16th CCP Congress, held in October 2003
2004	An amendment to the Constitution was made at the 2nd Session of the 10th People's Congress in March 2004 to ensure that private property was protected under the law

Source: Compiled by the authors based on various publications.

into mainstream Chinese political thinking and discourse before the new countryside strategy was formulated.

Interestingly, as a reflection of the Chinese political process, what is recorded in Table 4.1, especially those events that took place before the mid-1990s, is not simply an historical review but a set of real debates that took place among top-level policy advisers and researchers of the time. As mentioned, in the late 1970s and early 1980s a large proportion of urban-based CCP members still blindly followed the old ideological line set out by Mao and his followers. Therefore, Dengist reformers launched a nationwide debate on the criterion of truth at the start of the reform in 1978. During this famous theoretical debate, new reformist leaders encouraged CCP members to 'emancipate the mind' and 'seek the truth from facts', not stick to old thinking or ideological dogmas (He, 2010, p. 204). However, as listed in the first few lines of Table 4.1, the political circumstances of the late 1970s meant that the early debate about the role of market mechanisms in the economy was still started and undertaken in a rather religious manner, in which reformist theorists had no choice but to dig out a few words from Karl Marx to strengthen their ideological legitimacy. Marx's 'law of value' (*jiazhi guilu*) was retrieved and used to legitimise reformist efforts to introduce market mechanisms into economic management (Goodman, 1994; Fewsmith, 2010; Solinger, 2015).

China's market liberalisation has, since the 'law of value' debate in the late 1970s, gone through several main phases. What happened then was that while CCP theorists were debating whether Karl Marx had predicted the role of market laws, reformist administrative leaders had already initiated pilot programmes from 1978 to reform inefficient state-owned enterprises. Through a new policy measure of 'expanding autonomy and sharing profit' (*kuoquan rangli*) (Wu, 2004, p.114), the government hoped that enterprises and workers could be encouraged to lift their productivity, which China urgently needed at the time. The pilot programmes in Sichuan in 1978 were successful and in 1979 more programmes were quickly introduced in Shanghai, Tianjin and Beijing, China's top three economic centres of the time. This was the real start of China's reform of state-owned enterprises (SOEs), through which the economy could become more productive, and factories were rewarded with a larger share of their profits.

What then happened should be read along with the key reform measures listed in Table 2.2, through which a general trend in China's economic reforms can be clearly seen. The central leadership gained a range of positive experiences from the pilot programmes and decided to expand what they had learned to develop a more general management strategy, which was then called *fengquan rangli* (splitting powers and giving up some profits). Since then, as briefly mentioned in Chapter 1, there has been an overall trend called *minjin guotui* (the private sector has been advancing and the state has been retreating (Lardy, 2014)). In terms of the reform of SOEs alone, the entire process has been ongoing, but it went through four stages before Deng Xiaoping's southern China inspection tour in 1992 to accelerate and deepen China's economic transition. In addition to the very first 'expanding autonomy and sharing profit' reform pursued from 1978 to 1980, the second stage took place in 1981 and 1982, when an economic-responsibility system was introduced into the management of SOEs. The key words used to define this stage of reform indicate that this was very much a simple repeat of the successful use of similar practices in rural China, and the main idea was the introduction of contracts not only between workers and employers but also between government departments and SOEs. The third stage took place from 1983 to 1986, focusing on the relationship between the government and SOEs through replacing profit with tax (*li gai shui*). The fourth effort was made from 1987 to 1991, during which the responsibility system was further defined and SOEs were given more powers to manage themselves.

China's ongoing efforts to liberalise market forces have never been free from political tensions, reactionary responses and societal unrest. The reform's early emphasis on introducing contracts provided opportunities for motivated and able workers but posed challenges to millions of others, who had been told to firmly believe in socialist ideology and regarded their jobs as the 'iron rice bowl'. A few years after the urban reform, many workers realised that their livelihoods were threatened. Their resentments gave rise to a series of small-scale protests before the famous and massive protest in 1989, adding fuel to the already fiery debates over the ideological and political nature of some reform programmes. In the mid-1980s some inefficient SOEs were being privatised, while numerous factories were leased to individuals or collectives, which challenged the concept of state or public ownership – the core idea of the Chinese communist movement. Of course, these early industrial-reform measures were still relatively simple in comparison to those of the late 1990s and 2000s, and they were, therefore, supported by many urban residents, especially intellectuals. Their standpoint was that China needed to develop its economy, which should begin with alterations in the unfashionable egalitarian practice of 'eating from one big pot' (*chi daguofan*). The latter was regarded as the key obstacle in modernising China before egalitarianism gained momentum in the late 1980s.

Debate within the CCP over the ideological line of many reform measures dragged on until 1989, when thousands of students were deeply disturbed by the debate and marched out of universities. This refers to the so-called 'political disturbance of 1989' or the 'June 4 disturbance', according to the CCP's explanation; the event is, of course, also defined by other phrases in the West, such as 'massacre' and 'democratic movement' (He, 2010, p. 10). Leaving the details of the 1989 incident aside, what occurred in China in 1989 was predominantly a strong, but confused, societal reaction to these ongoing reforms. In fact, well before 1989, many Chinese researchers and policy analysts had already warned that China's economy was run on dual tracks – both the planned economy and the market economy, if not socialist and capitalist – which would unavoidably cause a great deal of disturbance (Gao, 1986; Wu, 2004; Buck, 2012).

As indicated in Table 4.1, the disturbance of 1989 did not derail China's reform agendas, and plans to lease out more factories and introduce market mechanisms were kept without revision. Two CCP plenums were held, in late June and early November 1989, after the most dangerous political crisis that the CCP had faced since the end of the Cultural Revolution. At the first post-4 June plenum, the CCP central leadership was replaced. More importantly, its second plenum in 1989 decided not only to re-emphasise its commitment to the reform policy but also to focus on market liberalisation. This decision was made because of strong internal pressure generated by the 1989 crisis, which made CCP leadership circles confront the serious issue of the legitimacy of their rule. The consensus reached among them favoured the reformist idea that further economic development and quickly improving the living standards of ordinary people would provide them with a new source of legitimacy. This political survival strategy guaranteed that the crisis of 1989 did not result in the discontinuation of China's reform programmes, especially rural industrialisation, which has been more essential to the formation of China's market economy or private sector than other reform policies. However, it was also true that the ideological debates before the 1989 crisis had clouded the minds of many leaders and bureaucrats, resulting in fewer reform measures being set forth and the debate over isms becoming more destructive to the reform agendas.

Another turning point in China's reform effort was Deng Xiaoping's inspection tour of several cities in southern China in early 1992, which aimed to turn the gloomy post-1989 mood of the country around. His tour tackled a series of general strategic issues, including explaining the necessity of having two stages of economic development, by which coastal regions were urged to accelerate economic reform to catch up with the 'Asian four small dragons' of South Korea, Taiwan, Hong Kong and Singapore (Tian, 2001, p. 84).[3] Deng even directly pushed the central leadership to take a more rapid and bold approach to market-oriented economic reform than had occurred in the late 1980s. For these reasons, he made the following very direct and blunt remarks, by Chinese political standards, on the protracted ideological debate about whether China's reform was socialist or capitalist:

> The fundamental difference between socialism and capitalism is not whether there is more planning and market. A planned economy is not equal to socialism, because capitalism also has planning; the market economy is [also] not equal to capitalism, because socialism also has the market. Planning and market are economic means. (Deng, cited in Jeffries, 1993, p. 198)

The push for bold market-oriented reforms without worrying too much about political labels resulted in the sudden emergence of a popular social trend of *xiahai* ('jumping into the sea [of commerce]' or 'taking the risk of entering private businesses'). Many bureaucrats and academics decided to leave their public-payroll jobs to start private businesses. That is, Deng's famous 1992 southern inspection tour not only accelerated China's transition to a market economy, achieving double-digit growth for several years, but also resulted in the rapid expansion of the private sector. This sector has since been diversified to include not only rural factory owners or operators but also many able and skilled people. At the same time, the central leadership made some bold decisions to further reform SOEs. A new company law, enacted in 1993, relaxed the requirements for setting up a company: there was now no need to have approval from government bureaus at central and provincial level; it was permissible to establish a joint stock or share stock company; and there was the right to merge, transfer and sell shares of a registered company. In 1995, another major policy of 'keeping the large [SOEs] and letting the small go' (*zhuada fangxiao*) was implemented, with the result that over 50 per cent of SOEs were privatised within a short period. Over the second half of the 1990s more than 80 per cent of SOEs were restructured, and by the end of 2001 roughly 70 per cent had also been privatised (Garnaut et al., 2006).

A major theoretical effort was made to respond to such a rapid expansion of the private sector. In several speeches made after early 2000, especially the speech marking the 80th anniversary of the CCP on 1 July 2001, Jiang Zemin, the then general secretary of the CCP, defined private entrepreneurs – who were a key target of the Chinese communist revolution – as outstanding elements of society. These capitalists, as they were called, are no longer the target of the revolution. Instead, according to Jiang's 'three represents' theory,[4] they are now regarded as people representing the advanced productive forces in China. It has since become evident that private entrepreneurs and the market economy cannot be disregarded. In fact, soon after the 'three represents' speech, the CCP decided to recruit 200 000 private entrepreneurs into the party. The country's rapid privatisation and marketisation have turned the ideological debate in a different direction.

The CCP is now no longer able to undervalue the important role of private entrepreneurs in China's economy, and any study of social mobilisation in post-Deng China, therefore, also needs to take them into account.

MARKET FORCES PARALLELING PARTY-STATE SYSTEMS

Despite the strong awareness of the increasing influence of the private sector or the market on various processes, including decision-making, policy implementation and social mobilisation, it is rather difficult to empirically examine various issues associated with market forces and related sectors in China. There are several reasons for this. First, as a newly emerged field, there are still insufficient data and accumulated knowledge on these issues. Researchers, especially those from outside China, are still paying more attention to two familiar ends of society – high-level institutions and grassroots social groups – than the rapidly maturing market, which has been vaguely treated as a massive whole that is difficult to observe and analyse. Second, commercial confidentiality and secrecy are often used to prevent researchers from gaining access to and collecting data on the issues being studied. This is a worldwide phenomenon, not just a Chinese issue. Finally, the fieldwork for this research project was done when China's anti-corruption campaign, launched by Xi Jinping, was sweeping not only across the whole country but also across all levels of the party-state bureaucracy. The campaign decided to eliminate both 'tigers' (corrupt senior officials) and 'flies' (corrupt lower-level officers). The campaign scared off many bureaucrats from acting corruptly, and many have also become very cautious about the way they interact with the private sector, let alone revealing their relations with it. Shandong is not immune to corruption, and local officials have all become very careful about answering questions concerning their links with the private sector.

Due to the above reasons, this discussion is based on three sources: the private-sector situation in Shandong, public official documents and corruption cases relating to senior officials in Shandong. Let us start with Figure 4.1, which is drawn based on information from the provincial bureau of statistics in Shandong.

What Figure 4.1 is unable to show is that the above-mentioned policy of 'keeping the large [SOEs] and letting the small go' resulted in a strong trend of privatisation in China nationally from the mid-1990s. Just like its GDP (see Figure 3.1), Shandong was ranked as one of the top three provinces from 1998 to 2008 in terms of private-sector share in the local economy, which was 82.5 per cent in 2008, only slightly lower than in

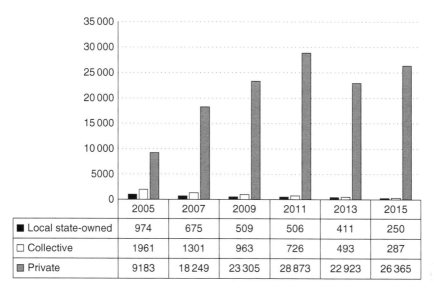

	2005	2007	2009	2011	2013	2015
■ Local state-owned	974	675	509	506	411	250
□ Collective	1961	1301	963	726	493	287
▨ Private	9183	18 249	23 305	28 873	22 923	26 365

Note: * The criteria for a sizeable enterprise were changed in 2011, increasing its annual core business income from RMB 5 million to RMB 20 million.

Source: Based on data from SPBS (2005, 2007, 2009, 2011, 2013, 2015).

Figure 4.1   Numbers of sizeable domestic enterprises in Shandong, 2005–15*

Jiangsu (87.8 per cent) and Zhejiang (85.6 per cent) (S. Zhao, 2013). According to Shandong's bureau of statistics, all sizeable enterprises in the province are divided into three main types: domestic; Hong Kong–Macao–Taiwan investment; and foreign investment. Leaving aside the last two types, because of their different relations with the government and market behaviour, domestic enterprises that employed roughly 55 million workers in 2005 are normally divided into eight groups: state-owned enterprises; collective-owned enterprises; shareholding co-operatives; joint-run enterprises; limited-liability companies; limited-shares companies; private enterprises; and other. Figure 4.1 clearly establishes that private enterprises in Shandong became much larger than local state-owned and collective enterprises during the rural building strategy's implementation period.

Figure 4.2 shows a different viewpoint to see the importance of the private sector, which has become the largest employer in the province while implementing the new rural strategy.

The above sets of statistics clearly support that, having been guided by the imported idea of 'big market and small government' (Lam, 2015, p. 268)

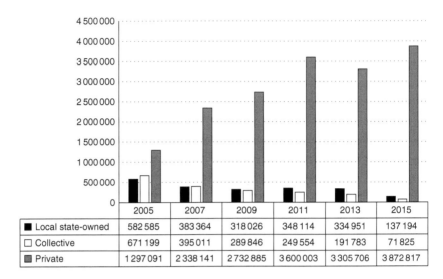

	2005	2007	2009	2011	2013	2015
■ Local state-owned	582 585	383 364	318 026	348 114	334 951	137 194
☐ Collective	671 199	395 011	289 846	249 554	191 783	71 825
▨ Private	1 297 091	2 338 141	2 732 885	3 600 003	3 305 706	3 872 817

Source: Based on data from SPBS (2005, 2007, 2009, 2011, 2013, 2015).

Figure 4.2   Numbers of Shandong people working in three types of sizeable domestic enterprise, 2005–15

and the self-created 'three represents' theory, China has achieved very high levels of marketisation and privatisation. Nowadays it is still accurate to say that China is under the rule of the CCP, but it is incorrect to say that the Chinese economy is socialist in nature. The above sets of statistics also reveal various possible socio-political ramifications. As far as implementation of the urbanisation policy was concerned, in a province with so many privately owned new enterprises it would have been impossible to simply rely on party-state bureaucracies for social mobilisation to execute the policy. In the words of some local officials, almost no enterprises and factories remain in the hands of government after so many reforms. Now the private sector has not only production lines but labour forces, which have made the sector as important as established party-state bureaucracies. Specifically, the number of its employees, ranging from blue-collar workers to professionals, and the human resources and networks it has established, have all made it possible for it to exert influence not only on government but also on its decision-making.

Table 4.2 shows another aspect of why the private sector has become so powerful: its financial strength. This set of figures proves that private enterprises in Shandong have far more financial resources than the other two types of enterprise, and therefore any analysis of local socio-economic policies and activities should take them into consideration. As will be detailed

Table 4.2   Annual business turnover of three sizeable domestic enterprises in Shandong (billion yuan), 2005–15

Year	Local state owned	Collective owned	Privately owned
2005	146.6	262.5	449.5
2007	132.6	240.7	1007.8
2009	191.2	244.9	1698.9
2011	280.3	274.6	2976.9
2013	357.7	327.3	4237.4
2015	131.3	179.9	6653.8

Source: Based on data from SPBS (2005, 2007, 2009, 2011, 2013, 2015).

next, many governments in Shandong have made use of their financial resources in mobilising the implementation of the rural construction scheme.

Chinese history from the late 1990s to the early 2010s was sensationally characterised by nationwide large-scale construction of buildings and infrastructure, such as freeways, airports and railways. The construction industry has, therefore, become a very important sector in China. When the rural building scheme started in 2005, Shandong province had more than 5670 construction enterprises, including 511 state-owned, 865 collectively owned and 1949 privately owned (SPBS, 2006). As early as 2005, the sector contributed RMB 250.9 billion to Shandong's economy and employed more than 2.5 million people. This sector in Shandong has now become more central than before, despite the national economic slowdown in recent years. In 2015 the sector's economic contribution increased to RMB 937.9 billion, almost four times greater than in 2005, and it employed no fewer than 3.1 million workers. The province's domestic construction industry now has 6046 enterprises, almost half of them (2916) privately owned, while state-owned enterprises have shrunk significantly, to 263 from 511 in 2005, and collectively owned enterprises have reduced dramatically, to 381 from 865 in 2005 (SPBS, 2016). Social mobilisation for the construction strategy was undertaken while the private sector in Shandong was not only rapidly growing its share in the local economy but also becoming a dominant part of it.

In adjusting to such new circumstances, Shandong's leadership at provincial and prefectural level has, from the beginning of the urbanisation campaign, taken a series of steps to involve the 'invisible hand' in the implementation of the scheme.

In spring 2005, when Shandong was drafting its plan to implement the strategy, it benefited from an inspection tour by Hu Jintao, the then

Chinese leader. Hu visited a famous village called Nanshan, where one of China's most successful rural industrial groups, Nanshan Group, was originally based. He made positive comments on the rural village development idea of *cunqi heyi*, the village-enterprise integration approach, which was advocated and supported by Nanshan Group. During the tour, Hu suggested that Shandong further perfected the market-economy system and made full use of the role of the market in allocating resources (Yantai Government, 2006, p. 14). Clearly, three key policy ideas could be drawn from Hu Jintao's inspection tour: the market economy; the market's function in the allocation of resources; and the village-enterprise integration approach created by Shandong's most famous private company. These ideas helped provincial leaders understand the extent to which they could make use of the private sector in implementing the rural construction scheme.

Once 'the emperor's sword' (*shangfang baojian*) was obtained, the local leadership felt politically protected and they then started working on the implementation strategy in Shandong. Since several practical issues to do with this process have already been detailed in Chapter 3, the discussion here pays attention to a new and challenging aspect of the policy's implementation at provincial and sub-provincial level: how to deal with the private sector. Despite its being called the 'invisible hand', local governments know the sector well. Our fieldwork revealed that ideological worries about private ownership are no longer common, but there is a high degree of alertness about the political minefields associated with connections to the sector. In general, China's party-state systems are believed to have insufficient experience and established practice in dealing with the market economy because of the country's revolutionary past. To handle such challenges, the provincial leadership tried to find more clues from the top leaders. They finally found another idea of Hu Jintao's. At the 4th Plenum of the 16th CCP Congress in 2004, Hu put forward the strategic idea of letting industry feed agriculture and letting cities support rural villages. Based on these principles, Zhang Gaoli, the then CCP secretary of Shandong, defined the provincial approach as 'integrating urban–rural socio-economic development, adhering to the policy of letting industry support agriculture and cities support villages' at the 2006 provincial conference on agriculture (Han, 2006, n.p).

The politically well-founded provincial strategy – or the well-articulated and clearly detailed provincial documents, in the words of several local officers – finally opened the door to the private sector, authorising government bureaus to invite various enterprises to attend meetings and discussions and allowing sub-provincial governments to work closely with the private sector. Among all these new approaches and novel ideas, a critical change was the principle of utilising the market, or market forces, in the allocation of resources. Leaving aside some details to be considered in the next section, the utilisation of the market in the rural urbanisation process has been widely called 'capital going down to the countryside' (*ziben xiaxiang*) by Chinese analysts; two of them have detailed this approach as follows:

> Capital going down to the countryside' has taken two main forms. The first approach is that investors take part in comprehensive enhancement projects that are related to 'rural-households-moving-to-apartments', and they, as investors, then gain construction-land quotas as surplus benefits. The second form is that social funds are used in the land-transfer process, better enabling the government to run the land transfer in scale, which is the key to the integrated urban–rural approach. (Zhou and Wang, 2015, p. 82)

The above process and its outcome represent the acceptance of the fact that market forces in China are as important as the initially dominant party-state system. However, utilising the market and implementing a new policy by means of market forces are politically complex. Ongoing reforms have gradually transformed and upgraded China's economic-management system and decision-making processes, which has also greatly changed the socio-political culture of the country. While ideology continues to be a topic for CCP institutions, dissatisfied people from both the left and the right, and foreign reporters, the Chinese people have become more concerned about how socio-economic and -political games are being played. The whole society seems to pay attention to the issue of 'transfer of interest or benefits' (*liyi shusong*) and various related schemes of sharing profits, transferring interests and turning public power into personal goods (Buckley, 2015).

To achieve both objectives of encouraging the constructive role of market forces in the economy, or in society in general, and preventing officials from abusing their power and acting unethically, various new supervision and disciplinary measures have been introduced. However, a small group of corrupt officeholders in Shandong acted as go-betweens between private entrepreneurs and government departments. These corruption cases disclosed a huge amount of information about the connections between the private sector and the government, and relations between some entrepreneurs and corrupt officials. Such information reveals that many private enterprises have taken steps to involve themselves in the building scheme as part of their commercial operations.

The first two provincial-level 'tigers' (corrupt senior officials) to be punished in Shandong were CCP secretary Wang Min and the mayor, Yang Luyu, of Jinan, the provincial capital. They had become connected with construction or building-material companies after 2004 or 2005 and, ironically, were directly involved in creating the provincial strategy of letting enterprises assist with agriculture and village development. Wang was the director of the provincial policy-research office, the top thinktank of Shandong, and Yang Luyu was on secondment from the central Ministry of Housing and Urban–Rural Development, at which Yang was the director of the Bureau of Standardisation. Because they had made a great contribution to the formation of the provincial strategy to cope with the demands of the rural urbanisation plan, they were promoted and worked as a team in the provincial capital. But they did not get along well, apparently fighting for better performance and more influence over various policies. Investigations by the Central Commission for Discipline Inspection (CCDI) of the CCP have revealed that they were actually engaged in a turf war over control of private enterprises. Wang was first accused by a developer from a neighbouring province (M. Li, 2016). He was then found to have acted on behalf of many business people to interfere with the bidding processes of major development projects and to have involved himself in many land-transfer deals. The CCDI investigation also found that Yang was involved in similar unethical conduct, receiving bribes of more than RMB 23 million between 2004 and 2016, higher than Wang's total of more than RMB 18 million, received between 2004 and 2014 (*Xinhua News*, 2016a, 2017b). Wang was sentenced to 12 years in prison and Yang received a jail term of 14 years.

In the latest big corruption case, Ji Xiangqi, one of Shandong's vice-governors, was punished by the CCDI in January 2018, making him China's second high-ranking tiger of 2018 (*Xinhua News*, 2018a). Ji became the director of Lushang Group in 2002, and soon decided to invest earnings from the group's retail businesses in the urbanisation-driven building project, which needed a substantial amount of working capital. Because of his success in expanding Lushang's business, he was even promoted to be one of its governors in 2012. Though he is still under investigation, he is now accused of embezzling public funds, transferring public properties and assets to associates, and seeking benefits for his collaborators (*Xinhua News*, 2018a). To some extent, the problems of all three officials are simply the result of inappropriate dealings with private businesses. But at the same time, these cases have confirmed that market forces in China are now so powerful that they can not only disrupt the country's whole economy but also disturb the political tranquillity and order.

MARKET FORCES ACTING AS A SOCIAL MOBILISER

Despite the above-mentioned corrupt conduct, much of which was spread as rumour among local people for years, the central leadership's attention to GDP and economic growth as indicators of decent governance and as a political strategy to maintain stability have driven further not only general marketisation but also the tactic of letting industry support rural development. As revealed in Figures 4.1 and 4.2, state-owned enterprises have been fast disappearing from Shandong's economy since the mid-2000s, and what has been vaguely called industry in official documents in fact refers to private enterprises, big and small. This section turns our discussion of the 'invisible hand' to the role of market forces in the implementation of the new rural building strategy and looks at the involvement of three types of private enterprise in the process of mobilising resources and support for the scheme. These enterprises include the construction industry, local enterprises and small-business operators, and demolition companies. Apparently, all involvement took place at the operational level, below the provincial level. That is, according to China's administrative divisions, these mobilisation roles were largely observed at or below the prefectural level. Discussion in this section should be read alongside related sections of Chapters 5 and 6.

The first and most obvious private-sector role was played by the construction industry. Two pieces of background information are worth mentioning at this point. First, as noted in the preceding section, the private sector in China was already large in the mid-2000s and the property market had also completed its early formation period. Second, China decided to fully reform its post-1949 welfare-housing system in cities in 1994, and since then no government at any level has been willing to assume the burden of looking after construction and allocating housing, especially the financing of so many building projects. For this reason, the construction industry was already seen as the key player in the property market before the implementation of the new rural scheme, and governments hoped that the industry would play its part in this round of construction activities.

In Laiwu, local officials tried hard to implement the idea of the provincial government to let enterprises help in the execution of the scheme. Among several real-estate developers, national and local, Laiwu identified one that was interested in some projects in the region. This was a comparatively small construction company called Lujian, which literally means Shandong construction. Lujian was established in 1995, and its early core business focused on structural engineering projects, specialising in large-scale demolitions, earth-moving jobs, major civil construction and building-foundation projects. Because of these business activities, its registered English name is Shandong Lu Jian Engineering Group. By the mid-2000s it had established itself in the local market and had accumulated adequate capital to support new projects, especially those that would help it expand into new seg- ments of the construction industry or additional business activities. There appeared to be a perfect meeting between demand and supply, but the link was in fact made through private contacts of a few village cadres, who were all under pressure from their superiors to mobilise villagers to participate in the scheme as speedily and numerously as possible. These village heads then became aware of the connections with Lujian.

The decision to contact Lujian and involve it in mobilising families to partake in the building project was not made without careful considera- tion. The project mobilisers paid particular attention to two factors. On the one hand, they had to introduce developers with a good record and reputation to ensure the quality of construction works. In the eyes of local officials, better word of mouth about a company could at least make their explanation and persuasion task less difficult. On the other hand, they also had to find and choose a sizeable company that was financially strong and able to invest some funds to jump-start the project. As will be detailed in Chapter 6, the mobilisers hoped that such a company could pay part of the initial cost of participating in the scheme. As an expanding company, Lujian would be inclined to take the financial risk in exchange for winning the bulk of construction contracts organised by local governments.

Lujian also made the decision according to its own procedures for investigating market conditions, which required a great deal of time and effort. This process was itself a rather efficient way of inducing villagers to consider their own position more seriously, as well as a way of draw- ing public attention to the project. Lujian sent its own teams to several villages many times to conduct preliminary studies, ranging from a field visit by senior managers to surveys by geological technicians to property valuations by experts and marketing teams. These visits and surveys had greater impact than township officials and village heads because they were undertaken by a specialist company. These meetings between villagers and Lujian helped ease villagers' two main concerns: which company will be doing the building work, and will the company be big and good enough to compensate villagers for losses if the project fails to deliver? Lujian pushed the social mobilisation beyond what township and village officers had been able to do, making the project a real and big topic among villagers.

The key issue in implementing the scheme was funding. A partial advance payment promised, and subsequently made, by Lujian was found to have a great mobilising effect by changing the minds of many villagers. In fact, after several rounds of surveys, investigations and other fieldwork,

Lujian identified construction in a few township areas of Laiwu as a viable business opportunity and decided to take on the project and persuade more villagers to sign up. Many township officials and village heads still remember that, to win more contracts, Lujian made two rather bold decisions, pressuring villagers to reach a decision quickly.

First, Lujian not only promised to pay partial land compensation in advance (and spread the message all over the place) but also made an offer of RMB 40 000 per *mu* for the land that each household would give up in exchange for a new apartment. This was done according to the national *zengjian guagou* policy, the details of which were given in Chapters 2 and 3. This offer was said to be much higher than villagers had expected. According to a couple of village heads, such a high offer even made some who missed the opportunity feel envious. Second, Lujian decided to rely on its own financial resources and started building a new residential area before many deposits were accessible. The company wanted the new development to indicate its determination in taking on the project and the quality of its construction. This strategy worked very well in the eyes of mobilisers, and the CCP secretary of a town called Fengyu praised it as follows:

> Once the construction started in a couple of villages, our tasks to explain the scheme and persuade fellow villagers to join became easier. We could only tell them to go to those villages and have a look [at the new buildings] and that the people in those villages were soon to move into those new modern apartments. This was very easy to explain, and people could also understand our point instantaneously. This was different from the start when there was nothing to show them, just relying on our lip-service. (Su, 2016, p. 126)

In addition to the above two decisions, Lujian took two less bold actions that were found to mobilise households to join the scheme. The company recruited many local workers, who witnessed what was happening on the construction site and were thus very confident about the quality of the new buildings. Partly because of the need to reduce transportation costs, Lujian also decided to use more locally produced building materials, such as sand, gravel and crushed stone, which benefited several local companies and workers. Policy-makers at different levels expected this socio-economic impact, but in terms of social mobilisation at village level it was helpful to have local factories and workers spread a positive report to potential participants in the scheme. It seemed to be that these people were better mobilisers than local officials and village leaders, and our fieldwork found that all the above actions, bold and otherwise, made the later stages of the project easier to promote.

Because all sides involved in the programme paid more attention to

funding than other concerns, and the construction industry consistently demanded favourable policies, governments at provincial and sub-
provincial level kept offering policy support for the scheme. To maintain
policy support, and improve policy-setting, the Shandong government
issued its directive No. 23 of 2009 to stress its policy of encouraging
private enterprise to participate in the scheme. In the same year, the then
Shandong governor, Jiang Daming, further emphasised this approach as
a pivotal strategy and novel mechanism for executing the scheme in his
speech at a provincial conference. Jiang also warned that government at
each level should regard the rural construction project and the rebuilding
of unsafe rural housing as the new economic-growth point in their region.
All local governments were therefore required to organise and guide
relevant enterprises to participate in the scheme based on the principles of
mutual help and mutual advantage (Jiang, 2009). Based on the Shandong
government's directive No. 23 and the governor's speech, the Shandong
Bureau of Land and Resources issued its notice No. 87 of 2009. The policy
of letting the market play a major role was not only emphasised but also
articulated in the document as follows:

> To innovatively manage land planning quotas and assist big land-users to be
> involved in the rural building, developers are permitted to gain the right to
> use surplus lands created by village renovations ... Support big land-using
> enterprises to finance the rural housing projects and surplus lands created from
> the projects can be used by the enterprises. (SPBLR, 2009, p. 2)

The above document once again confirms that private enterprises were
repeatedly encouraged not only to play their role as mobilisers in the
scheme but also to make use of their financial resources as efficiently as
possible to assist the execution of the strategy. This is an entirely new aspect
of social mobilisation of not only post-Mao China but also the country's
post-Deng industrialisation period. Such official documents have offered
policy support and guarantees for the market or private enterprises to be
further involved in the strategy from the perspective of social mobilisation.
However, these local approaches or strategies have also been considered
'state–business collusion', or 'government–business collusion' (*guan-shang
goujie*) and 'transfer of interest' (*liyi shusong*) (Tong, 2011; Nie, 2017).

The second type of private enterprise involved in the implementation
of the scheme consisted of local enterprises and small-business operators.
They knew what local governments were promoting, but many took a
wait-and-see attitude towards the scheme until Lujian started becoming
involved. What Lujian did in several township regions in Laiwu also
impacted on small local enterprises and even individual operators. In a
commercial market as highly active and competitive as that of China,

Lujian's involvement in building projects represented a disruptive force to market order, undermining the advantages of many players in the local market. All theories aside, no enterprise was able to stand up against Lujian's market expansion in the areas where our fieldwork took place, except a few big land users that needed more land for the cultivation of commercial crops. They contributed to the scheme by purchasing housing sites, which enabled some families to partake in the project. As will be further explained in Chapter 6, some local enterprises also acted as a work unit in a conventional way to help local governments persuade their workers to consider the scheme. Findings of this kind are important to our understanding of present-day China, as a work unit used to refer to a state-owned enterprise and was the basic socio-political and -economic unit to influence almost every aspect of the lives of its staff members. It seems to be true that private enterprises in China can still act in the way that pre-reform work units functioned.[5]

Interestingly, what was observed or heard from small-business operators was not helpful at all to the mobilisation effort. Of course, individual operators were not the main target of local governments' mobilisation efforts, but they had not only exerted their influence on the decision-making of some villagers but also acted in a way against the project because of their commercial interest. Until now, this analysis has not paid sufficient attention to the various forms of opposition and resistance to the scheme, especially those that were voiced by the private sector. In general, the emergence and development of the market and market forces have broadened the scope of social mobilisation and provided the mobiliser with more mechanisms and opportunities. At the same time, there are also new possibilities for complications. Our fieldwork revealed opposition and hindrances that were caused by various market forces. Leaving aside the issues caused by several enterprises due to commercial confidentiality, negative responses from some business operators showed that market forces could fight against anything that was believed to be unfavourable to their own business interests, and the effects of this opposition were contrary to the objectives of the implementation effort.

In one of our fieldwork areas, for example, one small-grocery-store owner and a fertiliser supplier were active and open opponents of building programmes in the area. They believed that those projects would result in the relocation of a large number of residents away from their service areas, which would be harmful to their businesses or would at least conflict with their way of operating their businesses. A new problem arising from this situation was that these private operators were outside the party-state system and relatively free from the influence of that system. However, the residents who were influenced by these operators were also influenced by others, and the opportunities provided by Lujian, for example, were tempting, which meant they had greater impact than the resistance of the operators. What the operators did may serve as evidence of an anti-mobilisation force in the private sector, which may indicate the level of development and power of China's private sector.

The third type of enterprise involvement was that of demolition companies. This was a relatively straightforward effort to let specialist companies do direct mobilisation in villages. Some of the practices used by demolition companies will be detailed in Chapters 6 and 7, so the discussion here will just briefly mention three aspects of the role played by demolition companies in the scheme. First, these companies could be quite efficient mobilisers and they played multiple roles in the campaign at village level. Our fieldwork showed that, because these companies were involved for business purposes, they worked not only diligently but also intelligently, trying various ways to persuade villagers. As private operations, they acted more freely and flexibly than local officials, and renegotiations with regard to payment and conditions even took place. Second, the involvement of demolition companies in the scheme was not unique to Laiwu but a national phenomenon. Due to the scale of the construction boom in China, the role of demolition companies expanded significantly, giving rise to special experiences, lessons and patterns. Many publications consider the role of such companies or that of the industry generally. In a Sichuan-based study, Xie defines their role in the scheme as a type of 'semi-formal governance' because the companies were found to have frequently assisted in settling housing-related disputes – doing what local governments were unable to do (Xie, 2014, p. 123). As recently as 2010, when the rural strategy was well under way all over the country, there were numerous forced-demolition incidents. Fuelled by extensive press coverage, especially online, there emerged the so-called forced-demolition development, which was articulated by a popular saying: No new China without demolitions. The latter will be discussed in detail in Chapter 7 because it was part of widespread collective resistance in China (M. Cai, 2015).

An additional point that is worth affirming here is the magnitude of infrastructure constructions, housing projects and related demolition works in China since the late 1990s, especially throughout the 2000s. Wade Shepard writes that such actions were so widespread that it became a common jest in Chinese social media to use the phrase *chai na*, which means 'in the process of demolishing', as the popular 'transliteration of the English name for their country' (Shepard, 2015, n.p.).[6] China was then called *chai na*, the place of tearing everything down, while all Chinese urban centres and towns, big and small, witnessed the destruction of old buildings and the construction of new ones (Lu, 2007). This background may help understand clearly why humble demolition companies could be regarded as crucial mobilisers in the campaign to implement a national policy, which could also indirectly explain how market forces have, step by step, become so powerful in policy implementation in China.

Of course, such government-initiated involvement of enterprises in the rural urbanisation scheme is potentially troublesome. Recently, the media in China have reported several cases involving allegations made by entrepreneurs against Shandong officials, who are accused of misleading enterprises, resulting in the loss of large sums of investment capital. Another round of the blame game has also started. Some are blaming local governments for inappropriately involving themselves in commercial operations, while others maintain that many entrepreneurs should blame themselves for their failure, as there is no guarantee of success for any business in a market economy. However, both sides agree on one crucial point: government–market relations need to be reviewed, reformed and redefined because both the market and the government have gone through the establishment phase of the market economy and have accumulated many years of experience (Fei, 2018). The social-mobilisation mechanism has been used in changing political, economic and social contexts that have not been clearly understood. The emerging challenges to government–business relations will further complicate the future use of the mechanism, which deserves ongoing attention.

NOTES

1. The arrest of the 'Gang of Four' took place on 6 October 1976, less than one month after Mao's death on 9 September 1976, which marked the end of Mao's Cultural Revolution. Although it was a type of military action that could well be defined as a 'palace coup' (He, 2010, p. 309) or 'palace revolt' (Barmé, 2010, p. 260), the arrest of these members of the CCP Political Bureau was welcomed and celebrated nationwide. In addition to the above-mentioned publications, readers can find more information about the 'Gang of Four' and the importance of eliminating their ultra-leftist influence on China's top-level decision-making in Baum (1994), Shapiro (2001) and Breslin (2014).
2. Numerous books have excellent discussions, and translations, of Deng Xiaoping's 'cat theory'. Leaving translations of this humble saying aside, as different translations are largely same in meaning, Susan Shirk once emphasised that Deng Xiaoping's 'cat' is a 'famous statement of pragmatism over ideology' (Shirk, 1993, p. 313). In addition to Shirk (1993) and Ju (1996), readers who are interested in Deng's political career and pragmatist thinking, or even the unsophisticated saying about the cat, are referred to Goodman (1994) and Vogel (2013).
3. The so-called 'Asian four small dragons' or the 'four little dragons of East Asia' refers to the rapid and successful industrial transformation of South Korea, Taiwan, Hong Kong and Singapore from the 1960s to the 1980s. Deng Xiaoping admired the achievements of these four small industrialised economies. He paid an official visit to Singapore as early as late 1978, in the year in which he returned to China's top leadership position, to personally meet with Lee Kuan Yew and see Singapore's economic achievements. In early

1992 he set a very specific goal for Guangdong to be the fifth dragon within 20 years. Interested readers can read more about this in Lee (2000), Vogel (2013) and Wong (2014).

4. Jiang Zemin and his 'three represents' theory were mentioned in Chapters 2 and 3. The core idea of this theory is that (1) the CCP should represent the development trends of advanced productive forces in society, (2) the CCP should represent the orientations of advanced modern culture and (3) the CCP should represent the fundamental interests of the overwhelming majority of the people of China. According to David Shambaugh, 'Jiang's odd-sounding theory was quickly dismissed by most Western analysts (and ordinary Chinese alike) as yet another propagandistic cliché ... Yet, upon closer examination, the Three Represents indicated an important, even radical shift in party philosophy, party composition, and party orientation' (Shambaugh, 2008, p.111). Although the theory has since been added to the CCP Constitution, the opportunity created by this bold theoretical attempt to reform the CCP was missed. In addition to Shambaugh (2008), readers can find more information about the theory in Zheng (2010), Guo (2012), Chun (2013) and Zeng (2013).

5. The so-called work unit is called *danwei* in Chinese. Like the concept *guanxi* (interpersonal relationships or contacts), it was once a very popular concept through which to consider complex and multidimensional Chinese socio-political systems and lives in the 1980s and 1990s. During those decades, in the eyes of many researchers, China simply meant *guanxi* and *guanxi* appeared to only exist and function in China. The concept *danwei* was also used by many China specialists in the same manner, for example *danwei* as a foreign word has appeared in several English book titles. However, while now more people have realised that interpersonal relationships and contacts are used in all human societies, not just China, the term *guanxi* is no longer as fancy as it was. But the concept *danwei* (work unit) is different and it remains a very relevant question in understanding how Chinese society is organised and managed at a micro level. Michael Dutton wrote that 'everyone exists in China in terms of a work unit' shortly before China's privatisation policies started taking effect (Dutton, 1998, p.43). Apart from Dutton (1998), interested readers can read more about *danwei* in Bray (2005) and Keith et al. (2014).

6. Precisely, this expression, or phrase, should be written as *chaina*, putting two syllables together. What is also worth noting is that some books and journalistic articles, as well as some academic articles, have not explained the meanings of *chai* (to tear down, to demolish, to destroy) and *na* (a grammatical particle indicating the present continuous tense) correctly. The main problem is the misunderstanding of *na* in the phrase, which should be a grammatical particle indicating the present continuous tense. Otherwise, the phrase does not make any humorous sense. In addition to the above-mentioned Lu (2007) and Shepard (2015), interested readers can find more information about this phrase and the demolition craze in China in the 2000s in Campanella (2008) and Visser (2010).

5. Mobilising policy support and resources at the prefectural level

Let us start this chapter with a brief note about the prefectural level, as it is now often expressed as the prefectural/municipal level. This refers to the first administration level under the provincial government, and it is, therefore, the third level of China's administrative system. This level was called the prefecture, which comprised several adjoining counties, but it has, in recent decades, been replaced by the term of prefectural-level municipality or city to implement the city-region idea. However, such an administrative region and arrangement cannot simply be called the municipal level as they are not entirely urban, and they all have several rural counties. The combination of rural and urban areas at this level has created the strange term of the prefectural-municipal level, which is also expressed as the prefectural/municipal level, to show our awareness of the problem with the phrase.

Early research attention on a range of issues relating to social mobilisation in China had, for a long time, been focused on two particular parts of the mobilisation process: China's central leadership and the various grassroots reactions to the rapid, unprecedented and extensive social changes taking place in this fast-industrialising country. The first focus on Beijing is so excessive that many educated Chinese believe, consciously or unconsciously, that they are personally implicated as being blindly obedient, and therefore of being incompetent and stupid. Spontaneous reactions aside, the overemphasis of the role of the central leadership in contemporary Chinese society contradicts known changes in central–local and state–society relations. The attention to the grassroots reactions, on the other hand, has been a significant advance in the field, adding a much-needed bottom-up viewpoint to the analysis of contemporary Chinese society, but discussions of this topic are often rather journalistic. What has not been adequately studied is the role of bureaucracies, and local CCP branches, at both the prefectural level and the county level, which may generally be defined as China's middle bureaucracy. In-depth research on these bureaucracies has not only been a challenge for non-Chinese analysts, but also for Chinese researchers, as it needs time and experience to clearly understand how they act, react and interact. Now, this book has also reached this vital middle point in both structural and conceptual terms.

As illustrated in Figure 2.2, China now has about 366 prefectural-level municipalities or cities, under which there are around 3000 county-level governments, including counties, county-level cities and county-level districts. Leaving aside the latter, which will be dealt with in Chapter 6, this chapter focuses on the role of the prefectural level of China's middle bureaucracy in social mobilisation. Since this is still an under-researched area in the study of contemporary China, and in view of the theoretical and practical importance of studying prefectural bureaucracies, this chapter will start with an analysis of the intermediary bureaucratic obstacle issue (*zhonggengzu*) that has frequently troubled China since the beginning of the reform era in the late 1970s and early 1980s. Though the issue was raised, and was also briefly discussed in this book's earlier chapters, a more systematic analysis of what has been undertaken to deal with this grave issue and what changes have occurred in the past decades is still required.

The analysis is followed by three sections that look at how the social mobilisation for executing the new rural scheme has been organised, managed and sustained in Shandong's smallest prefectural-level city, Laiwu, which has a population of only 1.4 million, as shown in Table 3.3. The second section of this chapter is, thus, a brief introduction to Laiwu, outlining local conditions that could affect the use of the social mobilisation mechanism. The third section focuses on how the tasks of mobilising local participation in the new countryside scheme are prioritised by the municipal leadership and its bureaucracies when policies are potentially beneficial. This discussion presents an understanding that is different from the theory of selective policy implementation, which may be used when new policies conflict with the interests of local officials (O'Brien and Li, 1999; Wu, 2014). The fourth and last section is devoted to a detailed examination of the project-driven approach that the city of Laiwu has virtually adopted to implement its various prioritised projects. In addition to revealing how the rural construction plan is being put into operation, this section will also look in detail at how the land finance (*tudi caizheng*) is utilised at the prefectural level as part of the mobilisation of resources.

CHANGING CHARACTERISTICS OF CHINA'S MIDDLE BUREAUCRACY

As mentioned, this chapter has a special section to consider the issues associated with China's massive middle bureaucracy. Since the 1990s, some non-Chinese China analysts have noticed 'the changing regional nature of the Chinese state' under the dual pressure of domestic reform and economic globalisation (Goodman, 1997, p. xi). Many efforts have also been made to understand what new characteristics the Chinese state has developed that are direct or indirect results of deep-seated and far-reaching changes in China (Bray and Jeffreys, 2016). As pointed out, however, China's middle bureaucracy is a difficult part of Chinese society to observe and analyse, especially for outsiders who are often unable to interact with many officials within the system. Therefore, this section will give more attention to analyses by Chinese academic and policy analysts than by outsiders. It is worth noting that this discussion is a continuation of what was introduced in Chapters 1 and 2. That is, it needs to be considered along with earlier discussions. Worth emphasising also is the parallel existence of at least two sets of macro political-economic mechanisms, which are two principal sets of driving forces, under China's central and provincial leaderships: the invisible hands of market forces analysed in Chapter 4, and the middle bureaucracy. The latter is the vital structure and basic mechanism used by the central and provincial leaderships to mobilise the whole party-state system and implement new policy initiatives. Of course, China could now do what is often described as *liantiaotui zoulu* (walking on two legs), relying simultaneously on the above two macro structures and mechanisms. Therefore, this analysis should be read with the understanding that new market forces are simultaneously playing their roles in executing the new rural scheme.

When the final part of the fieldwork of this study was conducted in 2015 and 2016, China's GDP growth rate reached new lows of 7.4 per cent in 2014, 6.9 in 2015 and 6.7 in 2016 (Yao, 2015, 2016; Magnier, 2016). In the words of Yao Yang, the current director of the National School of Development, Peking University, China's economy 'is in a period of recession' with Chinese characteristics defined simultaneously by both economic deflation and growth (Yao, 2016, n.p.). Consequently, the blame game has already begun, and the usual suspects responsible for the slow growth include the Xi Jinping-led central leadership, especially its tough anti-corruption drive, and the inefficient, irresponsible and inactive middle bureaucracy. The phrase *zhonggengzu* (intermediary obstructions) has once again become a frequently used term.

Outlook Weekly (*Liaowang*), an influential periodical published by the Xinhua News Agency, carried a long feature article in early 2015 entitled 'Four groups seen by Xi Jinping as *zhonggengzu* impeding the reform'. The article blames *zhonggengzu* at the prefectural and county levels for impeding the implementation of 500 or so reform projects in 80 main categories, which were proposed and approved by the CCP's new central leadership in 2013 and 2014 (Z. Chen, 2015). This article includes the following detailed analysis of *zhonggengzu* in terms of its nature and historical evolution.

> *Zhonggengzu* in early reform years was predominantly caused by limitations in thoughts and ideas, especially in ideology. Also included was *xiaoji zhengzu* [negative obstacles] triggered by uncertainties about reform prospects. However, having gone through more than 30 years of reforms, there are immeasurable fundamental changes in the interests [of different social classes and groups], which are evidently characterised by the regrouped patterns of [distributing] interests. The latter has also been noticeably reflected in the new differentiation of interest groups, resulting from various bonds of 'class identities'. Such new interests, of course, include not only economic benefits, but also political and cultural interests. (Z. Chen, 2015, n.p.)

This eye-catching article was obviously written based on Xi Jinping's speech at the Central Leading Group of Comprehensively Deepening Reforms, one of China's central decision-making committees, in February 2015.[1] It was the first time that Xi Jinping, as a political strongman in the words of some China observers (Brown et al., 2015; Tsang, 2015), admitted his frustration with the *zhonggengzu* issue that his father's generation of the CCP's central leadership encountered in early reform years.[2] What is hardly mentioned by China specialists is that Xi Jinping was away from Beijing a few years after the reforms began, and that despite his family's links with the central leadership, he may have no first-hand experience of how the issue was handled by the central leadership in the 1980s.

As mentioned in Chapters 1 and 2, China's reform was impeded from the beginning by its middle bureaucracy. After almost 30 years of Maoist experimentation from the early 1950s, China in the 1960s and 1970s was suffering from a serious lack of efficient connection between working people, in both rural and urban settings, and the work they do as a long-term outcome of collectivisation in villages and nationalisation in urban centres, big and small. Therefore, many ordinary people were not motivated to work or take responsibility for their work, except new cadres who had greatly benefited from centralised power structures. To motivate the entire population to work harder and produce more, reforms led by Deng Xiaoping started with initiatives to reconstruct the connection missing between people and production, for example the household production responsibility system in rural areas and the creation of various positions of responsibility in cities. Those working in bureaucracies, however, felt strongly that such fundamental changes deprived them of their privilege and political power to manage and control others. There were several years in which many new initiatives and strategies were unable to be executed quickly and correctly, which was soon identified as the *zhonggengzu* problem. This has since become one of the most crucial challenges that the central leadership must face, as it surrenders part of its authority to local establishments and retreats from its roles in various governance areas, demonstrated in the ideas of *fenquan rangli* (splitting powers and giving away some profits) as introduced in Chapter 2, and *minjin guotui* (the state retreats and the private sector advances) as noted in Chapter 1. In the past four decades, numerous efforts have been made by the central leadership to deal with various forms of *zhonggengzu*, caused not only by economic policies but also by different political measures aimed at intermediary bureaucratic obstructions.

First, the early efforts to inspire the middle bureaucracy to actively support reform programmes were mixed with traditional political education and economic incentives. The former was deployed at the time to ease the worries of numerous low-level leaders and rank-and-file members about the political nature of post-Mao reform, which was not so much about ideology, as maintained by the *Outlook Weekly* article, but more about how to avoid making political mistakes, which in Mao's era inevitably resulted in being removed from privileged official positions. The latter was the reformers' tactic to cope with the problem of cautious and unenthusiastic bureaucrats, which was characterised by a combination of the carrot of incentives and the stick of party lines and discipline. This was an early and experimental stage in which reform leaders were considering new remedies for bureaucratic resistance and inaction. Based on the CCP's experience, Deng Xiaoping put forward the *ganbu sihua* (cadre four modernisation) strategy first as early as 1980. The central leadership wanted to replace some officers with those who were revolutionary (which in fact means pro-reform, not pro-Mao), younger, educated and professional (Zhong, 2004; Guo, 2012). It was also in 1980 that the new leadership started considering what they called *tizhi gaige* (reform of the political system) (Talas, 1991; Fewsmith, 1994). Along with this idea, several efforts were made to bypass reluctant and resistant middle bureaucracies. For example, more autonomy was given to enterprises as early as 1980, just like what was done in agriculture (Li, 2001a). The bypass approach was also attempted to deal with prefectural leaderships because of the experience learnt from the Yantai case (discussed in Chapters 2 and 3). Early examples include the Sunan model,[3] indirectly showing that the market can be used to bypass middle bureaucracies.

The second approach to difficult and uncooperative middle bureaucracies was the use of a combined set of newly learnt management skills. The late 1970s and much of the 1980s were known in China as the decade of *sixiang jiefang* (thought liberation, or emancipation of thought), which made new management ideas a type of modern science. Therefore, the cadre management reform was driven further by the CCP's 'cadre four modernisation' strategy, turning the matter into a theoretically and practically crucial task. At the same time, a relatively relaxed, if not liberal, political climate also reformed many bureaucrats and their entire team, who had become more demanding than they were in Mao's era for help or support in terms of decision-making power, financial and material resources, and credit or recognition. While still vigorously pursuing the full implementation of the 'cadre four modernisation', central decision-makers also introduced some other new measures at different levels to deal with the growing demand from low-level bureaucracies. At the micro level, the performance-based cadre assessment system was introduced step by step; at the macro level, the previously mentioned *fenquan rangli* (splitting powers and giving away some profits) was developed further and upgraded into a system called *fenji baogan*, the multi-level contract responsibility system as detailed in Table 2.2, accepting local governments to be part of benefit-sharing arrangements, if they could achieve what was expected by higher-level offices.

Third, the criteria of selecting young leaders and the performance-based cadre appraisal practices had a profound impact on bureaucratic behaviour, both institutionally and individually, which resulted in the dilution of ideological control as early as the late 1980s, with utilitarianism becoming the main philosophical foundation for social transformation and an acceptable moral standard, especially since the mid-1990s. The political behaviour of the middle-level bureaucracy has therefore changed beyond the recognition of the observers who stick to outdated concepts and superficial topics. Direct observations have in fact already revealed many significant changes in bureaucratic behaviour and culture at different levels. From the policy implementation perspective, the behaviour of Chinese bureaucrats since the 1990s has become 'increasingly selective' (O'Brien and Li, 1999, p.167). From the position of China's political development, the middle-level bureaucracy has gone beyond being simply a demanding group of bureaucrats, and has become an interest group in present-day Chinese politics, actively seeking their own interests and their share of benefits, often in the name of local socioeconomic development.

Among various efforts to cope with the challenges imposed by the new political dynamics, one approach has its origin in China's traditional political culture and practices, which is the effort to restructure governmental arrangements at both the prefectural and the county levels. Although such territorial re-organisation was tried in the 1980s, such as the changes of *shiguanxian* (putting counties under the prefectural-level municipal governments) and *shengguanxian* (putting counties under the direct administration of provinces) (Zheng, 2007; C. Wang, 2016), the approach has been used more widely since the late 1990s and early 2000s. On the surface, these changes are nothing but responses to China's widespread urbanisation and, therefore, they have been considered by some analysts from a few modern perspectives, such as localism and government management. In more recent years, as will be reviewed next, such increasingly utilised territorial-administrative restructuring is often likened by many Chinese researchers to the traditional governance approach used throughout China's long imperial period (221 BC–1911 AD) and considered from the domestic political angle, especially political game theory. They see such trends as the formation of new forces and local interest groups that intend to carve up economic benefits and decision-making power with their superiors (Zhou, 2007; Jin and Yuan 2005; Qian and Ren, 2015). Because of this theoretical perspective, numerous interest groups have been identified. In the property market alone, for instance, the central government is now regarded as one of four key interest groups, along with local administrations, local developers and international investors (Huai et al., 2008).

Academically, leaving aside for a while other changing features of China's middle bureaucracies, China-based researchers introduced the social mobilisation concept into China in the early 2000s and, just like non-Chinese researchers before them, they started with some historical cases of social mobilisation. Since then, Chinese research on social mobilisation has gone through three phases of development. The initial phase was characterised by the simple introduction of the concept and the formation of an understanding of this perspective. With a few exceptions, such as Sun et al. (1999) and Sun and Guo (2000), the early efforts by Chinese analysts were to analyse pre- and post-1949 socio-political mobilisations, such as the land reform of the late 1940s and early 1950s and collectivisation (Liu, 2000; Lou, 2000; Zhang, 2003), or to discuss the concept generally (Zheng, 2000). Even though some analysts have simply accepted the Deutschian explanation of the concept, most Chinese scholars have regarded social mobilisation as a useful mechanism at an operational level, seeing it as a type of activity and process to achieve desired results (Gan and Luo, 2011).

The second main phase of Chinese research on social mobilisation coincided with the expansion of research activities in a range of areas, such as rural reforms, public policy and public administration reforms, mass politics and the mass media. As a concept borrowed from the West, also as an established analytical perspective, social mobilisation has quickly been adopted to analyse many issues since its introduction into the Chinese academic world. The extensive use of the concept by Chinese scholars is also because they are able to gather evidence quickly from a wide range of local sources. However, they have only considered the same topics as international researchers, ranging, as mentioned above, from rural reforms, to public policy and administrative reforms, to mass politics and the media. Certainly, their research is characterised by rich detail and applied nature.

It is also true that hardly any Chinese researchers accept that revolutionary politics or ideology, such as class struggles, are still behind social mobilisation (Zhou, 2008; S. Feng, 2011), because they all have devoted their attention to different policy initiatives (Yang, 2004; Long, 2005) and the routinisation of public governance (E. Chen, 2015). This second phase concluded with a shared understanding that traditional campaign-style governance was no longer dominant, and mobilisations in China were now being driven by multiple forces (Wen, 2017).

China's reform over the past four decades has resulted in multiple rounds of decentralisation and new forms of mass politics, and protests by students, urban and rural residents, which have attracted the interest of China scholars and observers, both inside and outside the country. It is because of these changes that Chinese research on social mobilisation has entered its third and current stage, which is characterised by a new understanding that social mobilisations in China now take place in the new context of non-unitary political orders.

In this third phase, Chinese scholars are well ahead of their foreign peers in conceptualising what social mobilisations are about in present-day China. The state capacity concept has led to a dynamic-interaction perspective, which emphasises that new initiatives are not one-sidedly based on a state strategy, but are often decided by 'day-to-day interactions between state agents of various levels and different social groups' in a wide range of arenas (Zeng, 2013, p. 24). To theorise why individuals can be mobilised to partake in mass protests when the state encounters serious problems in mobilising the whole country to achieve its goals, the notion of the 'microfoundations' of the macro-phenomena was formed. It stresses the importance of both the micro–macro connection and the new relations between the elites and the masses (Zha, 2015, p. 1). China's domestic politics has already been transformed, although many have not yet realised it, or refuse to accept it, entering what many Chinese, both academic and non-academic, have often called the new era of *boyi* (strategic game-playing) (Xu and Cui, 2011; Lee and Zhang, 2013), which is full of political bargaining and negotiating between various social groups at different levels (Liang, 2014). The hierarchical top-down process and campaign-style governance have been transformed and partially replaced by new and complex forms of social mobilisation. Although the concept of *boyi* may not be suitable to describe China's current political situation, the changes need to be considered when examining the use and role of social mobilisation.

The previously mentioned article from *Outlook Weekly* provides an official explanation of how China's middle bureaucracies have been affected, reshaped and changed recently by new political orders. Some characteristics discussed in the article represent the fourth category of changes that have taken place in the middle bureaucracy. The *Outlook Weekly* article argues that four types of *zhonggengzhu* (intermediary bureaucratic obstacles), should be dealt with urgently.

> Such obstacles can be divided into four general categories . . . The first type: powerful special interest groups interfere or 'misread' *dingceng sheji* [top-level design of reform] . . . The second form: selective policy implementations because of *bumen benweizhuyi* [selfish departmentalism or localism] . . . The third type: inactive local officials who either misuse allocated funds or refuse to act responsibly or cooperatively . . . The fourth category: fragmented interest groups join to form so-called 'opinion groups' and make use of fake 'public opinions' to undermine the environment and atmosphere of reform. (Z. Chen, 2015, n.p.)

In a new book-length report written by researchers from the Institute of Economic System and Management, a research organisation of China's National Development and Reform Commission (NDRC), six existing forms of intermediary bureaucratic blockades or hindrances have been identified (Zhang and Sun, 2017). It is worth mentioning that these six types of intermediary bureaucratic obstacle are identified and analysed while the report also criticises *dingceng sheji* (the top-level design of reform programmes) and openly blames faults 'in the thinking behind the top-level design' for the current 'tepid pace of reform' (Buckley, 2017, n.p.). Besides its criticism of central policy-makers, the report asserts that the following bureaucratic behaviours are responsible for the sluggish economy: substitutional implementation (*tihuanxing zhixing*) by which central policies are replaced by local counter-policies; supplementary implementation (*fujiaxing zhixing*) by which additional local specifics are inserted into central policies; selective implementation (*xuanzexing zhixing*); symbolic implementation (*xiangzhengxing zhixing*); partial or incomplete implementation (*pianmianxing zhixing*) due to lack of clear understanding of new national policies; and 'wait-and-see' implementation (*guanwangxing zhixing*) by which local officials consider the benefits and risks of new central policies before taking any actions (Zhang and Sun, 2017). It is worth remarking that all these have occurred while some scholars and advisers were still considering how to motivate middle-level bureaucrats to participate in policy implementations more actively and responsibly than before (Xu, 2016).

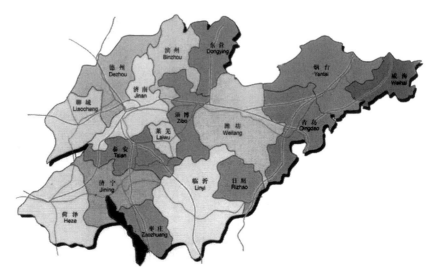

Source: Drawn by the authors of this book.

Figure 5.1   The location of Laiwu, Shandong province

THE PREFECTURAL-LEVEL CITY OF LAIWU

The city of Laiwu is where this research project is based, and as indicated in Figure 5.1, Laiwu is located right in the middle of Shandong province. It is one of Shandong's 17 sub-provincial regions listed in Table 3.3.

Laiwu is the smallest prefectural-level city or municipality in Shandong in both geographic and demographic terms. It has only a total land area of 2246 square kilometres, roughly 400 square kilometres smaller than the urban area of Shanghai, and more than 500 square kilometres smaller than the entire special administrative region of Hong Kong. Although it is a small place, Laiwu has been a reputable regional centre for many centuries, partly because it is perfectly located at the south foot of the Taishan range (or the Mount Tai range)[4] and in the southeast of Jinan, the provincial capital of Shandong. When the new countryside plan was about to be implemented province-wide in 2006, Laiwu had approximately 750 000 rural residents (60 per cent) and 500 000 urban residents (40 per cent). Ten years later, in 2015, when Laiwu's population had reached about 1.4 million population, its urban population had slowly increased to about 820 000 (roughly 58 per cent), and its rural population to about 570 000 (around 42 per cent) (SPBS, 2001, 2016).

It was also because of its small population that Laiwu was a county

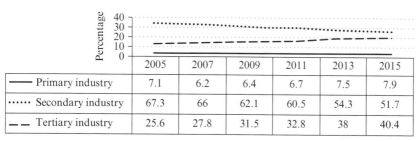

	2005	2007	2009	2011	2013	2015
—— Primary industry	7.1	6.2	6.4	6.7	7.5	7.9
······ Secondary industry	67.3	66	62.1	60.5	54.3	51.7
— — Tertiary industry	25.6	27.8	31.5	32.8	38	40.4

Year

Source: Based on data from SPBS (2016).

Figure 5.2   Shares of three sectors in Laiwu's GDP, 2005–15

until 1983, when it was upgraded to be a county-level city because of the growing importance of its industrial sector, which will be detailed below, but the left-hand part of Figure 5.2 indicates in part how substantial its industrial sector had been in the last decades of the twentieth century. For the same reason, Laiwu was given a special administrative status as a province-administered city in 1988. After only four years, in 1992, the city was upgraded to a prefectural-level city. However, even up to now, Laiwu has as little as two urban districts and 13 townships, the latter of which has declined from 15 in 2010. The two urban districts or suburbs now have seven *jiedao* (sub-district) committees, which has slowly increased from four of them in 2000 to five in 2002 and then to seven in 2012 (Zhang and Wang, 1998; SPBS, 2001, 2016; Ma, 2008; Yang, 2012a; L. Wang, 2016).

Despite being the smallest prefectural-level city and region, the overall education level of the Laiwu population is higher than that of several other sub-provincial regions, ranking seventh out of Shandong's 17 sub-provincial regions according to China's fifth census, conducted nationwide at the end of 2000 (SPBS, 2002). Such above-average educational attainments are partially because of Laiwu's local economic structure. In the mid-1960s, Laiwu was chosen to develop a new iron and steel production base because of its protected location by the mountains. According to this strategic national defence plan, many experts, engineers, mechanics and technicians, skilled workers, cadres and even military personnel were transferred from different places to Laiwu to participate in the project, which was then coded as Project 701 (Luo, 2017). As the project code indicated, the iron and steel production line in Laiwu was opened in January 1970 as a special project of China's 'third-front construction' plan in coastal provinces. The latter type was then called *xiaosanxian* (small, or minor, third-front) developments (Bramall, 2007; Luo, 2017).[5] Now, the iron and steel production is still Laiwu's main industry, and the city is often introduced, for example, by the HKTDC (Hong Kong Trade Development Council), to the outside world in the following way.

> Industry is the economic driver to the city, accounting for 46% of the GDP in 2015. Due to the abundant mineral resources, Laiwu's pillar industry is steel and iron, metallurgy. Other major industries include pharmaceuticals, food processing, textiles, construction materials and petrochemicals. (HKTDC, 2017, n.p.)

According to officials from the Laiwu Bureau of Land and Resources, the city's non-iron-and-steel district, Laicheng district, one of Laiwu's two urban districts, also had about 350 enterprises in 2012, producing auto parts and chemical products (Wang and Liang, 2012). These factories have implications for the implementation of the new countryside plan, especially for the land use and the land finance. For example, approximately 8000 *mu* of land was transferred to a few big industrial users;[6] these factories provided employment for more than 8000 local people. Adding to these challenges is the endless initiatives by the province to drive further growth. Before the new rural scheme, Laiwu followed a series of new policies and approaches to economic growth, such as *zhaoshang yinzi* (attracting business and investment) and *keji yuanqu* (high-tech park), creating a high demand for land.

Laiwu is also famous for a range of agricultural products. It is the main producer of ginger, garlic and Shandong green onions, although the sector's contribution to the local GDP, as shown in Figure 5.2, has stagnated at around 7 per cent, significantly lower than secondary and tertiary industries. However, the agricultural sector has provided more job opportunities in the region than the other two sectors, especially in the mid-2000s. In 2005, for example, the number of people working in the agricultural sector in Laicheng district (427 711 people) was about ten times that of the number of workers in the secondary industry (44 033 people). Even in Gangcheng district, the iron-and-steel district, 82 168 people worked in agriculture in 2005, while only 43 259 workers were employed by the secondary sector (SPBS, 2006). Laiwu's agricultural potential was also reflected in the high level of commercialisation and industrialisation of its popular products, especially its so-called 'three spices and one pepper' (Song and Ji, 2003, p. 32). In 2002, Laiwu had 995 factories to process ginger, garlic and other produce, and more than 100 temperature-controlled store facilities (Wan and Song, 2002). What is also important is that more land was used for rural housing than urban housing. When more people are moving to cities, there is a big potential in terms of the land finance. A group of analysts from Laiwu Bureau of Land and Resources estimated that the city's rural population (with 209 square metres per head) in 2007 was using about one-

and-a-half times more land than urban residents (with 130 square metres per head) (Cao et al., 2007).

In the first few years after the new rural scheme, the dominance of the iron and steel industry in Laiwu was causing structural problems in its local economy because of the strong competition from other producers, but the new rural building plan would assist in sustaining Laiwu's economic growth. An analysis by Laiwu Bureau of Finance revealed that the city's GDP was RMB 36.7 billion in 2007, and its financial income reached more than RMB 2.6 billion, growth of 16.9 per cent and 35.4 per cent respectively compared with the previous year (Laiwu Bureau of Finance, 2009). However, as argued by Yang Yixin, the city's mayor from 2011 to 2012 who trained at Beijing-based Renmin University of China as a land management specialist, the iron and steel market was overheated countrywide from 2004 to 2007, and since then, the huge drop of iron and steel prices 'had sent the entire economy of Laiwu into a tailspin' (Yang, 2012b, p. 6). This may well be the reason why a deputy director of a research division of Shandong Development and Reform Commission advised as early as 2006, before executing the new rural scheme, that the implementation needed new thinking beyond the sectoral division between industry and agriculture to find a way to sustain the growth (Sun, 2006).

Laiwu's economic problem caused by the massive drop in iron and steel prices in 2007 and 2008 was promptly dealt with by the actions of both the province and the city to hasten the implementation of the new rural building plan initiated in 2006, which was detailed in Chapter 3. Laiwu made various preparations in 2007, including the execution of the provincial document No. 111 of 2006 through the issue of the Laiwu government's directive No. 35 of 2007, and a more detailed guideline by the Laiwu Bureau of Finance and the Laiwu Bureau of Land and Resources on the land use policy of *zengjian guagou* (linking the reduction of rural construction land with the increase of urban construction land). Laiwu was then approved by the provincial government, in its No. 19 directive of 2008, to trial the new rural building programme (Su, 2016). A new opportunity was created, but the new scheme has been rather challenging from the beginning, requiring the prefectural leadership and their officials to be more strategic and innovative than before.

PRIORITISING SOCIAL MOBILISATION TASKS

Ma Pingchang, Laiwu's mayor from late 2006 to 2011, officially took the city's leadership position in early 2007, and as a university-trained accountant and experienced local official, Ma publicly promised in 2007 to increase Laiwu's annual GDP per capita quickly and substantially from US$3700 in 2007 to US$8000 in 2012, achieving more than 100 per cent growth in five years (Ma, 2008). In his public speech, he revealed six major policy measures, including a couple of political slogans that he mentioned repeatedly, such as building a harmonious society set forth by the then Chinese leader, Hu Jintao, and building *fuwuxing zhengfu* (service-oriented government), but local officers believed that two of the policies were his real intentions. His two new intentions were summarised by his cynical fellow officers as *zhuanbian fazhan fangshi* (change or re-orientation of the development model) and *tudi caizheng* (land finance). As discussed in Chapters 2 and 3, the land as a source of revenue to finance local governments and their growing expenditures was already widely used by many regional governments in the mid-2000s, and it has since become a considerable and dependable mechanism and a financial guarantee of achieving the transition to a new development model.

The two key points identified by local bureaucrats suggest a methodological approach to the analysis of the implementation of the new rural scheme in Laiwu, which is to identify what are the most critical steps in social mobilisation for the new rural building plan. This is very helpful because China's local leaders and bureaucrats excel at producing different types of paperwork, and many researchers become deeply confused by the overwhelming amount of documentation. What has also emerged is a similar analytical clue in relation to the different procedures that are often considered indispensable to social mobilisation. Three points are worth mentioning before looking at how social mobilisation for the rural urbanisation plan has been prioritised in Laiwu.

First, there seems no obvious or special need to mobilise personnel as often emphasised in previous studies. China has been in development overdrive for four decades, during which time its bureaucracies have been repeatedly reformed and well trained to cope with implementing numerous policy initiatives, including mobilising personnel resources for action. That is, the mobilisation of personnel was a factor in examining social mobilisations in China in the past, and is still important in other social contexts, but it is not a unique issue in present-day China. In the words of several local officials, China's economy has been on steroids, or as if on the so-called rooster-blood therapy (*dajixue*, or injection of chicken blood) in a similar Chinese phrase, for several decades and its bureaucratic teams have always been on high alert, permanently ready for mobilisation. The latter is not only massive, but also comprises two parallel organisational structures: the CCP and the government system.

Second, because of the permanent readiness for mobilisation, there is hardly anyone at the prefectural level who still places any emphasis on routine social mobilisation practices, such as document-reading sessions, cadre meetings and mass rallies. All these practices are still carried out, but they are more focused on the substance of the new policy than on other operational routines. Municipal departments and bureaus still must prepare written materials, such as meeting minutes, government circulars, booklets and explanatory notes, but as pointed out by a few local officers, all their attention is now drawn to how a new policy initiative could be better tailored to region-specific contexts and different local needs. To a large extent, frequent mobilisation exercises have familiarised local leaders and bureaucrats with textbook methods of policy implementation. They are so familiar with such routines that they can now turn most of their attention to the optimised utilisation, both politically and economically, of new policy initiatives, suggesting the urgent need for an analysis of social mobilisation from a new perspective.

Third, as mentioned, the initial trial of the new rural building plan was initiated in Laiwu in 2008, immediately after the city was formally approved to be a new region to trial the new rural scheme. To analyse out different approaches to different types of villages and towns, the second test programme was conducted in 2009. In the area where the sub-prefectural part of this research was carried out, three villages were selected to be part of the 2008 pilot programme, and two more were included in the 2009 programme. These were done with different aims in mind. In the eyes of some, the prefectural leaders must take action swiftly and perceptibly to avoid any possible blame from their demanding superiors, but they must also not overreact to new initiatives, or do anything beyond what they are expected to do, before forming a better and clearer understanding of how best to respond and how to act. Therefore, it has been a long-established local approach to organise a few test programmes first.

In the eyes of others, however, the above explanation is only part of the story, and in the case of this rural urbanisation drive, they consider that the local leaders and other key institutional and non-institutional players wanted to have more time to reflect on how this new initiative could be better used to assist local growth priorities, and meet the needs of the prefectural leadership and local interest groups, even though it meant putting aside some forms of personal financial gain that many cynical locals have repeatedly emphasised. Regardless of which explanation is closer to the truth, one thing is clear: the prefectural leadership needed to produce a workable plan that worked in their favour, and was also accepted by most of the parties involved. Such a tactical approach was sensible because all these were done at the same time as the massive drop in iron and steel prices struck the economy of Laiwu.

As mentioned at the start of this section, the prefectural leadership had at the same time developed a two-step approach for the municipal region to mobilise all relevant bureaus, departments and offices, sub-prefectural governments and other stakeholders to be involved in this multi-beneficial rural building project. The approach narrowed the scheme-related mobilisation down to two key actions: the development of a detailed action plan and a project-oriented approach to the implementation of priority projects. Putting aside the latter, which will be analysed in the next section, the rest of this section focuses on how the new rural development scheme has been localised and prioritised in Laiwu.

Shan Zengde, Laiwu's executive deputy mayor from 2006 to 2011, assisted Mayor Ma Pingchang with taking care of the government's daily business activities and the city's economic development, and published an article in 2011, shortly before being transferred to lead the provincial Bureau of Agriculture. In the article, Shan recapitulates what Laiwu's municipal government had been doing in mobilising various resources for promoting and activating the rural programme through a set of highly localised and prioritised strategies. According to Shan, Laiwu's urban–rural economic structures and its population–land ratio are different, to some extent, from many other regions. Its industry is better established than other regions, despite the need for restructuring in the mid-2000s. As introduced earlier, Laiwu's strong industrial foundation is due to its past role in China's *xiaosanxian* (minor third-front) industrial building project of the mid-1960s. Another advantage that Laiwu has is that its rural–urban gap in living standards is less than in many rural regions in China because of the higher level of commercialisation of agricultural production (Shan, 2011). Based on these advantages, and without mentioning other restrictions that many locals have identified, such as the limited amount of land available for the rural urbanisation scheme, Shan outlines Laiwu's overarching strategy for the new scheme in his article as follows:

> Based on its relatively solid industrial foundation, and its speedy advancement of agricultural specialisation and commercialisation, as well as other foundations and advantages, such as its relatively small urban-rural inequality in living standards, the city of Laiwu has opted to adopt an integrated urban-rural development strategy as the main policy thread [*zhuxian*], or policy conduit, for guiding the work of the entire municipal region. (Shan, 2011, p. 32)

A careful examination of speeches delivered by several key leaders of the government of Laiwu (including Shan, who was jailed because of seemingly bizarre extramarital relationships when the final part of the fieldwork of this project was carried out in 2015 and 2016 (Hu, 2015)), articles published under their names, data collected through fieldwork and other documentary sources have demonstrated that the entire set of strategies formulated by the prefectural government of Laiwu comprises three central components, one more than what Shan summarised in his 2011 article.

At the macro level, Laiwu adopted the integrated approach to deal with development of both rural and urban areas, not simply sticking to the original idea of building a new socialist countryside. It is true that this urban–rural integration strategy reflects a shift in the thinking of central decision-makers about how to deal with the rural issue, because the integration strategy was put forward by the new central leadership under Xi Jinping at the third plenary session of the CCP's Eighteenth Central Committee in late 2013. The Laiwu leadership realised the importance of this integration approach based on its situations, before it became official. The core idea of this approach was to combine two traditionally separate issues of rural and urban development. More specifically, the approach 'considers the city's total land area of 2,246 square kilometres all together and then develops an integrated plan for land use' (Shan, 2011, p. 32). Based on this localised general strategy, Laiwu formulated two guiding documents: *Fazhan gangyao* (Guidelines for the integrated urban–rural development in Laiwu) and *Zongti guihua* (Master plans of the integrated urban–rural development in Laiwu) in 2010. The latter also sets out some specific plans for action in 12 areas and ten sets of related policies, which will be considered next.

To broadly disseminate this contextualised strategy, a 16-character slogan, or directive, was put forward to mobilise and guide confused local officials and residents. This slogan says '*yigong cunong; yicheng daixiang; chengxiang hudong; xietiao fazhan*' (facilitating agricultural development through industry; advancing rural development through urban activities; correlating urban and rural growth; and developing co-ordinatedly) (Shan, 2011, p. 32). This badly worded slogan has been used extensively, and as a distinctive exercise in Chinese bureaucracy the catchphrase propaganda was not only used in this mobilisation, but has also been repurposed in this new socio-political context, to help promote a local approach to urban and rural development.

The prioritisation of the new rural scheme has been praised by main-stream researchers as an innovation in policy implementation and related mobilisation (Guo and Jia, 2012), but it has also been a cause for criticism from local officers and ordinary residents. Leaving the positive comments aside, because they come mainly from those who either benefit from this localised approach or are not interested in it at all, the criticisms mostly cover only a few objections. There are those who are unhappy that the policy is implemented gradually, according to priority (O'Brien and Li, 1999; Wu, 2014); those who regard the policy as a false innovation or pseudo-innovation (M. Cai, 2015; Jin and Yuan, 2005); those who see the change as part of *hemou* (collusion) between governments and businesses, or interest groups; and those who see such modification as typical cases of *boyi* (strategic game-playing, bargaining and negotiations) within China's party-state system.

While the critical comments can be sorted and classified into a few categories, the supporters of the prioritisation are more forthright in their arguments, focusing on two general changes that have taken place in China over the past decades. On the one hand, three or four generations of provincial and sub-provincial cadres have grown up with, and have also been trained by, Deng Xiaoping's work tactic of *zhua zhongdian* (grasp the main points), while also learning Deng's 'two-hands' approach (Dittmer and Chen, 1981). According to former Chinese vice-premier Bi Yibo, who became even more famous due to his son Bo Xilai's unsuccessful rivalry with Xi Jinping in seeking China's top leadership position, Deng Xiaoping was more skilful in using a *juzhong ruoqing* (to lift something heavy as if it is light) approach than his predecessor Zhou Enlai (Qiu, 2000, p. 258). Under Deng's influence, all tasks could be classified as important and urgent or otherwise. Therefore, a selective approach to implementing new policies according to local circumstances was allowed. On the other hand, the 'cadre four modernisation', which was discussed in Chapter 2 and the first section of this chapter, and China's reform have produced many well-educated and politically skilled cadres, especially good at justifying their actions and creating novel ideas, if not excuses, according to what has been called GDPism. All these have led to the new political *boyi*, with which local officials become very familiar, as they use it to deal with their superiors or superior institutions. This is what is now called China's *zhudong* (proactive) local politics (Yang et al., 2013).

Under Laiwu's over-arching and guiding plan of integrating urban–rural social and economic development, the secondary approach to the execution of the above primary strategy has also been set forth. As outlined by Shan Zengde, the prefectural leadership of Laiwu and its administrations have agreed to adopt *tongchou chengxiang tudi guanli* (coordinated management of land in both rural and urban areas) as the *qie'rudian* (point of entry) or *tupokou* (breakthrough point) for pushing the new rural programme (Shan, 2011). This is the very important part of Laiwu's prioritised approach to mobilisation for the new rural scheme and its implementation based on Laiwu's regional circumstances. The central idea of this so-called coordinated management of land use is to centrally control the land-use issue.

As early as 2007, in a policy analysis entitled 'Protection of arable land in the urban-rural integration progress and the coordinated use of land', several policy analysts of the Laiwu Bureau of Land and Resources argued for both the urban–rural integrated development policy and coordinated land utilisation. The policy recommendations were predominantly based on the following fact:

> Presently, the average arable land per capita in Laiwu is just 553 square metres (0.83 *mu*), which is the lowest municipal region in the province of Shandong, already below the alarming line of 667 square metres (1 *mu*) per capita that has been set forth by both the [CCP] Provincial Committee and the Provincial Government, and close to the alarming line of average 533 square metres (0.8 *mu*) that has been proposed by the Food and Agriculture Organization of the United Nations. According to forecasts, the average arable land per capita in the entire municipality [of Laiwu] will shrink to 400 square metres in 2010, when this average will be lower than 333 square metres in more than one-third of townships or district areas. This will lead to an even more serious imbalance between population and arable land than now in the municipality, posing a grave threat to socio-economic developments in the region. (Cao et al., 2007, p. 39)

The expansion of Laiwu's urban areas has been characterised by urban sprawl, expanding its urban area from 27.2 square kilometres in 1996 to 54.7 square kilometres in 2005 and 69.1 square kilometres in 2007 (Cao et al., 2007). In 2011, the sprawl increased to 78.8 square kilometres, and built-up township areas in the municipality had expanded from 2.7 to 26.2 square kilometres in 2011 (Guo and Liu, 2013). Such a rapid pace of expansion has put the local leadership on solid ground for answering any criticism on its plan of combining urban and rural land uses. Such criticism has been widespread, echoing the negative comments by many Chinese who see certain localised policies as the technique of *liyi shusong* (transferring benefits) to the collaborators of local leaders or officers. Despite the scepticism of many locals regarding the likelihood of the official-business collusion, Laiwu has developed strong arguments for considering the use of both urban and rural land together. This has also led to the drafting of another master plan for the use of both urban and rural land (*tudi liyong zongti guihua*), in which all 1070 administrative villages (*xingzhengcun*) in Laiwu are classified into four main types in terms of land use: new central urban district, key township, new rural village and normal residential area (Shan, 2011).

The core nature of this approach is what has been called *tudi caizheng* (land finance), which has indeed provided Laiwu with a massive amount of funds for local economic growth, including residential building. According to another team of analysts from Laiwu Bureau of Land and Resources, the land finance provided Laiwu with additional funds of only RMB 630 million in 2003, which was increased to about **RMB** 2 billion in 2007, and then an average of more than **RMB** 1.3 billion from 2009 to 2011, meaning the land-related revenue consistently accounted for more than 25 per cent of the total local revenue (Guo et al., 2014). In 2010, this percentage reached as high as 38 per cent, the figure of which has been used by optimistic officials to argue that land finance is in fact a new mechanism for mobilising institutions and resources for the new scheme. They insist that the prefectural region is sandwiched not only between the province and the central state, but also between their superiors and the market forces. Therefore, these local officials regard land finance as a creative and useful mechanism to guarantee the fulfilment of their *shiquan* (localised responsibilities or tasks) through local fiscal autonomy.

At the operational level, the entire set of strategic approach developed by Laiwu's leadership includes the third part that Shan Zengde did not mention in his 2011 article. This third key component is another set of localised policies for legitimising the coordinated use of rural and urban land, especially rural land that is, in theory, owned collectively by rural residents, or 'the collectives' in the words of the PRC Constitution (Rithmire, 2015). To make the coordinated use of rural and urban land legitimate, and therefore to make its own creative integrated approach achievable, Laiwu introduced a so-called *lianggu yijian* (two de-mutualisations and one establishment) approach, which was even praised by a few other provinces as a creative mechanism in managing rural land use (Cao and Jia, 2011). A typical result is that a few provincial bureaus of the Hubei Province organised a study tour to Laiwu to learn about its rural land-ownership reform.

According to a feature report published in *Hubei Nongye* (*Hubei Agriculture Weekly*), the third main component of Laiwu's integrated urban–rural development strategy is not only highly praised by interprovincial counterparts as a creative policy tool and implementation mechanism, but is also clearly summarised as follows:

> In recent years, the city of Laiwu has opted to take the deepening reform of rural [land] ownership as a key breakthrough point and primary focus in the implementation of its integrated urban-rural development strategy. In accordance with the action plan of both the [CCP's] municipal committee and the municipal government, the city of Laiwu has systematically introduced its *lianggu yijian* [two de-mutualisations and one establishment] (i.e. reforming the system of collectively owned rural assets through a shareholding structure, and reforming the right to contract and utilise rural land through a shareholding scheme, and establishing up-to-date rural organisations for economic cooperation), which have maximally activated rural resources elements. Having been guided by some government institutions, stimulated by various new policies, and influenced by some excellent examples, Laiwu has already put in place a range of new rural development mechanisms, typified by 'clear ownership,

distinct rights and responsibilities, trouble-free transition, and separation of government and business'. (Cao and Jia, 2011, p. 2)

This seems to be a typical case, as illustrated by an old Chinese saying, 'Outsiders can see clearly' (*pangguanzhe qing*), as there are hardly any other documents in Laiwu summarising its prioritised local strategies as 'two de-mutualisations, and one establishment'. Yet, there are also no local cadres who deny the ongoing implementation of the above reforms, apart from revealing possible self-promotion behind the coverage, hinting at the Mayor Yang Yixin's link with Hubei. In fact, these new local ideas were trialled as early as 2008, when more than 80 land transfers were done, involving more than 2000 *mu* of land (Shan, 2011). Based on the trial, Laiwu's leaders formulated regulations for the land transfer, laying a legal basis for the region-wide execution of the rural schemes in 2010 (Guo and Xu, 2012).

According to a local senior accountant, Laiwu pursued another 'establishment' alongside what Cao and Jia (2011) summarised, which was to establish the mechanism of transferring urban–rural land, while creating new rural organisations for economic cooperation (Xing, 2012, p. 189). Of course, the urban–rural land transfer policy was not created by Laiwu, but imposed on all regional governments by the central leadership through the still existing, and functioning, top-down mobilisation mechanism. What the accountant pointed out shows the new relationship between central policies and local choices. There has often been a wide divergence between policy design and local adoption, and Laiwu's 'two de-mutualisations and one establishment' are a set of localised tactics to execute the complicated *zengjian guagou* (bundling up the reduction of rural construction land with the increase of urban construction land), the state land-use policy (M. Cai, 2015; Meyer-Clement, 2016). New patterns and tactics of social mobilisation exist among the similarities and differences between central strategies and local adoptions.

It is worth mentioning that what Laiwu's leaders devised in the late 2010s to de-mutualise the rural assets and the land use, introducing different shareholding schemes, was a bold policy experiment, and it is only as recently as late 2016 and 2017 that this has been incorporated into national reform strategies. Recently, the rural asset-sharing reform has appeared, as a new reform initiative, in China's state-controlled media outlets, such as Xinhua News Agency and *China Daily* (*Xinhua News*, 2016b), which has, therefore, attracted the attention of the global media, such as Reuters and the *Financial Times*. In a typical journalistic manner, Reuters made the brief passing comment, 'No details were given' in its report on the new reform initiative (Yao, 2017, n.p.); the latter has already effectively assisted Laiwu in mobilising for the new rural building plan. Furthermore, the local prioritisation of policy-making and policy implementation has become not only part of China's new political reality, partly characterised by bargaining among different interests at different levels, but also a vital supplement to better governance, or at least a new way to deal with its 'management deficit' (Metcalfe, 1996, p. 43).

THE PROJECT-DRIVEN APPROACH TO IMPLEMENTATION

In a paper entitled 'The project system and mobilization of grass-roots government officials', published in *Social Sciences in China (Chinese edition)* alongside the journal's English translation, Chen Jiajian analyses the importance of *xiangmuzhi* (project-driven tactic or approach), a new form of social mobilisation, in mobilising local governments. He argues that the project-driven tactic has not only been extensively used in China's party-state system, but has also played an increasingly crucial role in mobilising its entire bureaucracy for implementing new policies (J. Chen, 2013). Having acknowledged the existence of the *boyi* (bargaining and negotiation) relations among institutions and interest groups in present-day China, Chen regards the project-driven tactic as the most noteworthy mechanism for mobilising local governments since the introduction of the highly praised *mubiao guanli zerenzhi* (target-responsibility system) in the 1980s and the tax-sharing system in 1994. Based on his study in Sichuan province, Chen identifies four new features of the approach: the direct channel of funding, the special power to make appointments, the prioritised status, and the ease of building a public profile (J. Chen, 2013). The same approach has, in fact, also been used in Laiwu.

In Laiwu, the prioritised implementation strategies discussed in the previous section gave rise to a construction boom, which was once defined by the Research Office of the Laiwu municipal government, a home-grown think-tank, as a *shuanglun qudong* (two-wheel-driven) economy. This demonstrates the important role of rural urbanisation and re-industrialisation in local development (Laiwu Research Office, 2013). Guided by all those prioritised tactics, Laiwu initiated 394 construction projects in late 2011 and 2012, all of which were worth more than hundreds of millions of Chinese yuan, and 71 projects were worth more than a billion Chinese yuan. Many rural construction projects were also started at the same time, and 106 projects were infrastructure developments, laying the groundwork for other projects that were part of the over-arching integrated approach to deal with rural and urban developments. In addition, Laiwu developed three-year construction guidelines. The government chose to focus efforts, especially funding, on building 'four urban centres and four districts', a specific design for its urban–rural integration plan (Laiwu Research Office, 2013, p. 65).

The large number of sizeable construction projects in such a small municipal region as Laiwu was partly due to the ambitious local economic plan, which was closely correlated with the local leadership change. Yang Yixin was transferred from Qingdao, where he held a deputy position for just two years as one of the so-called *guazhi ganbu* (a future leader on local secondment, or the young hopeful leader on job practice) of the central Ministry of Land and Resources, to Laiwu in mid-2011 to take over the leadership from both Ma Pingchang, the mayor, and Shan Zengde, the executive deputy mayor. The rumour about Yang's transfer led many local officers to believe that Yang was dumped from Qingdao, a far bigger and more economically important city than Laiwu, and that he would use the chance in Laiwu to reach the goal of the local secondment, which should be a promotion for one more level. Leaving the rumour aside, Yang had worked in the central Ministry of Land and Resources for 20 years after his undergraduate and graduate studies in land management and rural enterprises. Before being sent down to Qingdao, he was already the leader of the ministry's research office, which means that he was very familiar with land policies from the perspective of the central government. Moreover, Yang had studied at Beijing-based Renmin University of China, which was well known in China for promoting the planned economy.

Because of the obvious need for better performance records and policy innovations, Yang Yixin quickly identified four deadly problems in Laiwu's economy soon after commencing his new role as mayor. As discussed in the second section of this chapter, Yang took the huge drop in profit of more than 50 per cent from the iron and steel industry very seriously. In addition, he argued that Laiwu's resource-based economic structure had resulted in four structural restrictions on sustainable local economic development: an imbalanced industrial structure; an unsustainable supply of resources; considerable pressure on environment; and increasing social costs, especially rising unemployment in the steel and mining industries (Yang, 2012b). At the conclusion of his analysis, Yang identified rural development as a key priority and decided to stick to the integrated urban–rural development strategy. Therefore, the *lianggu yijian* (two de-mutualisations, and one establishment) mechanisms put forward by his predecessors were kept, but expanded to be *lianggu liangjian* (two de-mutualisations and two establishments), which included, as introduced in the previous section, the execution, if not construction, of the new urban–rural land transfer system in Laiwu (Xing, 2012; Yang, 2012a).

Acting in the established way of *xinguan shangren sanbahuo* (new leaders [often] light three fires, or a new broom sweeps clean), Yang decided in his first year as the mayor to launch several projects:

> The steady implementation of *Lianggu liangjian* will focus on the completion of the demutualisation of the rural land contract and management rights of 51 000 *mu* in 51 villages; the completion of the demutualisation of collective assets in 43 villages; and the creation of no fewer than 606 specialist farm corporates, for which 258 000 *mu* of land are planned to be transferred. The steady advancement of '*liangxin*' [two new] projects, is aimed at the completion of the demolition of urban villages [*chengzhongcun*] of 428 000 square metres, starting the construction projects of 76 new communities, and building 34 500 new dwellings. Greater efforts will be made for advancing infrastructure projects and expanding them to rural villages and towns, providing 95 per cent of rural households with access to tap water. (Yang, 2012a, pp. 59–60)

All these projects are believed by many locals to have had a very powerful impact on the execution of Laiwu's prioritised development strategies. At the same time, there were also numerous smaller rural construction projects planned and carried out in its rural areas. In 2012 alone, there were 243 rural building projects underway, including 102 clean water facilities, 529 kilometres of new roads, 101 sport facilities, and no less than 100 community centres, plus the contruction of approximately 7800 rural residences (Laiwu Research Office, 2013, p. 65). As stated in the same report produced by the government's research office, Laiwu's leaders decided in 2013 to focus on the building of central townships in its rural areas, through which they hoped to attract rural people wanting to be relocated to central townships. As part of its urban–rural integration strategy, the 2013 plan included 221 key construction projects, including building 44 new communities, 100 village renewal projects, upgrading power-supply systems for 125 villages, and water-safety projects in 41 villages (Laiwu Research Office, 2013, p. 68).

In addition to the various construction projects, which became the main economic activity in Laiwu from 2010 until 2015, the project-driven approach has also been utilised in restructuring its local economy. As summarised by two urban planners of the Laiwu Bureaus of Land and Resources, Laiwu's economic structure was transformed by what they call the 'four concentrations' (Wang and Liang, 2012, p. 48). This refers to the concentrations, or relocations, of enterprises in industrial parks, new projects in prioritised industries, rural families in newly developed communities, and movement towards the scaled use and management of rural land. Among these four strategic concentrations, the second one is a good example of driving the restructuring the local economy through a range of projects, on which the two planners provided the following details:

Currently, there are 350 sizeable enterprises in Laiwu's industrial areas, forming three main industries, namely the automobile parts industry, the advanced machinery industry, and the fine chemical industry ... The concentration of projects in prioritised industries will benefit the expansion of those leading industries, and lift the overall competitiveness of the regional economy ... To assist the expansion of the main industries, Laiwu had lately introduced 23 production lines of various automobile parts, including RMB1.1 billion investments in production lines of car transmission parts, RMB1.1 billion in automobile parts casting facilities, and another RMB0.8 billion in precision aluminium casting. (Wang and Liang, 2012, p.48)

The same project-driven approach has also been used to implement two rural development strategies, according to the summary by the two urban planners (Wang and Liang, 2012). As mentioned above, the two main rural strategies include the relocation of rural families into newly developed residential communities, and the realisation of the scaled use and management of rural land. To encourage the relocation, however, more efforts were made to transform Laiwu's rural economic structure and its long-established mode of production, which meant introducing the specialisation and commercialisation of various rural productions. As Laiwu was famous for growing ginger and garlic, and to support the expansion of ginger and garlic growing, which could in turn sustain the related processing industry, at least two mechanisms were developed and used to enable the transfer of more land to the ginger and garlic growers. The idea behind this was that creating more jobs in local industries could make the rural land transfer and the relocation of rural families, the core issues in the rural urbanisation, much easier to implement.

As early as 2010, two researchers from the School of Economics at Shandong University identified that three land-transfer models were in use province-wide in Shandong, all of which were related to the new local economic development initiatives that could disengage rural households from dependence on land (Bai and Zheng, 2010, p.76). In analysis of the three models, Laiwu was found to have attempted two of them. First, Laiwu was successful in using an enterprise-driven model, or the model driven by the so-called *longtou qiye* (dragon-head enterprises, or leading enterprises) in the words of Bai and Zheng. For example, Laiwu Manhing Foods, also known as Manhing Vegetables Fruits Corporation, one of the main producers and exporters of ginger and garlic in the global market, reached an agreement with more than 560 rural households in 2009 and took control of approximately 3000 *mu* of land through an innovative leasing system. These households have since earned reasonable incomes and benefits, while many have found jobs in the industry. Unused or under-used rural land has also been used for sustaining the main local industry.

Second, Laiwu also tried a centralised business operation model, encouraging and allowing some rural households to voluntarily lease their land allotments for fees, or other benefits, through negotiations with leading business operators in their areas. The example used by the two researchers is a famous tree grower from Zhailizhen, a hilly village in Laiwu, who successfully obtained the land-use rights through long-term leases with many households in several surrounding villages, involving more than 4500 *mu* of under-used land. Such deals have made his tree business a sizeable commercial operation and a big job provider.

Leaving aside details of business operations, both of the above methods were aimed at freeing land for development projects, but this goal was accomplished through project-oriented policies or projects themselves. Laiwu's experience in utilising the project-driven approach in its rural urbanisation mobilisation has suggested a few theoretical points about the new aspect of social mobilisation in present-day China, and one of them is that the project-driven approach has been used to break down the administrative barriers generated by China's complex multi-level governance structure. Differing from the four points summarised by J. Chen in his study (2013), as explained at the start of this section, the initial purpose of the project-driven approach was not to introduce anything constructive, but to interrupt the deadlock resulting from complexities of bureaucratic structure. A few local officials argue that the prefectural government is sandwiched not only between upper-level governments and counties, but also between their superiors and the market forces. Therefore, they are pushed by at least three different types of driving forces: the top-down push for the rural growth, the demand of market forces for expansion, and people's demand and financial ability for new housing. These factors have also generated a demand for better performance. Having confronted both the bureaucratic inactivity and the demand for better performance, the prefectural leadership needs to develop a strategic plan that is more specific than the one made by the province, and also find a workable way to implement it.

From the viewpoint of bureaucratic structure, there are at least two more levels of governmental bureaucracies below the prefectural-level municipal government in standard provincial governance structures in China. Thus, in theory, the prefectural leadership could rely on county leaderships to implement policy. The real situation in China now, however, is that prefectural governments are playing more direct roles in organising and handling the implementation of various major policy initiatives than other bureaucracies, because of the scale, complexity and speed of economic activity. In the case of Laiwu, as a small municipal region, its leadership and bureaucracies have been actual leaders in managing new rural building projects, that is, various activities of social mobilisation for implementing the new rural strategy start at the prefectural level. It is worth mentioning that many Chinese researchers, including many young scholars, regard the government as the main player in the new rural construction campaign and its related mobilisation (K. Chen, 2013; Wu, 2014), but fail to tell which level of government has been playing the most direct and crucial role in policy implementation in present-day China.

As mentioned, the last part of the fieldwork of this research project was conducted in 2015 and 2016, when the heat of the new rural drive was already cooling off, and local officials were starting to assess what they had done. As is often the case on such occasions, some people were optimistic and some were very critical. In the eyes of those who were optimistic, Laiwu had not only made a great effort to enthusiastically execute the new rural scheme, but had also done it in a creative way. In fact, the Laiwu government achieved many successes under unfavourable circumstances. As a small city in the province, and because of its heavily imbalanced economic structure, it was rather difficult at the start to simply promote and execute the new rural scheme without any modification of the central policy. Although some of Laiwu's local approaches were seen by some locals as selective, many others believed that both the prioritisation of the new rural scheme and the project-driven approach were essential and constructive. Some locals even argued that Laiwu's practices have contributed to the new national rural reform policy. Besides those noted at the end of the previous section, namely new rural shareholding schemes, a few other inventive policies, especially *tuichu sanquan* (withdrawing from three rights: the ownership rights, contract rights and management rights of rural land), that were tried in Laiwu have only recently become a topic among national lawmakers in China (*Xinhua News*, 2017b). This is because now is the 'time to unlock rights to rural land' (Ren, 2016, n.p.).

On the other hand, as mentioned, both the policy prioritisation and the project-driven tactic were seen by some critical locals as part of *gongmou* (collusion) between local governments and some businesses and interest groups. Such criticism is not completely unsupported. The social mobilisation for executing the new countryside policy in Laiwu, like many other regions in China, was accompanied by disciplinary problems and criminal offences. According to Shan Zengde, Laiwu's executive deputy mayor (2006–11), who was also jailed a few years after his appointment, Laiwu investigated more than 2000 illegal land-use cases from 2003 to 2011, which led to more than 20 people being charged, approximately 50 bureaucrats being internally disciplined, and the confiscation of more than RMB 41 million (Shan, 2011).

Ironically, Shan himself was also in trouble because of a seemingly adulterous affair, but according to a report in *Procuratorial Daily*, the institutional daily of China's Supreme People's Procuratorate, he was also found to have engaged in the following conduct:

> From January 2003 to October 2012, Shan Zengde had taken full advantage of being a standing committee member of Laiwu's CCP committee, the Director of the Personnel Department, the Deputy Mayor of Laiwu Municipal Government, and the Deputy Director of Shandong's Bureau of Agriculture ... to either seek benefits for others, or assist others in seeking improper benefits by making use of his positions or his contacts with other officials. He had illicitly obtained cash, bank and shopping cards, and other valuable items from 24 businesses or individuals, totalling worth of 7.37 million. (Lu et al., 2014, n.p.)

Although these disciplinary actions were seen by some local officials as measures to ensure smooth implementations of new rural strategies and ensure the success of integrated urban–rural development projects, critics have blamed the project-driven approach used by the local government for creating numerous commercial opportunities for those who are well connected in Laiwu or even beyond. In the eyes of many locals, Laiwu is a small region so the implementation of the new rural scheme should have no attraction for groups or individuals who wish to obtain illegitimate and unethical financial benefits from it through scandals. It is said that Laiwu had no record of acting against what central and provincial leaderships asked them to do. However, the local political culture has changed in recent decades, and various project-driven approaches utilised in the rural urbanisation scheme are considered by some to be the main reason for corruption in local political life. Reforms in China are always, in theory, accompanied by disciplinary measures or, more precisely, by punishment for disobeying certain laws and policies, violating of certain rules, and stepping over the red lines drawn by the central and provincial leaderships.

The different opinions suggest that the role of municipal governments in social mobilisation may be considered from another perspective, which is whether there are sufficient institutional resources and mechanisms at this level to carry out social mobilisation for executing new policies, and also to limit behaviours of local organisations and officers. The top level of China's party-state system has drawn a lot of attention from almost all sectors of Chinese society, which has thus given rise, unwillingly or willingly, to many new rules to guide and control the conduct of central and provincial bureaucracies, despite the insufficiency. However, China is still not a country where political mechanisms are perfectly developed and used at the prefectural level, such as an open leadership selection process, which might bring more political risks than benefits to China. Therefore, the real problem is that there are not sufficient *zhidu chubei* (institutional resources) at the prefectural level, even though it manages significant sections of bureaucracy and the economy. Hopefully, the issue will be partially solved through China's ongoing reforms to perfect its political institutions.

NOTES

1. This has been the CCP's long tradition of publishing some editorials, theoretical articles, commentaries or reports based on the speeches of the top leaders. They are normally published in several centrally controlled newspapers and political periodicals, for example, those institutionally managed, if not controlled, by the *People's Daily*, the Central Party School and the Xinhua News Agency. They should be able to be clearly identified, according to the seriousness of the issue, the uniqueness of the message, and even writing styles and unusual expressions. Mao Zedong was the best example in this regard, and he often contributed or was directly involved in revising and editing articles, editorials and opinion pieces. These publications are very useful in understanding what is happening in China, and skills to identify them and interpret the messages they carried should be a requirement for all those studying contemporary China. Interested readers can read more about it in Lieberthal and Oksenberg (1988), Stranahan (1990) and L. Liu (2010).
2. Xi Jinping's family background is widely known, but just in case readers would like to have a quick reference, his family background is as follows: Xi Jinping's father, Xi Zhongxun (1913–2002), was a senior and active member of the CCP central leadership under both Mao Zedong and Deng Xiaoping. Xi Zhongxun was promoted to be the secretary-general of the State Council (the Cabinet) in 1953 and a vice-premier in 1959 under Zhou Enlai. Xi Zhongxun was sidelined from 1962, but after the Cultural Revolution in 1978, he became a key provincial leader of Guangdong until 1981, after which he became the deputy chair of the Standing Committee of China's National [People's] Congress and a member of the CCP's Politburo and the CCP Secretariat in 1982. Readers can read more about Xi Zhongxun in Lam (2015) and Li (2016).
3. Sunan refers to the southern part of Jiangsu province, the region encompassing Changzhou, Suzhou and Wuxi, which are south of the Yangtze River and west of Shanghai. The Sunan model is normally regarded as the governance mode of TVEs (township and village enterprises), which has since the 1980s helped China solve its rural surplus labour issue through rural industrialisation. But it should also be considered as 'an organizational response to both the macroeconomic environment and local conditions', and the experiment to find an alternative way to adjust central–local relations (Xu and Zhang, 2009, p. 5). Interested readers can read more about the model and its institutional implications in White (1998), Whiting (2000) and Zhong (2004).
4. Mount Tai, or Taishan in Chinese, has been regarded by Chinese for thousands of years as the 'first mountain under heaven' (Harrist, 2008, p. 278) because of its historical and cultural significance. Mount Tai was used by many emperors since the Qin dynasty (221–207 BC) as the site of state rituals and ceremonies. It has since not only been considered as one of the five holiest mountains in China, but has also ranked as the first of the so-called five most famous mountains in the country. Interested readers can read more about Mount Tai in Wills (1994), Harrist (2008) and Yan (2017).
5. The so-called 'third-front construction', or *sanxian jianshe* in Chinese, refers to China's national industrial distribution strategy, but primarily its military industrial distribution and development, which the CCP leadership under Mao Zedong developed in the mid-1960s, after its political split with the Soviet Union, but before the Cultural Revolution. The key idea of 'third-front' strategy is to construct and locate, or even relocate, some industries in China's 'third-line' areas in southwest and northwest regions, away from the front-line regions (coastal provinces, northeastern provinces, and Xinjiang) and the second-front regions (middle-strip regions, between coastal provinces and the

Beijing-Guangzhou railway), because they could be targets of foreign invasions. As part of this major strategic industrial redistribution plan, some projects in the front-line region, such as Shandong, were called *xiaosanxian* (small or minor third-front) constructions. Readers can find more information about these in Bramall (2007), Naughton (1988) and Wang and Hu (1999).

6.   A *mu* is a Chinese unit of land area, equivalent to about one-sixth of an acre or about 667 square metres.

6. The awkward roles of county and township governments in rural urbanisation

The discussion up to now has revealed that each level of China's party-state bureaucracy above county and township level has shown a higher degree of influence and autonomy than was the case in the past in terms of decision-making or policy implementation. The same changes have also occurred in the social-mobilisation process. The power of influence and persuasion in Chinese society and in its political system has clearly been redistributed as a long-term effect of ongoing reforms and transferred to provincial and prefectural-municipal levels, as well as the market. More generally and abstractly, the government system in China has gradually been reduced to an arrangement of several major stakeholders in big strategic political-economic games. Higher levels of industrialisation, privatisation and urbanisation, and many other transformations have resulted in political power flowing to those with influence on production, the market, resources, innovation and even public discourse and public opinion. As an outcome of these important changes, it seems to be that each level of the bureaucracy has become more dynamic, influential, weighty and flexible in decision-making. Especially, local governments at provincial and prefectural-municipal level have been found to have more bargaining power because of China's emphasis on growth and GDP and its economic success in many regions. However, county and township governments are in a different position from other levels of government, and some researchers define this position as awkward (Bulman, 2014; Zhou and Tan, 2017). This analysis looks at the roles played by the county and township governments in Laiwu in mobilising local participation in the new-countryside campaign.

It must also be pointed out that there are some studies of the behaviour and roles of county and township governments from a policy-implementation perspective, but there are no sufficient studies on how they act, react and interact in the context of implementing major state policies. As noted in Chapter 1, the roles of these two lowest levels of bureaucracy have barely been considered in a broader context or in a systematic manner. The analysis of this chapter will place them in the entire party-state bureaucratic system and the whole process of policy implementation to analyse their roles as a unique feature of social mobilisation in present-day China. Structurally, this chapter has three sections. The first starts with a brief explanation of why governments at these two lowest levels have become awkward in policy implementation and the new rural construction campaign. The second section analyses the front-line roles of these governments in the campaign in Laiwu. The third section examines the more proactive and strategic roles these governments have played in the process.

THE AWKWARD POSITION OF THE TWO LOWEST LEVELS OF GOVERNMENT

The awkwardness of the roles of county and township governments in present-day Chinese political life can be observed or discovered from different angles. The headings of the second and third sections of this chapter, for example, suggest two of the most obvious ones, which are their front-line roles in policy implementation and the need to use both gentle and harsh approaches in local governance. In other words, these governments are the basic functionary units of China's massive party-state system, but they are not only squeezed politically and financially but also often forced into direct conflicts triggered by decisions made by their superiors. In terms of administrative structure, two special issues are worth noting at this point before we turn to how governments at county and township level have been mobilised and how they have then mobilised villagers to partake in the building scheme. These two special issues are the overall institutional uncertainty resulting from China's frequent, or frequently publicised, organisational reforms, and the smallness of Laiwu itself as both a city and a government system.

As listed in Figure 2.2, there are approximately 2800 county-level governments or administrative institutions in China, under which there are almost 40000 township-level governments or councils. Having been guided by the ambition to speed up its economic growth, the ruling CCP has, over decades, been identifying all the possibilities for improving production and management efficiency (*xiaolü*). Because of this attention to efficiency, all post-Mao leaders, and other political and economic elites as well, have been influenced by a newly introduced idea, namely that new and better management can boost performance and production, and therefore that it can also lift productivity. The desire for efficiency has led generations of Chinese elites to believe that management is a type of productivity, and this idea has guided China's economic development, if not nation-building, more directly than other isms. More relevantly, this doctrine has driven the CCP leadership to look for better management systems and practices. One of the conclusions of such active thinking and searching is governmental reforms, which have been called administrative reforms, organisational reforms or institutional reforms (*jigou tiaozheng*, or *jigou gaige*), as discussed in the second section of Chapter 2.

The first awkwardness of the positions and roles of county and township governments is the partial result of a series of efforts to reform the government system: these two levels, especially the county level, are always on the chopping block when policy researchers and advisers debate about how to improve administrative efficiency and local revenues. This is not an issue specific to China; the problem haunts other countries with multiple layers of government, such as the United States, and even those with smaller, simpler systems of government – for example, in Australia there are always bids to reduce the size of government, and one of the frequently mentioned options is to remove one layer of bureaucracy. Over the course of China's reforms there have been quite a few attempts to reform county and township governments, especially through the initiatives of *shiguanxian* (cities governing counties) and *shengguanxian* (provinces governing counties).

The *shiguanxian* (also spelt *shi guan xian*, prefecture-level cities governing counties) was the major administrative restructure in the 1980s (Yu, 2014). As China's early effort to drive economic growth through adjusting the administrative system, it started with the change of 'abolishing counties and establishing cities' (*chexian gaishi*). This was first introduced alongside the *li gai shui* (replacing profit by tax) reform in 1983 (see Table 2.2), and aimed to maximise the role of regional urban centres in economic development. The policy became very popular in the early 1990s, and greatly contributed to economic expansion in the post-Deng era. Because of its popularity, this policy has since been called the *shiguanxian* ('cities leading counties') plan (Cartier, 2005, p. 26). This administrative-reform strategy was put on hold for a few years after 1997, as it 'seriously restricted the scope of economic development at the county level', with the result that county and township governments became less able to provide various basic public services (Yu, 2014, p. 236).

In the early 2000s, a few years before the new countryside scheme, China also trialled a new governance approach to improve its central–local relations, which has been called the province-governing-county reform or approach (*shengguanxian*, which is also spelt by some as *sheng guan xian*) (Ahlers, 2014; Yu, 2014; Li et al., 2016).[1] The NSSFC (National Social Science Fund of China) even funded a major research project to study the innovative application of this new approach (Zhou, 2009). This approach evolved from the initial strategy of 'strengthening the county through empowerment' (*kuoquan qiangxian*), but it was put forward on purpose to rectify the problems caused by the then widely utilised city-governing-county model. The latter was already found to have destructively impacted country-level economies or, to be precise, their revenues. This widely debated strategy of bringing back the province-administering-county approach was even included in the CCP's 'No. 1 Central Document' in 2009 (Zhou, 2009), when the rural economy needed to be energised, as mentioned in Table 2.3. This policy attention to the role of the county government reflected the uncertainty felt by many county-level officials, and it has also been used to argue for the county-level-city approach (*xianjishi*). However, today China is a different place, and prefectural-level cities have become so powerful that they have made excuses – chief among them the importance of urbanisation – to prevent the possible restructuring of their roles.

All these creative ideas, practical or impractical, and policy changes have been used by China's central leadership to improve administrative efficiency, but they have also disturbed and weakened sub-provincial government systems, and alarmed many leaders and officials working in them. Frequent structural changes have also resulted in two types of government. The governments at provincial and prefectural or municipal level have become more capable of creating new policies to redistribute power and benefits with the aim of facilitating and accelerating local economic growth, on the basis of which numerous forms of personal achievement can be claimed. However, county and township governments have been left on their own, with substantially reduced influence on policy issues and decision-making processes but a considerably increased amount of managerial responsibilities and tasks. In many counties, these have even resulted in a vicious circle, in which counties turn to the township government system to finance their expenditures and cash deficiencies (Yang and Zhang, 2006). Currently, such problems are still a long way from being satisfactorily resolved, and they remain on the list of China's future areas for reform.

The second main awkwardness of the roles of county and township governments is specific to the municipality of Laiwu. As introduced in the second section of Chapter 5, Laiwu is the smallest city or prefectural-level municipality in Shandong in terms of both land size and population. Table 6.1 presents changes in the city's population and its distribution of rural and urban populations from 2005 to 2016 to show the most important aspects of the city's urbanisation. This should be read along with the second section of Chapter 5.

Laiwu was elevated to a prefectural-level city in 1992, when it had two district governments at county level. Since 2000 the city has seen more

Table 6.1   Laiwu's total population and urban–rural distribution, 2005–16

Year	Total (million)	Rural %	Urban %
2005	1.24	60.2	39.8
2006	1.25	59.8	40.2
2007	1.25	61.3	38.7
2008	1.26	60.6	39.4
2009	1.26	60.1	39.9
2010	1.27	54.0	46.0
2011	1.27	54.2	45.8
2012	1.26	48.8	51.2
2013	1.33	44.8	55.2
2014	1.35	43.6	56.4
2015	1.35	41.2	58.8
2016	1.39	38.9	61.1

Source: Based on data from LWTJJ (Laiwu Tongjiju [Laiwu Bureau of Statistics]) (2017).

frequent, almost yearly, rezoning, reflecting the need for more land for housing and industrial growth. Since the rural building scheme began in Laiwu in 2006 and 2007, the city has made more changes according to its integrated strategy to deal with the development of both rural and urban areas, as detailed in the third section of Chapter 5. During this process, Laiwu has quietly established two county-level special economic development zones: one is its high-tech industrial park and the other is its special economic zone, making the city of Laiwu the leader of four county-level governments. Despite such efforts, the smallness of Laiwu is still a special issue in terms of mobilising local people to partake in the scheme, as limited resources are available. However, it was in just such an awkward situation that sub-prefectural governments in Laiwu have managed to play their front-line roles in the rural building campaign, which are assisted by both the gentle and the tough approaches.

FRONT-LINE ROLES IN THE PROCESS

The new countryside campaign at county and township levels is simply called *nongmin shanglou* (to let rural households live in new apartment buildings or storeyed buildings). In the eyes of bureaucrats at these two levels, the project of *shanglou* (moving into new apartment buildings) starts from project design and application and ends when villagers have completed their relocation from their original houses, the land lot of which must be properly transferred. This is a lengthy process. To help clearly understand the process, it might be divided into two phases. The first stage takes much longer than the second, covering the period from project design and approval to the agreement being signed by villagers. The second main stage includes the completion of building projects and the relocation of rural households into apartment buildings, many of which should, in fact, be defined as landless units. Throughout these stages, our fieldwork showed that social mobilisation ran continuously, both internally and externally. The process at these levels is characterised by direct, and often confrontational, contact and interaction with villagers. These local people were often unable to contact any government offices or officials, except those at township and county level.

Internally, the process started with mobilisation within county and township bureaucracies, which was characterised by the allocation of tasks. This is a standard governmental operation at these levels, which has been repeatedly reformed and standardised through implementing the Dengist idea of the responsibility system. To some extent, many procedures and practices are like what must be done by bureaucratic teams at provincial and prefectural level, but this level is more concerned with policy implementation than policy-making. According to some local officers, there were three basic internal tasks to complete before going to the next phase, but two of them were not much different from what had been done by prefectural officials. Basically, meetings were repeatedly held not only to familiarise local officials with the plan but, more importantly, to motivate them to act accordingly. Repeated meetings or seminars are also believed to be the process by which work was divided among different governmental divisions and proper projects identified according to the procedure of the scheme. At the same time, a special leadership group was set up, and the roles and responsibilities of different governmental offices and branches were clearly set out. As a standard practice, the top leaders of local party and state bodies directly oversaw the leadership group. Because of the importance of the land issue for the entire plan, a more crucial role was given to the Bureau of Land and Resources than to other bodies.

A very special internal task, specific to the rural building scheme, was the project application and approval process, which was a strict policy-implementation procedure designed to avoid potential problems caused by ill-conceived design and corrupt behaviour. The procedure required that each county-level government develop a plan based on its own circum-stances, especially the factors of land, population and the local economy. A specific building project could then be identified and planned, if the government could meet the requirement regarding the *zengjian guagou* (rural land-use) policy: the balance between the reduction of rural housing land and the increase of urban housing-construction land. At this stage, mobilisation only took place among officials of the party-state systems at county and township level. It was only after the completion of these internal procedures that mobilisation could be carried out outside local bureaucracies.

Externally, once the project was approved, attention was turned to the implementation of the plan, and social-mobilisation efforts intensified, going beyond local bureaucracies. Through our survey, five general measures were found to have been more useful than others, delineating the front-line roles of county and township governments in the process.

First, endless meetings were held after the initial mobilisation within the government system to spread the message about the project. Although many recent research publications point out that sub-county organisational structures in many counties in China are no longer functioning, or even worse than dysfunctional (Zuo and Chao, 2007; Yu, 2009; Takeuchi, 2013), this study has not only seen functioning sub-county organisations but also identified the way in which such organisations play their role in rural projects. In general, county-government branches can always rely on township managerial teams, and the latter then make use of two formal organisational bodies: village (administrative) committees and village CCP branches. In the case of some towns or villages, influential individuals, such as local entrepreneurs, are often considered to be the third powerful force in local affairs.[2] The mobilisation meetings in Laiwu, however, were mainly held first among village CCP branches, which appear still to exist and work well for this purpose.

In a town known as Fengyu – a code name for this research project – there were countless meetings on this big issue, as members of the CCP branch were profoundly shocked by the new strategy at the first meeting, the fact of which shows that the nationwide publicity for the building initiative was not sufficient to mobilise the implementation of the strategy. In a clear difference from the Mao era, at early meetings local CCP members voiced no positive responses to the grand strategy set forth by the CCP central leadership. Mr Meng, the then secretary of the Fengyu CCP branch, described their mobilisation efforts as follows:

> At the start of the project, the township [CCP] committee and the township government held meetings of village [CCP] secretaries and heads of village committees frequently, virtually every two days. We received a meeting notification every day. What we had to do was to continually tell CCP members and other villagers that these projects are great, and that they would be able to complete them with great potential. (Su, 2016, p. 82)

Just like many other ordinary Chinese people, CCP members at the grassroots level are no longer obedient to their superiors and the policy and decisions made by their superiors. They have also become used to being able to complain and protest about whatever they dislike. Such regular meetings were, therefore, found to have been mainly used to generate pressure on CCP members to understand the rural building scheme favourably, through which other villagers could be influenced. In addition, frequent meetings served two other purposes. Governments at provincial and prefectural level used them to spread information about or revisions to the policy, although this is clearly less important than it is at higher levels. What becomes more critical at county and township level is feedback on the strategy and detailed local plans. From the perspective of provincial and prefectural governments, these grassroots meetings were a decisive step in implementing the strategy.

Second, sending working groups to villages was once again used in the campaign, because from the very beginning the scheme was not easy to accomplish once it had been presented to the mobilised. The decision-makers of the plan made every effort to emphasise the project as a new policy to modernise and beautify rural living spaces, but what they did not realise was that not everyone would be immediately attracted by what was portrayed as a new countryside, and that not everyone would appreciate its benefits within days or weeks. Having been confronted with uncooperative villagers, sub-prefectural bureaucracies were in a difficult situation – between the devil and the deep blue sea. To achieve their goals and guarantee the implementation of this national strategy, they turned their attention to conventional approaches used by the CCP in the past to promote new ideas and mobilise grassroots support. One such proven technique was to set up special working groups and dispatch them to villages, which is called *pai gongzuozu* in Chinese.[3] Despite the Maoist reputation of the expression *pai gongzuozu*, lower-level governments had no choice but to make use of the strategy.

The approach of sending working groups to villages may help achieve several goals, including calming antagonistic reactions, getting all possible conflicts under control, identifying solutions, and even helping with negotiations over compensation details. Some of these goals will be discussed as part of the normal roles of the county and township governments later in this section, but the discussion here focuses on how this tactic was used in Laiwu.

Setting up working groups and appointing team leaders was the first step. In the case of Laicheng, one of Laiwu's two districts, this process started soon after the project's application procedure, based on a long-term political understanding of enhancing leadership and strengthening guidance and supervision. What then happened in Laicheng district was typical, revealing the complexity of the process. The formation of working groups took place at two levels in Laicheng, but it could occur at more levels in a big region, or if a higher-level authority originated it. The county-level district government of Laicheng formed several groups, each of them looking after a few township regions, and each township government then repeated the process to form groups to take care of a few villages each. Overall, no village was outside the supervision of these working groups, let alone existing party-state systems. The sophistication in the use of social mobilisation in such a complex way brought back many people's memories of the Maoist era, but the party-state systems were promoting changes to rural living conditions, not an ideology. Practically, some locals regarded working groups as the use of person-to-person tactics in the promotion of the scheme. However, these tactics also seemed to them to have functioned well. The working groups helped spread information to each village quickly, informing residents that this was a serious project. On the other hand, the organisational structure of the groups was ready for a long and hard campaign, and from the local government standpoint, the strategy could at least guarantee that things would move in the direction anticipated by its superiors.

Each working group normally looked after a few villages, assisted by heads of village CCP and administration committees. This is what happened in Laiwu, but it challenges the concept of village-level self-governance that has been promoted in many Chinese villages for years. These practices seem to many researchers to be the return of top-down direct control. This observation is not baseless. Village heads appeared to simply act as contact persons, and they also relied on CCP members in their villages. Direct contact with each household, or door-to-door canvassing, was also regularly conducted. The groups contacted people who strongly opposed the scheme, and details of this will be discussed in the next section. However, local people did not seem to care which practices were used, and a project of such a scale appeared to warrant mobilising some officials before seeking to mobilise villagers.

The utilisation of various outdated social-mobilisation practices by working groups in this process seems to have been avoidable. Apart from the above-mentioned person-to-person approaches, our fieldwork has identified two other tactics that are not often used in China nowadays. In several towns there was widespread use of executive power, as will be further detailed in the next section, in asking those on the public payroll, including teachers, to persuade relatives or friends to participate in the scheme, or even sign up for new houses. As a teacher pointed out, this is because they were unable to challenge the authorities. In the process, working groups even made use of various propaganda practices. The most theatrical tactic was the use of publicity vans broadcasting through loudspeakers while driving around to distribute promotional materials. Clearly, these officials were also desperate to meet their job requirements.

Third, the compensation details for participating in the building project – or, to be precise, for giving up the *zhaijidi*, the existing site of each household – were a decisive factor in whether the project could continue. This concern was also behind the negative responses of village CCP members to the strategy and its policy. By the mid-2000s, a growing number of rural people were becoming aware of the value of their housing sites, because their land was required to support both industrial expansion and rapid urbanisation in many regions. Even in regions away from big cities, such as Laiwu, housing sites are the main asset of rural households. Villagers had to calculate the benefit to them of partaking in the scheme. This calculation was complicated by the possibility that a large amount of funding would be provided by governments at different levels. This assumption could be true: as noted in Chapter 1, in 2005 China decided to stop taxing agriculture. At the prefectural level, as shown in the last column of Table 6.2, many people heard that a comparatively large sum of government money had already been spent on rural roads, clean-water projects and so on. Such conversation topics spread the suggestion that governments would put their money into the new scheme.

Table 6.2   Laiwu's rural income and public investment in rural infrastructure, 2005–15

Year	Laiwu's rural income per capita (yuan)	Growth %	Engel coefficient	Public investment in rural infrastructure (billion yuan)
2005	4684	10.7	37.4	–
2006	5200	11.4	38.4	–
2007	5913	13.7	39.3	0.68
2008	6646	12.4	40.1	0.70
2009	7313	10.1	38.7	0.50
2010	8311	13.6	37.9	0.56
2011	9629	15.8	36.9	0.85
2012	10877	13.1	36.1	4.70
2013	12161	11.7	36.3	6.50
2014	13540	11.3	–	4.20
2015	13714	08.9	–	4.50

Source: Based on data from LWTJJ (2017).

The rural-income data in Table 6.2, on the other hand, supports another argument about villagers' initial resistance to the project and their hard bargaining for better deals. Specifically, the income of rural families in Laiwu was still low in the mid-2000s, and a large majority of them had no budget for rebuilding their houses at any time. They felt that the government had forced the rebuilding process on them, and therefore, if the government would like to see new, modern houses or units, the government should support their construction. Because of all this, rural residents and even CCP members bargained hard.

As a result, mobilisation for the new scheme was partly a bargaining process among villagers, township officials and decision-makers at prefectural level. Officials at township and county level held endless meetings, public and private, to discuss two issues: how to quantify the size of each family house and whether to take the style and quality of different houses into account when determining the level of compensation. The main disagreement on the first issue was whether to simply consider the main house or include additional buildings on the housing land. In Fengyu town, the decision was that only the main building was to be considered, and that it was impractical to treat different houses, built with various materials, such as brick or cement, and with a range of designs, differently. Villagers were given three new housing-design options regardless of the style or quality of their old house. They could have a new design of 96 square metres, 106 square metres or 116 square metres by paying RMB 47 000, RMB 59 000 or RMB 71 000 respectively. These options laid the basis for moving the project forward. This account should be read along with what was discussed in Chapter 4, where the role of local developers in the process was considered, which may be helpful in forming a fuller picture of the process.

Fourth, identifying breakthrough points was an ongoing task for officials at county and township level, especially at the early stages of the promotion of the scheme. Negative responses from village CCP members and hard bargaining by them and other villagers eventually drove mobilisers to pay attention to those who would be likely to participate in the project or accept the conditions offered by the township government. Attention was often given to those who already had plans to rebuild their houses or were financially able to consider rebuilding. Therefore, the more complicated relocation plan was presented to them first, and their participation could then be used to encourage others. Of course, this effort is different from what was discussed at the end of the second front-line role, which even made use of the administrative power to force those who were partly dependent on the government system to sign up for the project.

We found that the effort to identify and make use of breakthrough points was attempted at three levels. Apart from the efforts made to identify some individuals as mentioned above, the tactic was also deployed at the county-wide and township-wide level. The county government relied on the project application and approval process to determine the best place to start the scheme, and the project that should go ahead first or be encouraged and sponsored. The government's experience in managing a relatively large administrative area and huge population told it that once one project was successful it would be easier for it to encourage others to participate. At township level, the same strategy was also used. For example, there were 19 villages under the management of Fengyu township in the mid- and late 2000s. The Fengyu government and CCP committee identified one village that would clearly like to have some new buildings and another that was in desperate need of repair or rebuilding. The benefits that these two villages derived from the project fund, and local enthusiasm for the scheme, were then used in the scheme's promotion.

The utilisation of the influence of the so-called 'model village' is worth special mention, although it sounds like the above-mentioned roles of township and county governments. However, identifying breakthrough points appears to have had less impact on the policy's implementation than model villages. In the case of Laiwu, these two strategies were used at different stages to deal with different issues. Shangzhuang, a village in the area administered by Fengyu township, was set up as a model village, and used to show other villages and their residents what a new village would look like. A positive effect was observed at at least two levels. Heads of many villages learned how to organise their mobilisation and individual villagers could complete their calculations, from how much they needed to invest and what they must give up, to which house, and district surroundings, they would most like to be in.

Last, dealing with dissatisfied villagers who would be likely to be 'seeking an explanation' (*tao shuofa*) from higher authorities or filing complaints with, or petitioning, higher administrative levels (*shangfang*) was also part of the role of local governments. Despite the adverse reaction at the start of the campaign, Laiwu was mostly free of street-level protests and other forms of confrontational opposition. It is worth revealing here that, since the mid-1990s, China's local officials have been taking the street-level-protest issue seriously and trying very hard to resolve issues at closed-door meetings or through negotiations. However, petition events were still observed in Laiwu:

> When doing the fieldwork [in Laiwu], I saw petition incidents on two occasions. One took place right in front of the building of the municipal government. Villagers from a town called Gaozhuang took the issue of the building construction quality and the issue of heating facilities to the municipal government. The

other incident that I witnessed took place in the Fengyu township government, and the people from a village called Gujiacun were there to seek an explanation about unreasonable allocations of new apartments. (Su, 2016, p. 75)

While the above-mentioned first case was dealt with by the construction firm under pressure generated by the street-level action, in the second case the township government intervened and the answers that the government offered after discussions with a few government branches and offices calmed the petitioners down. Our fieldwork revealed that there were more protests than we could see on the streets – for example, protests carried out through writing or individual visits. We also found that preventing protests and similar public events has always been the most important and politicised task for officials at county and township level. To some extent, they are always on high alert for any possible street-level protests. Apparently, the roles of county and township officials in policy implementation are rather different from those of their superiors, and they must deal directly with dissatisfied villagers. To combat all these challenges, actual or potential, local officials have attempted to take a more strategic tack than their routine official roles normally require, and one of the best options here is the use of the carrot-and-stick approach.

THE CARROT-AND-STICK APPROACH

Since only limited strategies were available to governments at county and township level to mobilise residents to partake in the scheme, and also because of pressure from upper-level governments to meet deadlines and other requirements, county and township governments tried various other approaches to achieve mobilisation. These approaches are different from their routine work. A few researchers of rural China have used the Chinese phrase *ruanying jianshi* (utilising both gentle and tough approaches) to describe the complexity of their approaches (Sun, 2008; Hsing, 2010; L. Li, 2012). The meaning of this phrase is almost identical to the 'carrot-and-stick approach' in English. However, in present-day Chinese socio-political climates, 'carrot' approaches are always acceptable and politically safe, but 'stick' approaches can rarely be used as they carry too much risk for individuals and organisations.

This discussion, therefore, will use the English phrase as the section title but examine several new and nonroutine social-mobilisation tactics in reverse order – that is, we will start with the 'stick'. Specifically, this section will begin with a further analysis of the only hard-line method identified by this study, which will be followed by a brief discussion of why tours – a rather neutral tactic – were arranged for officials of party-state bureaucracies at township and village level several times at the early stage of the scheme. The rest of this section will focus on a range of strategically soft and tempting tactics, and attention will be paid to mobilisation of financial resources and utilisation of interpersonal networks among villagers in mobilising them to participate in the project.

A hard-line approach, as briefly mentioned in the previous section, was found to have been used only among those on the public payroll of lower-level governments. Therefore, this tactic very much relies on the executive power that the government can exercise over its staff members. Teachers, cadres and rank-and-file officers at township-government and village-committee level, and others in local public services were all asked to help persuade at least three families to partake in the scheme. This is a typical, if not political, form of traditional administrative mobilisation, because our fieldwork found that the use of this executive power also involved punitive measures, such as allegedly threatening to suspend employment or salary. According to reports produced by a few investigative journalists from China's Xinhua News Agency,[4] similar disciplinary measures were used in other regions in Shandong (Wang, 2010). Of course, in Laiwu there was a difference between the level of compulsion applied to those at township level and the compulsion applied at village level. Those at village level were clearly treated less harshly than those at township level because of the high degree of interpersonal relationships among village residents.

An interesting new phenomenon was observed in our fieldwork in relation to the use of hard-line internal disciplinary tactics: official denial of the use of punitive measures within party-state systems. In rural China there has long been a saying that 'the masses follow party members and party members follow leaders'. Therefore, in the eyes of rural residents, nothing seems to be wrong if cadres and CCP members are asked to set good examples in signing up for the new building plan. However, this campaign started when Hu Jintao's 'harmonious society' (*hexie shehui*) idea was guiding China. The strict policy of maintaining stability (*weiwen*) evolved into a mentality that made local officers extremely sensitive to anything that might be negatively interpreted as triggering instability.[5] Throughout our fieldwork, township officials and village leaders denied the use of disciplinary measures and any evidence about them, including internal documents, meeting minutes and audio recordings. Despite being unable to find other evidence, in our fieldwork we not only met several people who were pressured by their institutions to persuade their relatives to join the scheme but also discovered that all those on the local public payroll had registered their households for the scheme. More interestingly, most of them had moved into new houses earlier than other villagers.

A special soft approach used in several towns consisted of organised tours arranged for officials at township and village level several times from the early stages. This initiative came from county level, but behind the county offices was the Laiwu Bureau of Land and Resources, as the bureau played a coordination role in the scheme. It wanted to allow more officers at township and village level to learn what had happened in other regions and the tactics other regions had used. Of these two objectives, the first aimed to open the eyes of local cadres to more developed regions and let them see what new villages looked like. At the same time, these front-line cadres could learn how the scheme could be financed, which was central not only to the scheme but also to understanding its complexity. This is because the scheme involved a range of 'new tricks' that were never or almost never used, in the words of these local cadres. For example, the value of an original housing site was considered, and various forms of subsidy were also available. Visiting and learning are a conventional practice in China's social mobilisation, but what they wanted to learn in this case was very different and complex.

The tours were organised in three stages. First, the township government dispatched its leaders, demolition-team managers and members of working groups to pilot villages, and leaders of pilot villages to several counties outside Laiwu and some villages within the prefectural region of Laiwu. After the tours, meetings were held to compare those successful cases and identify key strategies for their own plan. Second, a selection of village heads, village-committee members and village resident representatives from pilot villages was sent to visit a few successful villages that were identified in the first round of tours. Last, for example in a few towns in the Fengyu area, all villagers who were believed likely to participate in the project were encouraged and financially assisted by village committees to join a study tour to see what a new house looked like. Many local cadres believed that newly built houses and units were much better than most existing ones and hoped that these new houses and units would help change the minds of their fellow villagers. What was more interesting than before were the many voluntary visits by families under the influence of early visitors. There were also many second or return visits with more family members. All these responses proved that visiting and learning is still a useful tactic for social mobilisation. Of course, there were also cases where families found excuses for not partaking in the project after seeing the new houses with modern facilities. The most commonly cited excuse was that the new houses lacked the space to keep farming tools.

The soft, 'carrot' approach adopted by the two lower-level governments took several forms. Some of these approaches were new and creative, especially that of mobilising financial resources by setting up projects, working

Table 6.3   Laiwu's public investment in rural infrastructure, new projects and housing units, 2009–16

Year	Public investment in rural infrastructure (billion yuan)	Number of rural infrastructure projects	New rural houses/ units built
2009	0.50	–	11 168
2010	0.56	52	15 000
2011	0.85	–	–
2012	4.70	243	8100
2013	6.50	221	8300
2014	4.20	167	6466
2015	4.50	142	6924
2016	2.40	136	4917

Source: Based on data from LWTJJ (2017).

with developers and making use of interpersonal networks. All of these are new features of present-day social mobilisation in China.

The first soft approach was the mobilisation of financial resources, or the utilisation of economic incentives, by setting up smaller projects through which to drive the entire scheme. The previous chapters outlined the background for the countryside strategy, showing that it was introduced at the right stage of Chinese socio-economic expansion. These favourable economic conditions are reflected in local investment in rural infrastructure. Table 6.3 shows how much Laiwu has spent on rural infrastructure projects in recent years, providing data for understanding why the mobilisation of financial resources was not only possible but also needed at county and township level.

While a huge amount of investment was available, even in a region as small as Laiwu, county and township governments needed to create mechanisms to obtain their share of this investment and turn it into financial incentives for mobilising villagers. Under China's present project-oriented management practice – which is also called the project-driven approach, as explained in Chapter 5 – no institution or region can simply put its hand up to ask for funding without ensuring any real project. After decades of administrative reform, local leaders and bureaucrats have been trained to be good at creating new projects and seeking public funding. As provincial and prefectural governments have often asked them to do, county administrations have contacted township governments, which have then applied pressure directly and more heavily to village heads or committees to propose new projects according to top-down policy initiatives. During our fieldwork, township officials and village heads were busy proposing and drafting funding applications for rural infrastructure, such as river maintenance, rural clean water, wetland protection, geological disaster prevention and new community services.

All these funds were allocated as part of the new countryside plan. However, township officials and village heads explained the usefulness of these funds to the mobilisation in two ways. The first, superficial account was that these funds could be used to modernise their regions, making them ready to be transformed into a new landscape. This diplomatic explanation established a sound link between applying for funding and mobilising villagers, but it was only partially correct. The second and more accurate account was also discovered throughout our fieldwork, and this was the coordinated management (*tongchou guanli*) of financial resources. As detailed in Chapter 3, the provincial administration tried to combine 130 or so central funds into fewer categories, in line with the provincial strategy. A similar tactic was also used at township and village level, but in a manner that is widely known in China as project packaging (*xiangmu dabao*). This refers to a frequently used practice of tying several projects together but naming the whole project and each sub-project differently according to need. In general, different project names could be used to apply for different funds, and the comprehensive project design could be used to reallocate funds based on local needs. That is, the mobilisation of financial resources is given a new meaning, and becomes more about the reallocation of funds for critical governmental tasks.

The second, and new, soft mobilisation approach was the use of market forces to incentivise villagers to take part in the scheme. Some details of this possibility and its utilisation were discussed in Chapter 4. Without repeating what was analysed there, this section will briefly explain how market forces were utilised by governments at county and township level. The ultimate reason related to the awkward position of these lower-level bureaucracies, which have limited financial resources and institutional capability. Although these governments sought external funding, such as through project packaging, villagers were still crying poor and asking for more financial help. At the same time, the objective had to be accomplished within a short period of time. A researcher from the Laiwu Bureau of Land and Resources identified the same problem in the region and described the awkward position of local administration teams as follows:

> The funding constraint is the main hindrance. The entire process, from demolition of existing houses, building new houses or units, to resettlement of all participating families, needs a huge amount of financial funding to support it. However, the district [county-level] government did not allocate 25 per cent

of start-up funding on time, making mobilisation at the village level awfully difficult. This situation is also complicated by the fact that some township teams have not made efforts to prepare some strategies for dealing with the issue or to raise resources from other external sources. (Y. Li, 2012, p. 67)

However, some township governments realised that more funding was still needed, even with the start-up funding from district management. For example, as detailed in Chapter 4, the Fengyu township leadership decided to search for other funding sources. They invited commercial companies to be involved in the construction phase of the project, with the hope of letting them cover part of the initial cost. Having negotiated with a Shandong-based construction firm, the Lujian Group, they finally reached a reasonable deal: offering Lujian the construction contract on condition that Lujian paid part of the project's initial costs. As discussed in Chapter 4, this deal greatly reduced villagers' risks in partaking in such a costly project and attracted many to sign up.

The third soft mobilisation approach used by Laiwu's bureaucrats at county and township level was a traditional one, which was to make use of personal contacts or connections to influence villagers. There were so many studies of the Chinese concept of *guanxi* (connections or social networks) before the mid-2000s that research interest in the issue has since slowly faded away. Once China simply meant a massive network of *guanxi* in the eyes of many China specialists, but the scale and depth of China's continuous reforms have turned attention to other aspects of its rapidly modernising society, especially its various institutional and policy issues. Fading academic interest in *guanxi* does not mean the disappearance of interpersonal relationships and social networks from Chinese social life. Instead, *guanxi* still exists and plays its usual important role. The only change that has taken place over the past decade is a change in the expression of the same social feature. Nowadays, more Chinese researchers are using the old Chinese concept of an 'acquaintance society' (*shuren shehui*) to define Chinese everyday life, while some young researchers argue that China has been transformed by industrialisation and urbanisation from an 'acquaintance society' into a 'semi-acquaintance society' (He, 2000).[6] The fact is that even the latter still believes in the existence and value of interpersonal contacts and interactions.

Leaving academic trends aside, no one can have a better knowledge of interpersonal relationships than lower-level officials in rural China. Over the process of mobilising villagers for the new rural scheme, two simple facts were in front of mobilisers from county and township offices and village committees. First, they were in a face-to-face social setting with the mobilised, which characterised the role of lower-level bureaucracies.

Through their direct interactions with the mobilised, it became evident that different people had different influences on their fellow villagers and that existing relationships, including those between relatives and friends, carried more credibility than the word of officials. This was still the reality in rural villages and mobilisers had to face that reality as it was. Second, and more practically, the mobilisers needed information about the financial circumstances of each household to decide their tactics, and the best way to get such information was through village networks. Having realised this fact, mobilisers tried to work out how villagers were networked in each target village before they made use of those networks.

Having mapped out interpersonal networks, mobilisers arranged small groups in each village to conduct the promotion and persuading separately. Each village head and active CCP member was responsible for directing a few small groups. Our fieldwork observed this grouping process in two villages, one of which was Gujiacun. In Gujiacun there were 356 households, which were organised into nine production teams according to the pre-reform village organisational structure. Therefore, village heads, representatives and CCP members were divided into five working teams. Each team was responsible for contacting and persuading a few financially able members from one or two old production teams. According to the original mobilisation plan, the mobilisers or each working team needed to tell villagers about a range of modern and gainful aspects of the new rural construction scheme, such as better housing quality, improved sanitary conditions, new facilities and healthier community life. Since the financial circumstances of each household and their willingness to partake were known through social networks, mobilisation efforts focused on those economically able participants and mobilisation costs were greatly reduced.

The fourth, and last, soft approach was an extension of the third tactic. It is defined by some Chinese researchers as mobilisation of affection, which refers to attention to interpersonal affections and communication in undertaking social mobilisation. Even though China is becoming a semi-acquaintance society, people who still live in villages are mostly influenced by traditional values and practices. Urban-based bureaucrats in their selection of mobilisation approach need to take such cultural variations and psychological factors into account. Throughout our fieldwork, the need to pay attention to affections and feelings was observed in two parts of the mobilisation effort. The first case involved the demolition of existing houses. The second case was about the use of language in the process – or the discourse of the new countryside, to use a stylish phrase.

Because it is widely known, and a universal phenomenon, that old family houses are sacred spaces, if not shrines, to numerous people in many ways and often associated with strong feelings, the demolition of old houses in many villages in Laiwu was found to have been conducted with a higher level of sensitivity and care. There were many delays in the demolition of old houses, despite signed contracts. There were even demands to re-negotiate compensation deals and demolition costs after demolition had begun. Since the government was concerned about possible emotional responses to demolitions, it appeared to us to act patiently and with great care. The only tricky strategy that it deployed was to set up a few demolition teams and purposely hire people with houses to be demolished. It explained this as giving these people an opportunity to earn additional income to cope with the change in family life. What it really hoped for, however, was that demolition would finish as quickly as possible, as payment would be made only on completion of the work.

While local bureaucrats exercised much caution and care in dealing with the demolition of existing houses, the official discourse of the so-called socialist new countryside was a challenge to them at the start of the campaign. For a political reason, or because of the laziness of some local officials, the original ideas of the scheme were relayed to all rural residents without appropriate modifications, and some of them were found to be not only inefficient but disturbing. Overall, four types of discourse were packaged and utilised, including ideological, scientific, modernist and rational discourses. When doing face-to-face promotions, the ideological meaning of the new rural strategy seemed easy to explain, as rural residents had already learned it through a range of channels, but its scientific aspect confused many, especially topics such as village relocations for geological reasons and the selection of different building materials. Obviously, despite the different details of the new rural policy, there was a huge gap between official discourses and what rural residents wanted to know. In the early weeks of the campaign some key points were soon ignored, and the language used was gradually changed by numerous down-to-earth questions from villagers. After that, the practical questions and personal concerns of villagers became the main and ongoing topics of interaction between the mobilised and the government-appointed mobilisers. The latter's timely answers and other responses to villagers' questions, which may be defined as rational economic discourse, helped peel off the superfluous decoration of the strategy and eventually moved the project forward towards implementation.

NOTES

1. This policy approach has been translated in several different ways, for example, the province-over-county, the province administering the county, the province-leading-county or even simply the province-managing-counties. Similarly, the city-leading-county

model is also translated as the city administering the county, the prefecture-level-city governing counties or the prefecture-over-county. Readers can find more information about these in Ahlers (2014), Yu (2014), Zhang et al. (2016) and Li et al. (2016).

2. The village-level governance structure in China and its function have been an interesting research topic, but readers are often confused by some analyses. For example, while many report that village-level governance systems are no longer functioning, or are even worse than dysfunctional, other researchers believe that self-governance and village democracy are emerging in many Chinese villages. In addition to the publications mentioned in the discussion (Zuo and Chao, 2007; Yu, 2009; Takeuchi, 2013), readers can find more information in Shi (2000), Xu and Zhang (2009), Schubert and Ahlers (2012), Ahlers (2014) and Wang (2014).

3. In the eyes of some Chinese, *pai gongzuozu* (sending working groups to the grassroots level to organise a political campaign) is a typical Maoist practice. In the early years of Mao's Cultural Revolution, when China was thrown into nationwide chaos, Mao decided to send teams of workers and PLA soldiers to take over the management of universities and research institutions, including Peking University and Tsinghua University. Because of this aspect of contemporary Chinese history, the phrase *pai gongzuozu* has not been used in China for a long time. Interested readers can find more information about this in Andreas (2007), Dittmer (1987) and Wheelwright and McFarlane (1970).

4. Investigative reporting on a wide range of domestic issues is another important role of China's Xinhua News Agency, and for this reason it has also published internally circulated newsletters. Shi Tianjian once mentioned that 'Xinhua and other major news organizations have daily internal publications to report the information provided by these letters to the authorities' (Shi, 1997, p. 65). Apart from Shi (1997), readers can find more information about this in Bandurski and Hala (2010) and Tong (2011).

5. According to Young and Guo (2007), Hu Jintao's 'harmonious society' (*hexie shehui*) idea was officially introduced in 2004 as a response to evident disharmony and an increasing number of so-called mass incidents. The political strategy of *weiwen* (maintaining stability) was then set forth to execute Hu's idea. The aim of *weiwen* is said to be to build a secure and creative environment for socio-economic development. This is important background to the new rural urbanisation campaign and important for understanding the behaviour of local officials in the 2000s. In addition to Young and Guo (2007), readers can also find more information about this in Fewsmith (2010), Saich (2011), Lam (2015) and C. Li (2016).

6. The term 'acquaintance society' is believed to be from Fei Xiaotong's book *Xiangtu Zhongguo* (*Rural China*, or *Earthbound China*), published in Shanghai in 1947 (Gao, 2013a). Partly because of the negativity of the concept of *guanxi* that was widely used outside China for a couple of decades before the mid-2000s, and partly because of the influence of Fei Xiaotong, a London-trained sociologist who became a national leader in his later life, the concept of the 'acquaintance society' has been recycled and further developed. Readers can find more information about it in Day (2013) and Ying (2013).

7. Participatory responses of villagers to initiatives

This last discussion chapter will look at villagers' responses to the construction scheme. In earlier chapters we have analysed how the strategy was executed at different levels of China's party-state system, including by means of market forces, which is of theoretical and practical importance in terms of updating our knowledge, but the ultimate objective of the campaign was the participation of rural residents in the building scheme. Therefore, this chapter sets out to answer the logical question of how villagers responded to the plan, and through this a fuller and clearer picture of social mobilisation will be obtained.

As noted in Chapter 4, the implementation of the strategy resulted in various forms of protest. Although Shandong was largely free from what many researchers and observers have defined as resistant incidents during most of the years of the implementation, and Laiwu was even better over the same period, there were numerous protests, either large-scale and collective or small-scale and individual, which were triggered by compensation and demolition issues in many regions. Because of the fast economic growth achieved in the 1990s and early 2000s, local leaders became more single-minded than when they were focused on GDP growth and, as briefly mentioned in Chapter 4, some even arrogantly shouted a catchphrase, 'No new China without demolitions'.[1] It is also true that the speed, scale and complexity of China's reform programmes from the late 1990s to the 2000s had confused many people, including analysts and researchers. Such prevalent and deep confusion became even more puzzling and problematic because of the increasingly marketised, if not liberalised, Chinese media. The latter helped disclose numerous forced-demolition incidents and vulnerable victims of unfair compensation, but at the same time the journalistic need for headline-grabbing drama and sensation often overemphasised one aspect of the incidents at the expense of others. Frequent protests against involuntary demolition and unfair compensation in the 2000s and exaggerated and sensationalised media coverage of the issues have together given rise to a range of misinterpretations of grassroots redevelopment- or construction-related protests. Zhou Xueguang, a Chinese American sociologist, and his Chinese collaborator, Ai Yun, also consider that this phenomenon is a problem in this type of study, and one of the key problems they have identified is that various forms of protest or resistance have been 'interpreted as the resilience to the authoritarian state' (Zhou and Ai, 2016, p. 446). Theorisations of this type are far out of context, and in need of research.

As indicated in the chapter heading, this analysis considers various forms of grassroots reaction and protest to the rural building strategy from a participatory perspective, which aims to offer a new account of frequent and widespread protest in China. This analysis will be conducted in three steps. The first section will continue what has been discussed here in this brief introduction to detail how reactions to various rural developments have been inadequately theorised, through which this analysis will be placed in a theoretical context. The second section will discuss what we discovered in Laiwu, detailing how rural residents considered the scheme according to their own circumstances, demonstrating their participatory responses to the campaign. The third and last section will examine actions taken by households to protect their own interests or seek more benefits as a result of taking part in the scheme.

GRASSROOTS RESPONSES AND INADEQUATE THEORISATION

Despite being portrayed as an authoritarian state, and being ruled by a single political party, contemporary China has never been entirely free of public discontent, social unrest and protests. Similarly, despite being seen to be 'timid, introverted, reserved, inactive, and obedient' (Gao, 2013b, p. 189), the Chinese people have not only never stopped voicing their discontent but also never paused their protests, big and small. China is full of resentment and protests. In 2014 the Chinese Academy of Social Sciences (CASS), a ministerial-level thinktank, published an analysis of what has since the late 1990s and early 2000s been called *qunti shijian* (collective incidents or mass incidents), taking place from 2000 to 2013. Because there were so many collective incidents, the CASS report divides them into four big categories: incidents involving more than 100 people; those involving 100 to 1000 people; those involving 1000 to 10000 people; and those involving more than 10000 people. While there were only ten incidents in the fourth category over those 14 years – just above 1 per cent of all incidents, which is very different from the exaggerated media coverage – the second category accounts for more than 67 per cent of all incidents. The CASS report also reveals that incidents in the fourth category – the main concern of the party-state system – were predominantly caused by

Table 7.1   Mass protest incidents in 17 categories, out of 871 cases, 2000–2013

Category of mass protest	Number of incidents	%
Traffic-incident triggered	25	2.8
Business-operation related	21	2.4
Mass fights	11	1.2
Labour disputes	267	30.7
Medical disputes	16	1.8
Consumer disputes	33	3.8
Resource-allocation related	21	2.4
School-fee and service related	15	1.7
Inter-village conflicts	15	1.7
Enterprise-operation related	14	1.6
Improper law enforcement	174	20.0
Forced demolitions and land acquisition	97	11.1
Environmental pollution	37	4.2
Petitions	53	6.1
Violent resistance to law enforcement	11	1.2
Indignation or resentment between officials and the public	37	4.2
Other	24	2.8

Source: Based on data from CASS (2014).

two increasingly serious social problems: pollution issues (approximately 50 per cent) and labour disputes (above 36.5 per cent) (CASS, 2014). The report states that there were only 871 incidents involving 100 or more people over those 14 years. Table 7.1 shows that demolitions and land acquisition were the third-biggest reason for these incidents, responsible for 97 mass protests nationally.

Of course, many other efforts were made by Chinese researchers throughout the 2000s and 2010s, and their research yielded more evidence about the scale and impact of widespread forced demolitions and land acquisition. In late 2012 the Center for Monitoring Public Opinions (*Yuqing Jiance Zhongxin*), a research team of China's *Legal Daily*, the Beijing-based newspaper 'under the supervision of the CCP's Central Commission for Political and Legal Affairs', released a report entitled *2012 Research Report on Mass Incidents* (*Legal Daily*, 2012).[2] The report focuses on six key reasons for mass incidents: environment related (8.9 per cent); forced demolitions and land disputes (22.2 per cent); official–citizen con-

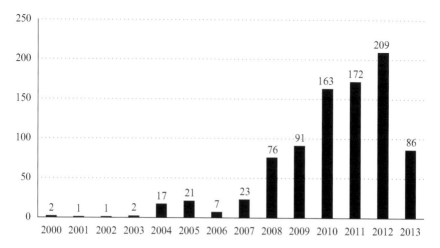

Source: Based on data from CASS (2014).

Figure 7.1   *The increasing occurrence of mass protests, out of 871 cases,*
            2000–2013

flicts (13.3 per cent); police–citizen conflicts (22.2 per cent); social disputes
(24.4 per cent) and ethnic-group related (8.9 per cent). It shows once again
that forced demolitions and land-acquisition-related disputes are one of
the top three categories of mass protest (*Legal Daily*, 2012).

Figure 7.1 shows that these incidents predominantly occurred after
2004, and especially after 2008 when the rural building strategy started its
implementation phase. This trend has been documented in many publications, but various confusions are also obvious. For example, Li Lianjiang
believes that the number of mass incidents had already increased from
8706 in 1993 to 87000 in 2005 – a tenfold increase (Li, 2006). Because of
the lack of a unified definition, other studies have documented 313773
mass incidents in 2005 (Chen, 2009). Even analysts at CASS have been
using different numbers of collective incident in their research publications
(Stenslie and Chen, 2016). Of course, the 2014 CASS report not only made
the definition very clear but also evidently established the connection
between the rural scheme and the increasing number of incidents.

The numbers used in Figure 7.1 are self-explanatory; incidents involving
fewer than 100 people are not included because of the consideration of
their impact in terms of China's overall population size. An event involving
100 people in China is equivalent to an event involving fewer than two
people in Australia, fewer than three people in Canada and fewer than

five people in the UK. This is also because CASS is a ministerial level thinktank, paying attention to the socio-political impact of any mass incident, not just local law-and-order issues. Undoubtedly, there is also a large group of observers who have treated all incidents seriously regardless of the number of participants, because they believe that every incident has its reason. In other words, in addition to reports produced by larger institutions such as CASS, there are many other types of statistics or estimates concerning collective incidents in present-day China. Among the widely cited figures are those from the VOA (Voice of America) website, quoting the comment of a Singapore-based researcher and claiming that there are as many as 500 collective protests per day (VOA, 2016).

It is worth briefly mentioning how the countryside strategy and the sudden increase in mass incidents are linked. On the surface there has been a simple time correlation between them, signifying that many recent mass incidents took place during the implementation of the strategy nationwide. Many analyses stop at this point and start commenting on how badly rural residents were treated and so on. In fact, there has been a crucial link or mechanism between the strategy and the rise in protests: *tudi caizheng* (land finance), which was considered in almost all the preceding chapters of this book. There are many analyses of the recent increase in government dependence on revenues from land transfer. Figure 7.2 is drawn based on analysis published on the website of the China Land Science Society, a top professional association affiliated with China's Ministry of Land and Resources.

In response to the growing number of collective protests, many efforts have been made to theorise these events as a new socio-political scene and

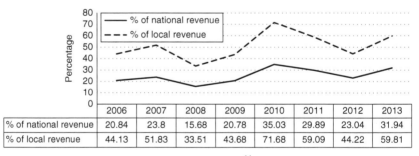

	2006	2007	2008	2009	2010	2011	2012	2013
% of national revenue	20.84	23.8	15.68	20.78	35.03	29.89	23.04	31.94
% of local revenue	44.13	51.83	33.51	43.68	71.68	59.09	44.22	59.81

Source:　Based on data from Zhao et al. (2015).

Figure 7.2　The growing dependence of governments on revenues from land transfer, 2006–13

its implications for China in many aspects. Such academic efforts, however, have been influenced, one way or another, by both the long-standing and powerful intellectual tendency to consider almost all non-official collective protests or events in China as politically driven or revolutionary action, and the extensive media coverage from a tabloid and sensationalist perspective, especially coverage conveyed via the internet and related technologies. Because of this, recent studies of such new issues have repeated the mistakes of the past. According to Xie and Cao (2009) of Shanghai Jiaotong University, most studies in the area have been guided by three theoretical frameworks, namely social movement, revolution and contentious or protest politics. As stated at the start of this chapter, Zhou and Ai identify two 'discernable lines of research', one focusing more on the specific institutional context and the other paying more attention to the various political aspects of mass protests (Zhou and Ai, 2016, p. 446). Interestingly, Zhou and Ai also point out that many Chinese studies belong to the first category, but they make no clear comments on the second type.

The difference identified by Zhou and Ai has been made clearer by some Chinese scholars who consider that non-Chinese research on the issue has been inadequate because excessive attention has been given to the antagonistic effects and politics of social movement. When commenting on various studies from these foreign points of view, Ying Xing, a Beijing-based sociologist, points out the following problems with internationally widely used theoretical frameworks:

> First, there are very strong emotions and certain values and morals involved in [*their*] studies, which may unavoidably influence our understanding of profiles of grassroots protestors, resulting in the idealisation of these partakers. Second, [*their*] studies have overly exaggerated the organisational characteristics of peasant protests, especially their political nature. Although we believe in the depth and authenticity of many fieldworks conducted . . ., [*their*] political enthusiasm and value orientation have eventually made [*them*] quickly jump to such a conclusion: present-day Chinese peasant rights-defending is on the way to being politicised.[3] (Ying, 2007, p. 5)

Leaving aside whether differences exist between Chinese research and non-Chinese research, the critical problem associated with this area of inquiry is theoretical orientation or perspective. The above quotation is one interesting piece of evidence showing that some analysts in China also view protests from politicised perspectives, while the author makes sweeping comments about the problems of non-Chinese research on the same issue. In fact, long before the contextual point of view became accepted and dominant in Chinese academic circles, some non-Chinese researchers already suggested using rational-choice theory to consider why many protests happen during periods of rapid economic growth, and an idea of considering the costs and benefits of various reforms was recommended (Mason, 1994). A warning was also given that now is the time to say 'farewell to revolution', when widespread protests caused by forced demolitions and land disputes reached their climax in China (Perry, 2007, p. 1). However, despite all these efforts, the general tendency mentioned by Zhou and Ai (2016) remains rather persistent, and the theorisation of mass protests and resistance remains incomplete. The process of gaining a clear understanding of these issues has also been regularly affected by the media, because analysts inside and outside China rely on them for information about recent events. The problem is that media coverage of grassroots mass protests in China is often sensationalised for commercial gain.

Among existing theoretical approaches, the contextual approach has been widely used by analysts in China in recent years despite being articulated in different ways. Various forms of this approach share a crucial new methodological trait, which is to place each collective incident in a specific context without over-politicising it or drawing any overstretched conclusions irrelevant to that context. In practice, however, the approach still seems to be insufficient to examine many types of grassroots mass-protest events, and its methodological insufficiency appears in at least two aspects.

First, this widely used approach does not pay sufficient attention to the motivations of participants, which has made it difficult to consider the goals protesters want to achieve. This could well be the reason that many researchers could only draw a simple direct link between two extreme ends of a continuum of socio-political process: governments as policy-makers versus victims of the policies. The people affected by certain policies are assumed to have no other demands and to take no any other action than fighting against governments or the entire political regime. Any conflict between two sides is also seen to be irreconcilable. In the words of some Chinese researchers who believe that rural people in China are suffering from *biaoda kunjing* (predicament of articulation, or articulation problems) (Wu, 2007), the lack of consideration of motivation in many analyses appears to be the real reason for such difficulty. What also needs to be considered is a different type of everyday politics based on the status and identity of vulnerable people. Such a politics has not only been identified by some Chinese researchers but also been found to have been used as a weapon in playing strategic games (*yishi boyi*) (Dong, 2008, 2010). As pointed out, Chinese politics and China's political power structure have been transformed, entering what many Chinese have called the era of *boyi* (strategic game-playing). A crucial consideration in game-playing is the motivation of each side.

A second methodological insufficiency of the contextual approach is that it does not pay adequate attention to process factors or dynamics, overlooking the process by which people make up their minds on questions as grave as the demolition of their houses, and how people evaluate and calculate the costs and benefits of taking part in a particular scheme. Many earlier studies did their surveys in a journalistic fashion, noticing how emotional or even angry people could be when dealing with new policy-driven schemes, but offering less insight into the approaches of the people affected. Although this methodological insufficiency has been raised (O'Brien, 2008; Liu, 2015), it remains a key problem in this type of study.

In view of all the above problems, this analysis will consider responses of villagers to forced demolitions and land disputes from a participatory perspective, paying more attention to why some villagers refused to partake in the new scheme and why some even openly protested against it. This viewpoint implies that socio-political participation has become a very normal part of everyday life in China, and that this participation could occur in abnormal ways, including protests, petitions and even bribes, as has been suggested by some Chinese analysts (Wen, 2009; Ye, 2009). The participatory perspective seems at least to be able to correct the above two problems associated with this type of study, in that it avoids treating villagers and other rural residents as passive victims of certain policies, and it does not exclude their motivations and actions from the analysis.

RATIONAL CORRELATIONS BETWEEN MOBILISATION AND PARTICIPATION

The discussion here is based on data gathered from a township region code named Fengyu. As mentioned in Chapters 4 and 6, Fengyu is one of Laiwu's 13 township-government regions and once managed more than 50 villages scattered all over the district. As early as 2008, three villages were selected to be pilot sites, and a few more were chosen afterwards. By 2010 there were 19 villages listed in the new rural plan. Because of the participation of so many villages, this township region has, as mentioned before, generated various types of experiences, both successful and not so successful, in the implementation of the construction strategy. This includes the successful involvement of a local construction company in the building projects, as discussed in Chapter 4. Several rounds of interviews were carried out in nine villages in the Fengyu township region in 2014 and 2015, and observations were also conducted in several villages. The latter aimed to look at the general condition of family houses and village development as part of the research effort to find out why some villagers opted to participate in the project and some did not.

We read many research publications on how rural residents in China had responded to new government policies, especially those related to land use and housing sites, and we were influenced by ideas from those early studies, but the impression that we formed from the first round of fieldwork was very different from what we had read. The effect of that first impression was twofold. First, the mobilised, or village residents, were not passive objects of the campaign, and their responses did not automatically end with a simple yes or no. Second, what eventually occurred, while neither immediately confirming nor precluding their participation, was that almost all households calculated the costs and benefits of participation and looked for all possible ways to optimise their gain from it. At the same time, what they were unable to accept was clearly set out, and this, as will be explored in the next section, was the likelihood of losing what they already had.

There seemed to be no simple positive correction between villagers' actions, either welcoming or opposing, and government initiatives and policies. Rural residents were not faithful supporters of the CCP and its initiatives, as they were portrayed in many publications of the 1950s and 1960s, nor did they act as challengers to authoritarian rule, as they were depicted in publications of the 1990s and 2000s. After a few decades of economic reform, villagers have become neither supporters nor opponents but rather experienced calculators of self-interest. Such a calculation is evidently economic in nature, and it can be made alongside other considerations, such as intra-family relations, nostalgia for traditional village life and social networks. In the case of this new building scheme, there was clearly a different type of correlation – a rational one – between the government's proposal and each family's decision to partake or not.

Such rational calculation was found to be very comprehensive and detailed in the Fengyu region. It was entirely based on each household's circumstances, with no evidence showing that any villager still took support for government plans into consideration. Villagers seemed not only rational but also family-oriented. Our interviews in nine villages identified six – five plus one special, different one – motivations or reasons to consider participating in the scheme. All these considerations were important, and helped to develop an updated understanding of how people react to a new national policy and how the rationales of mobiliser and mobilised could be played out in a mobilisation campaign.

First, straightforward support for the scheme came from those whose houses were rundown but who had some savings towards building a new dwelling. In the Fengyu region numerous houses were built in the 1980s to cope with increased housing demand from the birth cohorts of the 1960s. In the 1980s rural China was still very poor, and the houses built then were very basic and unable to last for a long time. Despite this, the first response from these households focused on a key point of the reasoning of ordinary Chinese: was the building project *huasuan* (financially worthwhile)?[4] Despite being expressed differently, *huasuan* is the key concept used by ordinary Chinese to evaluate whether a thing is worth doing, and one villager offered more details about its meaning as follows:

> Having considered it at home, I believe it is *huasuan*. Our house and many others in the neighbourhood were all built in the same period, more than 30 years old. They have already become very rundown, if not the most uninhabitable. If we were rebuilding it by ourselves, it could cost more than one hundred thousand [yuan], as one of my brothers spent over one hundred and fifty thousand [yuan] on his new house. I also like the arrangement, and I simply pay less money than my brother did and let the company do the construction. Now I also need a new house because my daughter has a boyfriend, and we need to make our house presentable. (Su, 2016, pp. 146–7)

Second, villagers who had two or more housing sites responded favourably to the project. This was an atypical phenomenon in rural China because the country's 1998 *Land Act* defines land as a scarce resource, laying down the rule of *yihu yizhai* (one household, one housing site). The practice of applying for a new housing site for a newborn but not for a deduction when a family member passes away has enabled some families to have more than one housing site. Because of growing wealth, some rural households have also acquired a second housing site through other legal channels, such as purchasing, transferring or inheriting land. Roughly 20 per cent of families in the Fengyu region had more than one housing site at the time the project was promoted. From the perspective of land-title holders, the value of rural land is entirely dependent on development opportunities, and the new countryside project was a heaven-sent one. In other words, such ownership situations already partly ensured at least minimum success for the scheme.

Third, people who already worked outside their villages or outside the agricultural sector, but kept their rural household registrations and therefore kept their housing sites in villages, usually had a welcoming attitude to the scheme. Though these people were hardly involved in discussions with their fellow residents, most of them were willing to rebuild their houses. In a village called Guchun, approximately 20 per cent of the households that registered to purchase new apartments belonged to this category. These residents were mostly interested in keeping a dwelling in their home village and in long-term capital gains.

Fourth, well-off rural residents who wanted to enjoy modern life in a rural setting were also supportive of the plan. These villagers were almost all in their fifties or sixties and had at least one adult child working in a city. These people had no financial difficulties about participating in the project, but they were mainly worried about whether the design was modern enough to suit their family's needs, especially whether the dwellings would include a range of modern facilities, such as gas or electric stoves and flush toilets. These people considered these facilities to be necessities for attracting their urban-born, or city-living, grandchildren to visit them more often and more conveniently. By the 2000s it was no longer taboo to admit that old-style facilities in rural China were not acceptable by the standards of many urbanised young Chinese, and that they prevented them and their young families from visiting their home villages on a regular basis.

Fifth, support was given by those who were open-minded and progressive, especially those who were familiar with what had been happening outside their village or even outside rural areas. For many years reforms have resulted in a constant and massive flow of rural–urban migration. Villagers have been witnessing all these changes and the moving out of many of their neighbours, and many have even become familiar with the fashionable term urbanisation. Rural Laiwu, like many parts of rural Shandong, has not seen empty villages and substantial uncultivated land, as has happened in several other provinces. However, it was a strong trend that villagers were moving away from rural life into rapidly growing urban centres, big and small. These changes have not only benefited those moving out and making a good fortune but also changed the minds of some who had decided to stay. Through all these life experiences, these people had become more sophisticated in their understanding of social trends and the direction of socio-economic development. Villagers with such a broad-minded attitude towards social change were ready recipients of the messages of the campaign.

Last, as noted earlier in this section, the sixth group of those who supported the building project consisted of a special type of village resident: those on the local public payroll, such as township-government staff members, some teachers, and some village-committee cadres. As discussed in Chapter 6, they were under pressure from the party-state systems at county and township level to not only support the scheme but also sign up for the project. Many of them did not want to participate, because their better and stable jobs and incomes, by village standards, had already ensured that their houses were in good condition. However, they had to do what they were told to do, including urging relatives and others to participate.

In addition to the above six affirmative responses, our interviews in nine villages identified a set of adverse motivations or reasons on the other side of the correlation equation. Figure 7.3 is drawn to show an overall view of where the main challenges to the mobiliser were from.

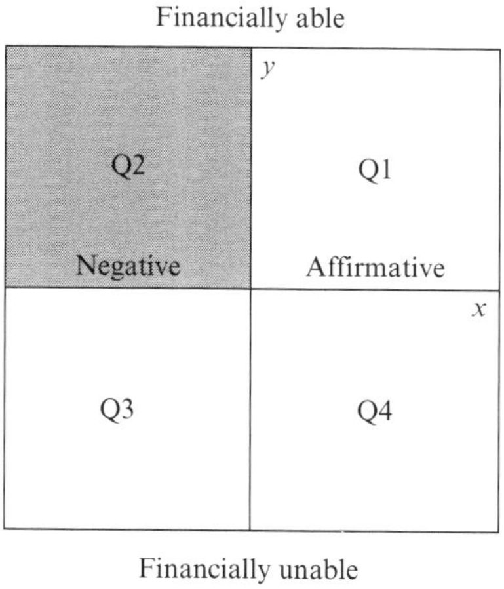

Financially able

Financially unable

Source: Based on interview data.

Figure 7.3   Four types of responses and the most difficult groups

As illustrated in Figure 7.3, villagers' responses could be considered at the intersection of two perspectives: whether respondents were financially able to partake in the rebuilding scheme, as indicated by the vertical (y) axis, and whether respondents were willing to buy a new house, as represented by the horizontal (x) axis. According to these two key considerations, villagers could generally be divided into four types. Of the quadrants of Figure 7.3, Q1 represents those who were both financially able and positive in attitude. What we discussed in the first half of this section is primarily based on this type of villager. People in the Q4 category were positive about the scheme but unable to afford it. Efforts were made to help some of them and inspire them to participate. Q3 refers to those who were not only financially unable to partake but also negative towards the project. As highlighted in Figure 7.3, Q2 shows where the main challenges to the mobiliser were from, as it refers to those who were financially able to participate but negative towards the scheme.

Because of the above categorisation, special attention was given in interviews to those who were classified in Q2. Due to their success in accumulating wealth, these villagers were regarded as smart, diligent people. Therefore, their responses, and the calculations behind their decisions, were very interesting. Our interviews identified five main reasons behind their negative responses.

First, because of their higher incomes, these families already lived in relatively new houses with some modern facilities, such as solar hot-water systems and heating systems. Of course, their response was also partly because they did not have a second housing site, in which case they would have responded quite differently. Our interviews also confirmed that, in addition to the above two main points, some people did not like the simplified property-valuation policy, which disregarded building type and quality when determining the level of compensation. This last issue was found to be very upsetting to many of those classified in Q2 in Figure 7.3, lowering their interest in participating in the project.

Second, the new urban-style centralised apartment housing was not convenient for those who still mainly worked on their allocated land to grow various crops. In theory, they supported the strategy to reduce rural housing sites and save more arable land from housing, as well as the grand idea to modernise rural living conditions. However, their lands were usually allocated near the place where they originally lived, and the house relocation would not only increase their daily transport costs but also make their lives less convenient.

Third, many villagers strongly believed that the old courtyard-style house still suited the level of rural development and the existing way of life. Basically, they wanted to express that rural activities had not been developed into a factory-style production system, and their current main activities were still household based, which may never completely change. In other words, many village residents were still peasants, and they still worked and lived as peasants. Unlike factory workers, those villagers working on the land had various special needs. About half a dozen such special needs were repeatedly mentioned throughout the interviews. A couple of them were specific to the location. For example, as it is a famous region in which to grow ginger, ginger growers would need an additional piece of land on which to do what they normally did in their family courtyard – including germinating seeds before planting them in a field – if they moved into new apartment units. This need also applied to the drying process after harvesting and the temporary storage. There were also some other general concerns, but all focused on the absence of a courtyard. In addition to space for parking machinery, requirements for which have increased significantly as a result of rural reform and development, some households were worried about space for storing crop residues, or straws and stalks, which are still used in rural China as free household fuel for cooking and heating. This latter issue was targeted by the strategy in some regions to reduce the level of air pollution.[5]

Fourth, some villagers were influenced by the strong sense of affection they had for their old family houses or even old housing sites, especially those who had inherited houses from their parents or grandparents. As introduced in Chapter 3, Shandong is the homeland of Confucius and many other central contributors to the Confucian tradition. In a region with a long history and a traditional heritage, the heavy cultural baggage of this place obviously influenced many villagers. In the eyes of some, the demolition of a house implied cutting off their roots. According to others, their houses carried deep and profound memories of their past lives and hard work, feelings that were found to be much stronger among villagers who had earned their fortune through work and effort.

Last, the fifth main reason to prevent a group of households from participating in the project or even considering it favourably was related to China's strong urbanisation trend and the likelihood of relocating a family from a village to a city. These villagers were at least considering how to financially support their urban-working children, if not themselves, to move out and purchase an apartment in a city. This has been one of the most frequently discussed topics nationwide in China, because some families want to take advantage of urbanisation to move out of smaller places, especially villages. With hundreds of millions of Chinese people moving into bigger urban centres over the past decades, it was a legitimate excuse for delay in making up their mind about what to do or to simply say no to mobilisers of local building projects. This was complicated by the fact that China had implemented its one-child policy about 35 years before our fieldwork, and this had greatly altered the way people planned their family life. Unsurprisingly, many families had to consider their children's long-term plan first. What was astonishing was that the gender factor was not only still playing its role in all these decision-making processes but also clearly forming a new pattern in many rural regions, including the Fengyu region. This pattern was that families with a son needed to purchase a new apartment or house before their son's marriage. Without making any further comment on such social norms and practices, it was evident that the decision-making of many rural households was greatly influenced by the long-term effects of the one-child policy, which ended shortly after our fieldwork in Laiwu.

Based on the above two sets of reasons or motivations, there was a clear indication that villagers did not act against the new rural strategy and related projects, and that they were responding to the mobiliser of the new scheme. However, lack of opposition to the policy and its projects does not mean participation in the project. Leaving aside those on the public payroll, who were obligated to partake in the project, the attention of all the villagers we interviewed was focused on several key issues, including financial advisability, effects on daily work engagement, quality of daily life and intra-family relationships. There was a clear correlation between the mobilisation campaign and participation, but ultimately positions were decided rationally by each mobilised villager or family based on their own circumstances.

PROTESTS AGAINST POTENTIAL LOSSES

It is known to ordinary Chinese people, who have experienced many changes, one after another, over the last few decades, that any new major reform initiative can have negative effects on some members of a community while providing others with better benefits or opportunities. Protection of their own interests and rights, therefore, has been a constant part of the daily life of those who feel affected by policy initiatives. Objections and protests have also become part of not only popular discourse but also the Chinese socio-political scene. In the process of continuous reform and a never-ending push for economic growth, largely characterised by the redistribution of power and interests, it seems to be inevitable that some unethical and illegitimate behaviour, by groups and individuals, will take place. Such actions worsen uncertainties caused by policy changes, making some people feel even more deprived, disadvantaged and angry. On the other hand, governments at different levels often discriminatorily push for the speedy implementation of policy initiatives and hope to complete certain objectives of their new strategies. Such an approach can also cause those who feel deprived to react more strongly than usual to the drive to execute initiatives. However, our fieldwork found that grassroots responses did not comprise just two extreme types: positive and supportive reaction, and negative and destructive objection; there were many other types of response between these extremes.

The last point mentioned above is of some theoretical significance, especially in examining grassroots protests in rural China, which have been sensationalised for various reasons, such as the need for headlines or the need for theorisation. What we observed in our fieldwork reminded us not only that various responses from villagers cannot be considered as simply positive or negative, but also that protests even at the negative end of the spectrum cannot be regarded as a single type that takes place at only one stage. More specifically, responses of the mobilised were found in this study to have taken different forms, ranging from positive reactions to angry street protests. Protests alone were found to have multiple types and to have taken place at multiple phases. For analytical purposes, these protests might be classified as invisible or visible, or non-public or public. To elaborate this point further, this section discusses the grassroots protests observed in Fengyu region in two parts: some occurring on a small scale without too much publicity, and some taking place outside villages as collective incidents.

The first type of protest was largely overlooked due to their small scale and the fact that they often had no publicity. However, mobilisation efforts were often made in this area to deal with this type of protest because of their strong, often emotional, negativity towards the project and their direct, powerful influence on other residents. From the viewpoint of outsiders, these protests were invisible, but their impact – or, to be precise, their potential to cause more difficulties for the policy's implementation – was not much less than that of angry street actions or collective petitions outside the offices of county or municipal governments. Moreover, the number of these invisible incidents was found to be far greater than that of visible incidents. Some village residents reacted to certain practices of the mobilisation campaign more angrily and sensitively than they did to others, due to their perception of possible unfairness or even losses. This then also caused adverse reactions by other villagers.

Two main triggers for these adverse responses were identified through our interviews: the property-valuation policy and practice, and the house-demolition process. As mentioned, valuations of existing properties did not take building type and quality into consideration when determining compensation, which made some villagers very upset and angry. However, valuations were conducted before villagers signed up for the project, and participants could refuse to proceed if valuations were not acceptable. Therefore, any bad feelings caused by the property valuation were less overwhelming than those caused by the demolition, which was normally done after the contract was signed, making many villagers feel that they had no choice but to accept it. Although the demolition company was partly utilised, as discussed earlier, by the township government and village committees as a mobilisation force to persuade villagers to partake in the scheme, its practices made some villagers very upset. One furious resident made the following comments:

> Demolition companies are all devil and have no moral conscience. They knew that we have signed the contract and must move out of the old house very soon, and that the old house is no use to us any more, they have then started playing dirty tricks on us to shrewdly lower the prices of [valuable] salvaged items that they can collect from demolishing our house. If you wanted to bargain with them for fair prices, they would then stop the work and tell you 'to get somebody else to do it for you'. (Su, 2016, p. 141)

Apparently, the demolition process was notorious and caused trouble all over the place during China's construction boom of previous decades, partly because demolition could destroy other things connected with old houses or buildings. In the case of the scheme in Laiwu, the troubles caused by demolition were worsened by the surge in the market price of housing over the period between the signing of the contract and the actual demolition, which made villagers feel deprived and angry. Because such negative responses could be exacerbated into collective protests outside the village, many of these small-scale, invisible protests were found in the Fengyu region to have been dealt with by what is usually called proactive persuasion in China. In practice, such proactive persuasion was not undertaken through official channels, which would have worsened the situation. Instead, personal kinship networks were mobilised as part of the strategy to calm heated disputes and negotiations. All of this happened in a rural society in which people are still more closely related to each other through traditional ties than through modern ones, and often kinship networks are still helpful in dealing with disputes. In the latter circumstance village heads, who were sandwiched between superior governments and village residents, were found to have often turned to kinship networks for help in preventing disputes from worsening and spreading beyond the village.

What was briefly discussed above also confirms that, alongside the official channel through which a social-mobilisation campaign may be organised, at least one more non-official channel can play a vital role. This channel consists of various traditional networks among villagers. A special role that village heads can play in such a dual-track system is to establish a link between the two channels, and to decide when to make use of one of the two systems. It seemed that village heads were fully aware of the limitations of administrative mobilisation, which could alienate those residents who were already hesitating and doubting. Many of the latter still put more faith, trust and confidence in people in their close kinship or traditional networks, believing that only people from these networks would consider issues from their standpoint. As mentioned earlier, greater effort was made by mobilisers to deal with small-scale protests. The reason for this was that local leaders and bureaucrats would generally devote greater attention to preventing large-scale mass protests than to other issues.

The second type of protest, visible and held outside villages, was also observed in the Fengyu township region, despite the above-mentioned efforts by mobilisers. This is the type that has attracted a great deal of journalistic attention and scholarly interest, but our observations in the region confirm that these protests were triggered by problems of local participation in the scheme and operational procedures. In other words, these mass protests, as our analysis would like to stress, are participatory responses; they are not uncooperative or even antagonistic, resistant and oppositional, which would make mobilisation impossible. Throughout our fieldwork, a few protests were found to trouble mobilisers and the execution of the project, and interestingly, all these protests resulted from issues that had not been dealt with properly by mobilisers. Two incidents were found to have dragged on for longer than other incidents, which is worth examining in this section. During our fieldwork, the first mass protest was called the Gujiacun case, and the second incident was called the Xiazhuang case.

The Gujiacun case resulted from improper conduct by the head of the CCP village committee, who was found to have sold assets that were collectively owned by registered village residents and administered by the village committee and its members. This is a complex ownership issue, as the assets were passed on from the old People's Commune system but were still officially defined as collectively owned. According to current Chinese law, the village committee can sell or lease collectively owned assets left untouched by rural decollectivisation or other reform measures. In numerous less-industrialised regions, old production-team office sites, courtyards and storerooms have remained in collective hands, which is to say the hands of the village committee. In the Gujiacun case, the secretary of the CCP's village committee sold the remaining 56 old storerooms belonging to the village to as many as 17 families without going through the proper procedure of discussing it with other committee members, let alone with villagers.

Informal information networks in Gujiacun village revealed this big sale, and protests started immediately. Officials from the township government believed the excuse made by the secretary, which was that the deal aimed to increase the number of participants in the new building project, which would be unable to start if those 17 households did not sign up. On the other hand, all other villagers and party members felt trapped by the secretary, even suspecting that he had derived personal gain from this bold and illegitimate decision, which must have been at the cost of other residents' interests. To deal with township-government officials who were unwilling to take a tough stance on the issue, a few members of the village's CCP committee decided to rally non-party support to fight against the sale and recover the losses in both monetary and reputational terms. Once everyone in the village became aware of the secret sale, responses became stronger than before and demands increased. Villagers made two demands at meetings: to resell what the 17 households purchased, and to discipline the secretary. Collective action took shape, and one CCP member even proposed the following tactic to make the issue bigger that it was and thus push their demands with the government:

> In my opinion, this issue would be extremely difficult to solve, or impossible to resolve, without making it bigger and more serious [than now]. It might need

to be taken to the district government, or even to the municipal government, but we might need to give the township government more time to deal with the trouble. It might not be a good idea to involve higher-level governments in it from the very beginning. (Su, 2016, p. 170)

The township government was given a few months to handle the issue, but villagers could no longer be easily satisfied by the removal of the CCP secretary, as all attention was on the property sold to 17 families. Having negotiated many times with the township government without success, the action ended with a large group of frustrated villagers storming a meeting attended by county-level leaders. With the direct intervention of higher-level governments, prompt action was taken by several government offices, including the police. The sale of the properties was revoked, and all 17 titles were reallocated through a traditional lottery system and sold to village residents.

The Xiazhuang case represented a different problem in the implementation of the policy that also resulted in mass protests. As noted in Chapter 6, the construction-quality issue was observed in several villages in the Fengyu region, but the one in Xiazhuang dragged on for a long time without a satisfactory solution as several issues were involved, resulting in mass petitions up to provincial level.

Xiazhuang is in the central area of a geologically unstable district, as revealed by local geological karst surveys. For this reason, the village was chosen to be one of the few villages to be rebuilt and relocated. However, construction was delayed due to a shortage of land, and Xiazhuang residents were unable to move to their new houses at the promised time. Collective resentments started surfacing and some suggested challenging the township government to explain why they were treated differently from several other neighbouring villages. Apart from the repeated delays, another trouble emerged when a vice-governor of Shandong, while inspecting villages, was overheard by villagers to ask whether each household had already received RMB 30000 compensation for relocating from karst-stricken areas. The media team accompanying the vice-governor on his tour asked the same question. Speculation and theories spread quickly and provoked deep confusion and furious responses. This was a huge sum of money that no villager had ever heard throughout the process, but the vice-governor and the media people appeared to them to be the most reliable information sources. The key issue of the collective protests was altered, and investigating where the money had gone bonded more villagers together than before. After village leaders and township officials all denied the existence of such funding, a group of village activists decided to organise a collective petition to the provincial government.

This petition action and several protest meetings outside a few provincial-government bureaus had received no constructive reply a few months after our fieldwork in the region. We were told that the provincial bureaus had all promised to investigate the issue, and another geological survey was organised and subsequently carried out. Fortunately, or unfortunately, the new survey confirmed the need for compensation, which further complicated the issue. A few provincial departments and bureaus then decided to let the Laiwu municipal government take full responsibility for resolving the dispute. However, once the responsibility was handed down to bureaucracies at lower levels, the decision-making process would once again be influenced by these bureaucracies, resulting in what is called *ti piqiu* (kicking the ball around, or kicking the issue back and forth like a ball): endless wrangles over the issue.

Many villagers regarded these two protest incidents as actions to protect their interests or to prevent, or reduce, their losses in such a huge and radical socio-economic change as the new rural plan. While no one denies the important role of collective protests in rights protection, the above cases also reveal the different dynamics involved in the mobilisation mechanism in present-day China. In addition to the above-mentioned point regarding the participatory nature of many grassroots protests, a few more points can be drawn from these two protests. First, losses of material interests or benefits, real, imagined or expected, were triggers for collective protest. In response to such losses, local people had very limited means to argue for themselves and defend their interests, other than to make use of petitions, public protests and other forms of collective action. These options have been widely used in numerous rural regions in recent decades, and despite support from emerging channels of communication, such as tabloid newspapers and social media, multiple layers of bureaucracy have prevented smooth and efficient communication and negotiation between concerned citizens and decision-makers, making policy implementation more difficult. Second, a high proportion of participants took part in protests because of their strong sense of equality and fairness. The very traditional Chinese idea of *bu huangua, er huanbujun* (less concerned with paucity, but more concerned with inequality) still influences many villagers, who might not hope to gain any material benefit from taking part in collective protests but really want to maintain even or impartial distribution of goods, benefits and opportunities. Third, our fieldwork found that a small proportion of protesters intended to reap more benefits from the project, as the government was obviously behind it and some additional benefits were thought to be likely to come with it.

Last, as partly mentioned above, the two collective-protest cases hinted that trouble seemed to be resolved with no big hurdle when the party-state system was in the position of umpire, as in the case of Gujiacun. However, as suggested by the case of Xiazhuang, a solution was difficult to reach if the issue challenged the party-state system, or even if it involved relations among various parts of the party-state system in local trouble. This distinction seems to explain what happened in the Fengyu region and why one of the above-mentioned issues could be resolved after a while, but the other still had not seen any real resolution several months after our fieldwork.

NOTES

1. The original Chinese version of 'No new China without demolitions' is *Meiyou qiangchai, jiu meiyou xin Zhongguo*, which is also translated as 'without demolitions, there is no new China'. This new saying is clearly based on the sentence pattern of one of the CCP's most frequently used propaganda slogans over the past few decades, which is *Meiyou Gongchandang, jiu meiyou xin Zhongguo* (Without the Communist Party, there would be no new China). This propaganda expression is part of the lyrics of a popular song, which is entitled with the same phrase. This song has been sung and spread widely to promote the CCP leadership since 1943, well before the CCP's takeover of national power in 1949. In China, people's familiarity with the song is believed by some educated Chinese to be comparable to Westerners' familiarity with the 'Hallelujah' chorus from Handel's *Messiah*. Interested readers can find more information about the song and the slogan in Hua and Nathan (2016) and Mei (2018).
2. This commission is also translated as the Central Political and Legal Affairs Commission, and in Chinese it is simply called *Zhengfawei*. According to Xu and Yang (2015), it is a very powerful party organ that straddles the CCP and the government system. It is 'the paramount institution overseeing public security, armed police, state security as well as courts, the procuratorates and the prison systems. The Ministries of Public Security, State Security and Justice are concurrently members of the commission and are under the leadership of the commission's secretary, who has no official position in the government' (Xu and Yang, 2015, p. 86). China's policy of 'protecting stability' (*weiwen*) has been the main task of this commission. Apart from Xu and Yang (2015), interested readers can read more in Sullivan (2012) and Lam (2015).
3. We have used four pairs of square brackets in this quote, three for *their* and one for *them*, to replace *his* and *him* respectively, which were used by Ying Xing originally in his journal paper. This is because Ying Xing mentions the name of a popular Chinese male researcher here as an example of oversimplifying and politicising recent peasant protests. There are two reasons for making these minor changes: one is to avoid confusion, and the other is to emphasise that Ying Xing is commenting on two general theoretical problems in the field, not making a personal criticism. Just in case readers would like to know more about this debate, Yu Jianrong is the person mentioned by Ying Xing. Yu Jianrong is a high-profile researcher in China because of both his research on grassroots workers and peasants and his long-term online activism. He currently works at CASS. Interested readers can find more information about Yu Jianrong in Smith (2013) and Negro (2017).
4. Please note that *huasuan* does not always mean financially worthwhile but could also be used to mean worthwhile politically and socially. Google simply translates *huasuan* as cost-effective, but six entries for the term are listed in the *TPS Frequency Dictionary of Mandarin Chinese*, including: to calculate; to weigh (pros and cons); to view as profitable; worthwhile; value for money; and cost-effective. Similar expressions have already been used in English publications, for example *huadelai*, as used in Zhou (1994) and Zhang (2010). As noted, this is a very important but less-discussed concept, helpful in understanding the minds of ordinary Chinese people, and helpful to some analysts in

avoiding the mistake that tends to link the actions of many ordinary Chinese to certain big political or even religious issues.

5. During our fieldwork in the Fengyu region we noticed that many families who had moved into new apartment units had taken their old-style stoves with them so that they could keep using free stalks and straws as fuel. On several occasions when officials from high-level governments came to do inspections, village heads had to repeatedly make announcements, often using loudspeakers, warning residents not to burn stalks and straws on the days when government officials would be in the village.

8. Towards an updated understanding of social mobilisation in China

This is the only book-length study written in English in recent decades that looks systematically at the use of the social-mobilisation mechanism in post-industrial China. The preceding chapters have examined a series of aspects of the mechanism when it was used to help execute the new socialist countryside strategy. In the eyes of some China analysts, both Chinese and non-Chinese, the enthusiasm and attention devoted to the strategy have already faded from media coverage and most current discussions among bureaucrats at central and local level. Other observers also share such impressions. It is only partially true that the rural strategy was put forward under the Hu Jintao leadership (2003–13), which was succeed by the Xi Jinping leadership in late 2012 and early 2013. However, as indicated in Table 2.3, rural issues remained the subject of the so-called No. 1 Central Document in the first term of the Xi Jinping leadership from 2013 to 2017. In early February 2018, China's Xinhua News Agency released a report confirming that the focus of 2018's No. 1 Central Document was still on the rural-development issue. The following passage shows that the issue has become even more important than before:

> The strategy of rural vitalization was first proposed as one of the major aspects of developing a modernized economy in a report delivered to the 19th National Congress of the [CCP] . . . In this latest document, the strategy was described as a 'historical task' essential to accomplishing China's modernization goals and building a moderately prosperous society. (*Xinhua News*, 2018b, n.p.)

According to this latest No. 1 Central Document, the rural strategy is articulated in a slightly different manner, and more explicitly as part of long-term national development plans or policy frameworks. To better understand the continuity and improvement, it is worth mentioning the three timetabled goals set by the current Chinese leadership to execute the rural-vitalisation strategy. By 2020 a new institutional framework and policy system will be established. By then, rural productivity and agricultural supply should be substantially improved, and no rural residents should be living below the existing poverty line. By 2035 decisive progress will have been made towards the objectives of achieving basic modernisation of agriculture and rural areas. All people in rural areas and urban centres will have equal access to basic public services. Then, by 2050, rural China should have strong agriculture, beautiful countryside and well-off farmers. China's reforms have been reasonably successful in modernising cities, and now is the time to devote more attention to rural areas. In other words, China has a clear understanding of the need to prevent less-developed rural regions and sluggish rural progress from dragging down its overall performance in socio-economic development, and it has a coherent strategy to prevent this outcome. Improved socio-economic development is practically the only political basis for the CCP's ruling legitimacy.

While many rural construction projects and schemes are still in the process of execution in rural China, its rural development strategy has become more comprehensive than rebuilding houses. For example, in 2017 Xi Jinping himself authored a front-page article in the *People's Daily* urging rural regions to revolutionise their toilets. Now, many township governments have a special office, called the three major revolutions (*sanda geming*) office, driving and guiding revolutionary changes in the management of drinking water, rubbish and sanitation in rural China. Analysts have underestimated China's determination to modernise rural regions partly because of the country's recent focus on the anti-corruption campaign, which has indeed not only restrained economic activities in various regions but also diverted media and public attention from these activities. In fact, rural construction has continued without pause, and China's urban population has reached a new high, totalling more than 813 million at the end of 2017 and accounting for as much as 59 per cent of the population, according to official Xinhua reports in early 2018. In other words, China's rural urbanisation is still going on at a rapid rate, and it remains the main theme of its recent reform programmes.

This final chapter of the book has three key tasks to complete. First, it will sum up what has been analysed in earlier chapters with regard to a range of social-mobilisation activities and approaches that have been utilised in China's new countryside campaign. This is one of the major tasks that all large-scale studies must undertake as part of the effort to further identify what is absent from our knowledge and what is new to our understanding. Second, this chapter will include a further theoretical discussion, focusing on more general issues in the field than the above summary, and aiming to offer some theoretical insights into how to analyse social mobilisation in post-industrial China. This discussion is necessary, as the scale, complexity and rapidity of China's ongoing transformations have already rendered much of our understanding of the country obsolete and made many researchers feel that it is difficult to identify vital clues to understanding these changes and the characteristics of present-day Chinese life. The last section of this chapter will put forward some suggestions for future research directions on this topic.

SUMMARY OF FINDINGS

As pointed out earlier, social mobilisation has long been regarded as a major characteristic of Chinese life and, more recently, a key aspect of China's state capacity and its task-oriented management. The research focus on social mobilisation emerged in the 1960s, when a worldwide wave of socio-political activism was intensifying and spreading. China was no exception to this trend, becoming a subject of academic study soon after the social-mobilisation thesis was put forward, even though China was in the throes of the Cultural Revolution and in the worst period of a prolonged internal power struggle. However, there are few countries in which social mobilisation has been as frequently utilised as a socio-political mechanism during economic expansion. The existing literature on the topic is characterised by studies of pre-1978 – or pre-reform – China and also by small-scale and disconnected cases.

To rectify the problems identified in a review of the literature, this study implemented two analytical strategies. First, the analysis of social mobilisation had to be thorough and complete, taking all participants, institutional and non-institutional, at all levels into consideration. This should be a requirement when analysing mobilisation to implement a policy intended to make grassroots changes, such as in villages, in factories or in other small work units. In this case, it was important that the analysis of the building campaign did not disconnectedly pay partial attention to what the central government wanted to achieve or how some village residents responded to the policy. Instead, it had to consider the influence of each official or non-official participant on the entire process, including governments at central, provincial, prefectural-level municipal, county and township level, village-level committees, and individual villagers or households. These were all involved in the campaign as mobiliser or mobilised. Since partial consideration of the indivisible whole was found to be the main flaw in previous studies of social mobilisation, this study chose to include all parties along the vertical chain of social mobilisation. Our book project benefited greatly from the co-authorship arrangement, combining the knowledge and experience of two authors to enable this analysis to look at the complex social-mobilisation process thoroughly and systematically.

On the other hand, second, this analysis also considered various recent socio-political developments resulting from China's decades-long economic reforms. For example, as early as 2005 a key research project funded by the National Social Science Fund of China (NSSFC) pointed out that China's continuous decentralisation reforms, especially the decentralisation of various tasks and duties and the development of extra-budgetary financing, had not only noticeably mobilised local enthusiasm for socio-economic growth but had also made many fundamental changes to the foundation, structure and process of China's post-Mao national leadership system and decision-making. Its current state governance is generally believed to be full of complex strategic games played by different stakeholders (Jin and Yuan, 2005). Subsequently, in addition to the vertical thoroughness detailed above, this analysis also expanded horizontally to include various new sectors and players emerging from outside the party-state system, or outside the known pathway of social mobilisation, from top-level decision-makers to grassroots mobilised or common targets. The exploratory discussion of the 'invisible hand' in Chapter 4 is one such theoretical attempt.

This analysis also took into consideration some of the helpful ideas from what Chinese researchers call *boyi* (strategic game-playing) theory. As explained, rapid and far-reaching transformations in China have added many new topics to the field and interested many scholars, producing a large and increasing number of publications on a range of issues. Research on China has become very diversified, going beyond existing dominant interpretations and paradigms of the country. Game theory-oriented studies are one type of such new academic efforts and have generated hundreds of books and journal articles in China. One of these studies' main arguments is that China's domestic politics, political structure and power relationships have been transformed in recent decades. Contrary to the widely held view that China is an authoritarian state where political power is in the hands of the ruling CCP, this new perspective argues that the government system in China has gradually been reduced to one of many stakeholders engaged in major political-economic games. According to this viewpoint, higher levels of industrialisation, privatisation and urbanisation have already resulted in political power flowing to those with influence on production, the market, public opinion and even innovation. It is widely accepted among Chinese researchers that large groups of powerful developers and private business owners, and many other key players, have transformed China into a multi-player society. China's new interest groups became more powerful in the early 2000s, and their emergence has been characterised by tension between established interests and emerging interests (Cheng, 2006). For this reason, social mobilisation is no longer understood as a simple top-down linear process in which higher-level authorities are seen to be the only force to drive a campaign. Currently, the process is seen to have evolved into a dynamic one in which bargaining and negotiations take place among interest groups and social forces at different levels.

As detailed in Chapter 1, the theoretical and methodological strategies that we have applied in this research project can be defined as a holistic-dynamic approach. The purpose of deploying this integrated approach is to correct past methodological deficiencies and consider the roles of different forces in the mobilisation drive from an interactive viewpoint. This new approach makes it possible to identify many new mobilisation methods and procedures while still taking traditional practices into consideration. Such a combined research approach accurately reflects what has occurred in post-industrial China: old and new coexist, with endless surprises. It is also worth emphasising here that the new rural building campaign was based on a strategic national policy of land use, *zengjian guagou* (linking the reduction of rural building land with the expansion of urban construction land) (Looney, 2012; M. Cai, 2015). This strict policy has made mobilisation for the campaign very intricate, as the restriction has been both the driving force for partaking in the scheme and an institutional barrier to mobilisation at an operational level.

Guided by the above approach and theoretical thinking, this book has six discussion chapters and explores the following aspects of social mobilisation in post-industrial China. Chapter 2 focused on the changing role of China's central decision-maker in utilising the social-mobilisation mechanism to launch new policy initiatives and how this role has evolved over the years. It is generally accepted that, in addition to economic development, China's reforms have transformed its central–local relations for the better, from centrally dominated authoritarian rule to a mixed, interactive central–local political structure. Numerous issues and challenges faced the CCP regime in post-Mao China, but the core issue was the need to maintain and strengthen its political legitimacy. The decades-long succession crisis, including the Maoist Cultural Revolution, resulted in almost no economic progress, which almost completely depleted the legitimacy earned by the CCP before 1949. Economic development was, therefore, identified as the political strategy by which to resolve the problem of reduced legitimacy. To achieve economic growth the mobilisation of local enthusiasm became a very useful mechanism, although it has often been articulated as 'two enthusiasms', of both the central and local governments. A set of new decentralisation measures have been used to encourage such enthusiasm, while making efforts to eliminate *zhonggengzu*, intermediary obstacles in its party-state system.

Maintaining political stability and a high level of economic growth is not an easy task, requiring a constant effort to identify new growth areas and develop new strategies and polices. The rural urbanisation strategy was developed based on the so-called three rural issues (*sannong wenti*). China in the early 2000s entered a new era in terms of state leadership and economic development. In late 2002 the new Hu Jintao leadership identified rural socio-economic development as the top priority in China's new economic strategies. At the time the rural–urban income disparity had become so large that the state leadership had to take it seriously. The rural strategy was developed as a way to kill several birds with one stone, maintaining GDP growth and reducing political instability. To mobilise local support for the plan, the fiscalisation of land use (*tudi caizheng*) was generally used by local governments while imposing the restriction of *zengjian guagou* (linking the decrease of rural construction land with the increase of urban building land).

Chapter 3 turned to the politics of social mobilisation at the provincial level, based on the case of Shandong. At this level, we found that social mobilisation was conducted at the intersection of two decisive roles that the provincial bureaucracies usually play in China's party-state systems: policy implementation and policy innovation. The first role is their basic function of implementing the policies decided by the central government, and the second role is played to satisfy local needs and interests. Several traditional mobilisation methods were found to be still in use, including communicating central documents; holding work conferences; media promotion; training key project leaders; arranging personnel; arranging resources; and gathering feedback. Creative implementation and local decision-making by provincial bureaucracies generated various types of dynamics that directed and drove policy implementation in Shandong province, so this approach was found to be particularly important for understanding social mobilisation in present-day China. Five creative measures were utilised by the province and were also found to be very provocative to its bureaucrats. These measures were a round of province-wide planning; province-wide classifications of rural areas; identifying and selecting local pilot regions; introducing coordinated management of financial resources; and making use of market forces in the new rural building scheme. Through such local, innovative policy-making processes, the new rural strategy was eventually translated into political power, action and a form of new local politics in Shandong, during which the entire provincial bureaucracy became highly mobilised.

The role of newly emerged and established market forces in social mobilisation was the focus of Chapter 4. This is a completely new angle compared to previous studies of social mobilisation in China, as a consequence of the country's decades-long socio-economic and socio-political transformations. As explained at the start of Chapter 4, it may confuse some readers to discuss the role of market forces – which are called the 'invisible hand' in China – at this point. Such confusion seems to be caused by two factors. First, many people still believe that China is a planned economy run by the party-state system and controlled through state-owned enterprises. We argue that this is not accurate; an assessment supported by the figures and charts contained in this book. Second, the growing role of market forces is an under-studied phenomenon, and many analyses are influenced by a conventional understanding of China's power-ful party-state system.

Despite this being an exploratory analysis, two novel perspectives were discussed in detail in Chapter 4 of this book, based on a thorough review of the market liberalisation that has taken place in China since the early years of its economic reform in the late 1970s and early 1980s. First, as a direct result of China's effort to cultivate a market-oriented economy, market forces have been expanding without pause and their influence has been spreading into every aspect of Chinese life. This chapter based its analysis on the socio-economic conditions in Shandong – virtually the most politically correct, if not conservative, Chinese province – and argued that market forces have now become so powerful that they must be seriously seen as new socio-economic and -political forces paralleling party-state systems. Second, from the viewpoint of social mobilisation, market forces, or local private companies, in Shandong were also found to have acted as mobilisers in the new building programme. It must be admitted that evi-dence to support these arguments is very difficult to obtain because of the guise of commercial confidentiality. This also explains why there are hardly any studies of this important issue by non-Chinese researchers. This study benefited immensely from China's current anti-corruption drive, which not only provided us with clues and evidence concerning the above second point but also presented us with information proving the above first assessment.

Chapter 5 analysed the role of the prefectural level of China's huge bureaucratic system in social mobilisation. This level is now normally called the prefectural/municipal government, or administration, due to China's recent administrative reforms in response to fast and massive urbanisation. As the level that is right in the middle of China's five-level governmental structure, the prefectural-level municipal government is believed to have become increasingly important in managing and organis-ing everyday life in Chinese society, but previous research attention to the two extreme ends of the Chinese bureaucracy – namely, the central leader-ship and grassroots protests – has prevented analysts from conducting sufficient studies on this level. Because of the latter reason, this analysis paid attention to the role of the middle bureaucracy in social mobilisation, especially to how the intermediary institutional- or bureaucratic-obstacle issue (*zhonggengzu*) has been dealt with in more recent times. Among many measures, decentralisation, or frequent changes in central–local relations, is the practical strategic approach to making social mobilisation possible.

In addition to the link between the intermediary obstacle and social mobilisation, we found that the Laiwu municipal government made two special mobilisation efforts. The first municipal-level effort was to prioritise and rearrange tasks for mobilising local participation in the building scheme. There is hardly any prefectural officer who still pays serious attention to routine social-mobilisation operations. All the routines are still carried out, but the municipal-level leadership devotes all its attention to how the strategy could be better used to meet the needs of local growth priorities and interest groups, including the prefectural leadership. Due to increasing local autonomy, Laiwu was found to have prioritised various implementation tasks and also to have combined the building strategy with its own urban-development plan. This integrated approach allowed it to utilise land and financial resources freely. The second municipal-level effort was to adopt a project-driven approach to the implementation of its priorities. By using an approach clearly associated with the Dengist responsibility system, administrative barriers could be bypassed easily and the performance results required by local officials could be achieved more quickly than by using other tactics.

The mobilisation roles of the next two bureaucratic levels – namely, county and township level – were combined in Chapter 6 and discussed as one system. As suggested by the chapter heading, the county and township governments were in an awkward situation in mobilising local support for and participation in the scheme. Their awkward roles are a pointer to two features of mobilisation in present-day China: frequent changes in its bureaucratic management and goal-oriented performance tied to various reform programmes. Specifically, these two lowest government levels are the basic function units of China's huge bureaucracy, but they are not only squeezed politically and financially but also are frequently forced into various direct conflicts triggered by decisions made by upper-level governments. Of course, as pointed out in Chapter 6, Laiwu, as the smallest city and region in Shandong, was also the reason behind the awkwardness. Because Laiwu is small, sub-prefectural governments had to play their front-line roles with no power and no financial resources to do anything decisive and bold in the building campaign. However, their basic mobilisation role was identified, and this included holding endless meetings; sending working groups to villages; deciding levels of compensation; identifying local participants in the building scheme; and dealing with unhappy villagers. While undertaking the above mobilisation roles, county and township officials were also found to have utilised more strategic methods than their routine practice, and these strategic methods may be defined as the carrot-and-stick approach. Some 'carrot' approaches were new and creative, for example mobilising financial resources through setting up new projects; involving local developers as mobilisers; and making use of interpersonal networks and affections.

Chapter 7 considered an issue that has been repeatedly explored but seriously misinterpreted by numerous analysts from the perspective of conflict revolution theory: grassroots reactions and protests. These responses were once seen by many as resistance to China's authoritarian regime, based on which a range of imaginative interpretations, such as China's coming collapse or democratisation, have been put forward. To divert our attention from the long-standing and powerful intellectual tendency to see almost all protests in China as politically driven or revolutionary actions, our analysis adopted a participatory standpoint from which to look at various rural protests in China and their role in social mobilisation. This participatory standpoint proposes that socio-political participation has become a normal element of everyday life in China, and that this may even take place in atypical ways, in the form of demonstrations, marches, petitions and other acts of civil disobedience.

Having been guided by the above participatory perspective, our analysis examined how rural residents considered the building scheme according to their family circumstances. Villagers were found to be very different from the loyal followers of the CCP they were described as being in the publications of the 1950s and 1960s, and they did not act as rivals to authoritarian rule, as publications of the 1990s and 2000s depicted them. They are now very experienced calculators of self-interest and economic benefit, and their responses to the rural scheme were predominantly influenced by their circumstances, not in terms of supporting or opposing the government. On the other hand, it seems true that protests can be divided into invisible and visible types, both of which were found to have focused on two key issues of the construction scheme: property valuation and house demolition. Disputes on these money-related, or pecuniary, issues and subsequent bargaining or negotiations often happened in an invisible way, but some angry villagers opted to take them to the streets and higher authorities when issues were not solved to their satisfaction.

A BETTER UNDERSTANDING OF SOCIAL MOBILISATION

As mentioned in Chapter 1, the research literature published in English in the past few decades on the topic of social mobilisation in China can be divided into two main categories: pre-1978 studies and post-1978 studies. The first type was largely influenced by the ruling CCP's long revolutionary past and the Maoist idea, and often analysed various mobilisation-related issues from the revolutionary perspective. The second type, therefore, has simply been regarded as a reflection of the post-revolutionary Chinese political process. However, considering that significant changes have occurred in China in recent decades and that numerous mobilisation-related studies have been undertaken, these post-1978 studies should not be simply, if not inadequately, defined by either a temporal period or the non-revolutionary characteristics of that period. As the first systematic examination of social mobilisation in China in recent decades, this study identified a range of more theoretical and abstract ideas and questions than those considered in earlier chapters. Many of these theoretical issues are related to the key deficiencies and problems of the existing literature, and are therefore helpful in guiding future studies on this important social mechanism.

The most obvious difference between social mobilisation then and now is that social mobilisation in China is no longer a simple top-down process that is one-sidedly initiated, determined and directed by an authoritarian power. The latter has become a thing of the past, as China's political power structure has been decentralised. This point of view carries many implications. First, as stated earlier, mobilisation is no longer based on ideological principles, and even if some people wanted to launch an ideology-based social-mobilisation campaign or political movement, it has now become extremely difficult, if not impossible, to do so. Any study of China according to non-indigenous ideas and non-traditional politics could destructively limit our knowledge of the world's most populous country and fastest-growing economy. Second, what has united political elites in post-Mao China is Deng Xiaoping's famous judgment and governance principle that 'development is the only hard truth' (Kroeber, 2011, p. 204), which in effect means that economic growth is the only political answer to challenges and future problems. This has been the main consensus among Chinese elites, and it is firmly based on the logic linking economic expansion and betterment to the legitimacy of their rule. This logic has been interpreted by some as the Party promoting economic growth and stability in order to rally and renew widespread support for itself. That is, it would be self-deception to consider social-mobilisation-related matters in China from any other standpoint, especially the various ideological notions suggested in some old publications.

To accomplish and sustain a comparatively high level of economic expansion, which also needs to be done in a sustainable manner, many other changes have been made to the Chinese way of managing socio-economic and socio-political activities. Such efforts have focused on a very special issue that troubles China more severely than other countries: a massive bureaucratic system. At least two changes have been made to tackle this problem. One was to reform the government system itself, and the other was to bypass administrative hurdles by allowing, encouraging and nurturing a market-oriented economy. These calculated changes have resulted in a different political power structure and the dynamics of multiple interplays. All recent social-mobilisation pushes, including the new countryside campaign, occurred under these circumstances. In terms of the change to the government system, repeated efforts have been made to reassign powers previously held by higher-level governments to lower-level ones in order to activate and sustain their enthusiasm for economic development, many details of which were analysed in Chapter 2. Such efforts have also expanded from the power to make local policy to the right to share, allocate and channel material resources and benefits, among which numerous rounds of financial decentralisation have been important for keeping and renewing the state's capacity to use the mobilisation mechanism.

As an outcome of decentralisation efforts, a different set of relations and dynamics has gradually emerged within China's governance system. There is still a clearly arranged leadership relationship between the central and local party-state systems and their functionaries. However, careful examination shows that this relationship is no longer based on ideological beliefs, loyalty, faithfulness and obedience. China's long transition from a post-revolutionary political order to a post-industrial society has added new dynamics to its political life. Its pivotal central–local relations, as well as state–market and state–society relations, now include bargaining and negotiations taking place among various regions, sectors and priorities. It has become acceptable, if not encouraged, for local and sectoral leaders to seek and maximise their share of material benefits and even decision-making powers. A large part of present-day Chinese social mobilisation is based on such dynamic processes of bargaining and negotiations, through which the patterns of utilising social mobilisation in the post-industrial environment can be fully explored and understood.

Some commentators have put forward the very general and abstract *boyi* (strategic game-playing) theory. Partly based on the traditional Chinese notion of *boyi*, and partly based on game theory, this perspective enables attention to be paid to conflict, bargaining and negotiations among different social forces or interest groups in different sectors and at different levels. It insists that *boyi* bargaining relations occur not only between the central and local governments but also in many policy-making processes. It also argues that China's party-state systems have gradually been reduced to a system encompassing many major stakeholders engaged in big, strategic political-economic games, as higher levels of industrialisation, privatisation and urbanisation have already resulted in political power flowing to those with influence on production, the market, public opinion and techno-economic innovation. According to this analytical framework, social mobilisation not only is still possible but also has become rather dynamic due to the involvement of diversified interests. A recent impulse to deny such newly upgraded power-sharing and benefits-distribution structures has met with strong resistance from various social forces and groups, revealing the existence of major strategic political games in China.

The other fundamental change resulting from China's restructuring efforts is the marketisation of economic systems, which has paralleled the above-mentioned administrative reforms and is worth mentioning here as a brief reminder of its theoretical importance in understanding social-mobilisation issues in China. Because it is still an under-studied area, the importance of which will be further stressed in the following section, two key points need to be made here. First, this book's analysis of the role of market forces in the rural construction campaign was an entirely new endeavour, since the Chinese economy has become highly marketised and privatised. The development of market forces is a double-edged political sword: it helps open an additional channel for implementing new policies and achieving what governments want to achieve, but it often complicates the whole process because of various demands. The 'invisible hand' of market forces is quite difficult to define and analyse at this stage, but one point is very clear: market forces have a role to play in mobilising resources and people. Second, from a broad economic perspective, the building campaign can also be regarded as an economic-growth strategy, since China has also been challenged by how to maintain its level of growth. As noted in Chapters 2 and 3, the building plan has, therefore, been regarded as *jiuming daocao* (the last straw to clutch at) in keeping the economy afloat and people working, while solving China's three rural issues. That is, this study examined the implementation of a complex strategy that was designed to kill a few birds with one stone.

As for whether decentralisation – which has taken place both vertically and horizontally, and both inside and outside the party-state system – has made China weaker or stronger in terms of utilising the social-mobilisation mechanism, different studies offer different answers to this question. At first sight, researchers who emphasise the power of central authorities and ignore the impact of intermediate bureaucratic hurdles, as well as market forces, on social mobilisation believe that China's party-state system remains strong and efficient. However, it would be different if researchers simply paid attention to sectoral and local politics and resistance. What we have analysed in this book was a rather successful process in terms of mobilising people and resources from central to village level, but the reason for its success was not the governmental capacity to carry out such a campaign but the campaign's various benefits, material and non-material, direct and indirect, for all involved. These benefits created common ground and new pursuits for all, establishing strong and potentially beneficial relationships between mobilisers and mobilised. Therefore, the nature of social mobilisation is now key, deciding whether a powerful campaign is possible.

The above issue can also be considered according to how a social-mobilisation campaign is organised, or what approach to conducting a social-mobilisation campaign is used. There have been debates among Chinese analysts over the nature and strength of contemporary social mobilisation. Some argue that China's traditional campaign-style governance is still in use, since there have been no fundamental changes to the country's political system, while others believe that there have been many changes and that public governance has been largely normalised and standardised. The debates have also considered the use of project-oriented mobilisation, believing it to be rather effective in realising a strategic goal. All these may help partly answer the above question about whether decentralisation has made China weaker or stronger, but the other part remains unanswered to this day, which is reflected in the following comments:

> All these debates have enriched our understanding of campaign-style governance, but unfortunately, the notion of 'campaign-style governance' used in these debates is rather descriptive. Precisely, they [researchers] have all observed and described the 'campaign nature' of campaign-style governance or a governmental action, but they have not ably explained the differences among different 'campaign-style governances' or used the idea to further analyse other more general socio-economic phenomena and events. (Xu et al., 2005, p. 24)

All the above theoretical clues and debates are not a denial of another key aspect of the recent use of social mobilisation in China, which is the institutionalisation of mobilisation practices. What we have analysed in this book may be considered along with divisions between three main domains: the government system, the market and grassroots people. The latter is now often called civil society, which is a major misunderstanding of Chinese society in the field, but that is beyond the scope of this analysis. While the market and the interplay between the market and the state are in obvious need of more reform and regulation, the present bureaucratic uses of social mobilisation in China are highly institutionalised. Such institutionalisation has at least two meanings. First, mobilisation approaches and practices have been standardised or bureaucratised, being clearly assigned and allocated to different levels and divisions of bureaucratic institution. Second, all related procedures and actions have also been clearly defined, detailed and routinised. As compared to the pre-reform years, the above institutionalisation has been advanced with quite a high level of flexibility, if not liberalisation or democratisation, because of the openness of decision-making processes and the many other changes in policy implementation.

In short, all the above theoretical points suggest that studies of new forms of social mobilisation in China must be full and systematic, and must be expanded into newly emerged socio-economic and social-political areas. They are also the reason that the holistic-dynamic approach was adopted in this study project. As mentioned, the co-authorship of this book made the thorough and systematic examination of the entire new countryside campaign as a complete social-mobilisation operation achievable. This is because one of us is very familiar with China's party-state systems and their political behaviours and the other is very familiar with what has occurred at township and village level. Such a blend of experience, knowledge and skills suggests a methodological choice that fits well with this type of complex analysis and helps develop a better understanding of the use of social mobilisation in post-industrial China.

FUTURE RESEARCH POSSIBILITIES

Some comments and suggestions in relation to future research have already been mentioned, directly and indirectly, in earlier discussion sections. In Chapter 1, we detailed that this analysis is placed at the intersection of China's current new countryside building campaign and the use of the social-mobilisation mechanism. Future research directions should also take note of the need to clearly understand the circumstances in which studies are to be conducted. Based on all our analyses in this book, it has become abundantly clear that China has entered its post-industrial phase with a highly privatised economy, the reality of which represents a huge theoretical challenge to researchers and has a range of analytical implications. Therefore, this section will focus on these emerging realities in contemporary China, where the one-party governing system remains unchanged despite many other fundamental changes, and the likely impacts of these realities on the future use of the social-mobilisation mechanism. Specifically, this section suggests that attention should be paid to three aspects of China's changing realities: the market, the connection and collusion between the market and the bureaucracy, and the rapidly changing behaviour of the state bureaucracy.

First, the roles, and the behaviours as well, of China's recently formed and largely matured market in relation to social mobilisation should be a priority topic for future research. Our book has made a preliminary analysis of this increasingly important fact, but the significance of the issue is so great that not also should further in-depth studies be made but also the scope of these studies should be broadened to include all influential factors, variables and interactions. Since market forces are new in China, more studies comparable to ours should be considered the first step in providing deep insights into the role and means of market forces in relation to social mobilisation. As stated, social mobilisation in China is no longer a simple top-down process but is achieved through negotiation with various stakeholders and agencies, and among these the most powerful is market forces.

There are at least two types of obstacle that can make it difficult to study the role of the market or might interfere with examining it. First, because of different ideological and political stances, there has been a strong denial of the full development of the market economy in China. The denial was originally part of international trade talks but has since become wide-spread and politicised by the sensation-hungry media. At the same time, numerous analysts have been susceptible to second-hand or processed information about what has happened in China. Therefore, many China specialists and researchers might not believe in the existence of the market mechanism along with the party-state system. Second, as mentioned above, the notion of commercial confidentiality and related practices can be utilised not only as an excuse for diminishing transparency but also as a method for circumventing serious research attention. As many other scholars have pointed out, such widely used excuses and practices can also be employed to hide corrupt acts and deals. However, this is not an issue specific to China, and new Chinese entrepreneurs and private business owners have in fact learned these practices from other capitalist counties. That is, this is a global issue – a key challenge to the capitalist system – but it is complicated in China by various local factors, such as lack of public supervision, and official–business collusion.

The second obstacle is that, while the relationship between the market and the government, either constructive or undesirable, has been a research topic for more than a decade, the fast expansion of market forces has rapidly made much of our knowledge outdated. The speed of market formation and maturation in many Chinese regions has been confirmed by higher privatisation levels and the increasingly massive scale of the Chinese economy. In the vast grey area between private enterprises or businesses and government systems, there are many cases or incidents revealing new but often non-standard relationships between the two sides. Research attention to such empirical clues has often been diverted by China's long-term focus on GDP growth, while the academic research tradition, within the boundary of established topics and norms, has also prevented many researchers from examining emerging issues. We have seen some studies of the relationship between the market and the government, but there are no sufficient studies on how they act, react and interact in the context of implementing major state policies. There are also many other players in this massive grey area, which has made study of the issue difficult. China's reforms have changed the power structure, producing various new forces, such as entrepreneurs, public intellectuals, and a large group of princelings (*taizidang*) – children of national leaders and veteran revolutionaries. These players have often blurred our understanding of the transformations in state–society relations, as well as the relationship between private businesses and government systems.

A third key topic for future research is the changing role of the party-state system in utilising the mobilisation mechanism, though its influence is believed to have been reduced by its own reforms that aimed to boost economic expansion. We make this point not to deny the importance of the state bureaucracy but to stress its changing role. There are at least two broad perspectives from which future studies can look at the changing nature of this long-established system. On the one hand, there is an urgent need to accurately assess the central but changing role of the state bureaucracy. For example, it is evident that the state can perform well in intervening in the market, while giving up some power to private sectors and lower-level administrations. What is urgently needed first, therefore, is an updated understanding of the leading role of the party-state system. On the other hand, an assessment must be made of the crucial changes that have taken place in the government's capacity to mobilise new nationwide campaigns. In this book we have argued that decades-long reforms have significantly transformed China's party-state bureaucracies, generating various new norms, behaviours and morals. In practice, however, the details of these changes remain largely unexplored. Attention needs to be paid to the consequences of such administrative and political restructuring.

We would like to conclude this section, and the book, with two additional points that deserve attention from China specialists and other researchers. First, after our fieldwork in Shandong, and while we were finishing this manuscript, the CCP publicised its first intra-Party accountability regulation, in July 2016, and started implementing new rules that aimed to hold its leaders and other officials nationwide accountable for bad leadership. In fact, since Xi Jinping took over the leadership in late 2012 there has been a strong and ongoing campaign against corruption to prevent the CCP from further corrupting. Xi has been helped by Wang Qishan, who was the head of the CCDI (Central Commission for Discipline Inspection), and therefore Wang has been regarded as a formidable anti-graft tsar. Because of this, Wang's recent appointment as the PRC's vice-president even broke the CCP's newly formed retirement rule for national leaders. As China's most powerful strategist of the Xi Jinping era, and as the only current national leader involved in national politics since the early 1980s, Wang recently made the following comment on the use of social mobilisation:

> A thousand campaigns of mobilisation are in fact not as good as looking into who is responsible once. The vitality of institutional systems lies in the implementation, and the key in implementation is people. The Party's leadership is concrete, not abstract. Leadership means setting a good example first and guiding others. Guidance means discovering problems and rectifying them without delay. Whether the new accountability system works will depend on whether the Party's organisations and leaderships at all levels take it seriously and whether they keep their vitality. (Q. Wang, 2016, n.p.)

The second final point we would like to make is that, while Wang Qishan's above speech might be seen to indicate the return of neo-authoritarianism to Chinese politics, nothing is more significant for future research and research directions than the historical shift that occurred recently when China entered its post-industrial era of economic development. This is an important factor in analysing not only the utilisation of the social-mobilisation mechanism but also other contemporary issues of Chinese society. From a macro-historical perspective, China has finally achieved the industrialisation that it has dreamed of for more than a century, during which it has tried to learn from several industrialisation models, including Russian and Western practices. Now, China has no established model to follow or copy but must rely on itself. At the macro-economic level, the incomes of many ordinary Chinese have increased substantially, and their happiness has also become greater than ever before. However, until now, not many people have realised that there is virtually nothing left in China's toolbox to drive further socio-economic growth. China has utilised all the methods that it has learned from others, including the Leninist-Stalinist approach and neoliberal economic teachings. China has no more trump cards (*zhupai chujin*) in its long-term strategic game. All these changes will have a profound impact on the country's future use of the social-mobilisation mechanism.

References

Aglietta, Michel and Guo Bai (2013), *China's Development: Capitalism and Empire*, Abingdon: Routledge.

Ahlers, Anna (2014), *Rural Policy Implementation in Contemporary China: New Socialist Countryside*, Abingdon: Routledge.

Ahlers, Anna and Gunter Schubert (2009), 'Building a new socialist countryside: Only a political slogan?', *Journal of Current Chinese Affairs*, 4: 35–62.

Anderlini, Jamil (2016), 'The return of Mao: A new threat to China's politics', *Financial Times*, 30 September 2016, accessed in March 2017 at https://www.ft.com/content/63a5a9b2-85cd-11e6-8897-2359a58ac7a5

Andreas, Joel (2007), 'The structure of charismatic mobilization: A case study of rebellion during the Chinese Cultural Revolution', *American Sociological Review*, 72(3): 434–58.

Apter, David (1965), *The Politics of Modernization*, Chicago: University of Chicago Press.

Ash, Robert (2001), 'China's agricultural reforms: A twenty-year retrospective', in Chao Chien-min and Bruce Dickson (eds), *Remaking the Chinese State*, London: Routledge, pp. 76–100.

Bai, Nansheng (2010), 'Urbanization and movement of rural labor', in Qiang Li (ed.), *Thirty Years of Reform and Social Changes in China*, Leiden: Brill, pp. 117–70.

Bai, Qing and Yeqiu Zheng (2010), 'Tudi liuzhuan moshide bijiao ji xuyao zhuyide wenti: Shixi Shandong moshi' (A comparison of land-transfer models and issues worth studying: An analysis of Shandong model), *Market Modernization*, 5: 76–7.

Bandurski, David and Martin Hala (2010), *Investigative Journalism in China: Eight Cases in Chinese Watchdog Journalism*, Hong Kong: Hong Kong University Press.

Bao, Tong (2015), 'How Deng Xiaoping helped create a corrupt China', *The New York Times*, 2 June 2015, accessed in March 2017 at https://www.nytimes.com/2015/06/04/opinion/bao-tong-how-deng-xiaoping-helped-create-a-corrupt-china.html?_r=0

Barmé, Geremie (1999), *In the Read: On Contemporary Chinese Culture*, New York: Columbia University Press.

Barmé, Geremie (2008), *The Forbidden City*, Cambridge: Harvard University Press.

Barmé, Geremie (2010), 'For truly great men, look to this age alone', in Timothy Cheek (ed.), *A Critical Introduction to Mao*, Cambridge: Cambridge University Press, pp. 243–72.

Barnett, Arthur Doak (1964), *Communist China: The Early Years, 1940–55*, New York: F.A. Praeger.

Baum, Richard (1978), 'Review of *Revolution at Work*', *Journal of Asian Studies*, 38(1): 151–3.

Baum, Richard (1994), *Burying Mao: Chinese Politics in the Age of Deng Xiaoping*, Princeton: Princeton University Press.

Baum, Richard and Frederick Teiwes (1968), *Ssu-Ch'ing: The Socialist Education Movement of 1962–1966*, Berkeley: University of California Press.

Bell, Daniel (1976), *The Coming of Post-Industrial Society: A Venture in Social Forecasting*, New York: Basic Books.

Bennett, Gordon (1976), *Yundong: Mass Campaigns in Chinese Communist Leadership*, Berkeley: University of California.

Bernstein, Thomas (1967), 'Leadership and mass mobilisation in the Soviet and Chinese Collectivisation Campaigns of 1929–30 and 1955–56: A comparison', *China Quarterly*, 31: 1–47.

Bernstein, Thomas (1977), *Up to the Mountains and Down to the Villages*, New Haven: Yale University Press.

Bislev, Ane and Stig Thøgersen (2012), *Organizing Rural China: Rural China Organizing*, Lanham: Lexington Books.

Blecher, Marc (2003), *China against the Tides: Restructuring through Revolution, Radicalism and Reform*, New York: Continuum.

Bo, Zhiyue (2015), 'Provincial politics', in David Goodman (ed.), *Handbook of the Politics of China*, Cheltenham, UK and Northampton, MA, USA: Edward Elgar, pp. 95–103.

Brady, Anne-Marie (2008), *Marketing Dictatorship: Propaganda and Though Work in Contemporary China*, Lanham: Rowan & Littlefield.

Bramall, Chris (2007), *The Industrialization of Rural China*, Oxford: Oxford University Press.

Bramall, Chris (2009), *Chinese Economic Development*, Abingdon: Routledge.

Bray, David (2005), *Social Space and Governance in Urban China: The Danwei System from Origins to Reform*, Stanford: Stanford University Press.

Bray, David and Elaine Jeffreys (2016), 'New mentalities of government in China', in David Bray and Elaine Jeffreys (eds), *New Mentalities of Government in China*, Abingdon: Routledge, pp. 1–11.

Breslin, Shaun (1996), *China in the 1980s: Center–Province Relations in a Reforming Socialist State*, London: Macmillan.

Breslin, Shaun (2014), *Mao: Profiles in Power*, Abingdon: Routledge.

Brown, Colin, Scott Waldron and John Longworth (2005), *Modernizing China's Industries: Lessons from Wool and Wool Textiles*, Cheltenham, UK and Northampton, MA, USA: Edward Elgar.

Brown, Kerry (2015), *Contemporary China*, London: Palgrave Macmillan.

Brown, Kerry, Peter Cai and Benjamin Herscovitch (2015), 'The rise of China's imperial president', *CIS* (Centre for Independent Studies) *Event*, accessed in June 2017 at https://www.cis.org.au/app/uploads/2015/10/Speech-150413.pdf

Bruun, Ole (2013), 'Social movements, competing rationalities and trigger events: The complexity of Chinese popular mobilizations', *Anthropological Theory*, 13(3): 240–66.

Buck, Daniel (2012), *Constructing China's Capitalism: Shanghai and the Nexus of Urban–Rural Industries*, London: Palgrave Macmillan.

Buckley, Chris (2015), 'Graft offensive may expose something more vile in China: Factions', 6 January 2015, *New York Times*, accessed in June 2017 at https://cn.nytimes.com/china/20150106/c06factions/dual/

Buckley, Chris (2017), 'In rare move, Chinese think tank criticizes tepid pace of reform', 27 March 2017, *New York Times*, accessed in June 2017 at https://www.nytimes.com/2017/03/27/business/chinese-economy-reform-critical-report.html

Bulman, David (2014), *First in Command: Leaders, Political Institutions, and Economic Growth in China's Counties*, PhD thesis, Baltimore: Johns Hopkins University.

Burns, John (1988), *Political Participation in Rural China*, Berkeley: University of California Press.

Cai, Jiming (2016), 'Chengxiang jianshe yongdi "zengjian guagou" de zhengce xiaoying' (The policy effects of *zengjian guagou* of urban and rural construction land uses), *Chinese Cadres Tribune*, 6: 65–8.

Cai, Meina (2015), '"Flying land": Institutional innovation in land management in contemporary China', in Jessica Teets and William Hurst (eds), *Local Governance Innovation in China: Experimentation, Diffusion, and Defiance*, Abingdon: Routledge, pp. 60–83.

Cai, Yongshun (2010), *Collective Resistance in China: Why Popular Protests Succeed or Fall*, Stanford: Stanford University Press.

Cai, Yongshun (2015), *State and Agents in China: Disciplining Government Officials*, Stanford: Stanford University Press.

Cameron, David (1974), 'Toward a theory of political mobilization', *Journal of Politics*, 36(1): 138–71.

Campanella, Thomas (2008), *The Concrete Dragon: China's Urban Revolution and What It Means for the World*, New York: Princeton Architectural Press.

Cao, Shangxue and Mingchen Jia (2011), 'Shandong Laiwushi nongcun chanquan zhidu gaige gongzuo kaocha baogao' (Study tour reports the rural land ownership reform in Laiwu, Shandong), *Hubei Nongye (Hubei Agriculture Weekly)*, 8 November 2011: 2.

Cao, Zirong, Yong Wei, Changping Li and Xiangzhong Xu (2007), 'Chengxiang yitihua jinchengzhongde gengdi baohu he tudi jiyue liyong: Yi Shandongsheng Laiwushi weili' (Protection of arable land in the urban–rural integration process and the coordinated use of land: The case of the city of Laiwu, Shandong), *Shandong Land Resources*, 23(11): 38–42.

Cartier, Caroline (2005), 'City-space: Scale relations and China's spatial administrative hierarch', in Laurence Ma and Fulong Wu (eds), *Restructuring the Chinese City*, Abingdon: Routledge, pp. 19–33.

CASS (Chinese Academy of Social Sciences) (2014), *Annual Report on China's Rule of Law, No. 12*, Beijing: Social Sciences Academic Press (China).

CDRF (China Development Research Foundation) (2013), *China's New Urbanization Strategy*, Abingdon: Routledge.

Cell, Charles (1977), *Revolution at Work: Mobilization Campaigns in China*, New York: Academic Press.

Chan, Chak Kwan, King Lun Ngok and David Phillips (2008), *Social Policy in China: Development and Well-Being*, Bristol: The Policy Press.

Chan, Kam Wing (2015), 'Five decades of the Chinese *hukou* system', in Robyn Iredale and Fei Guo (eds), *Handbook of Chinese Migration: Identity and Wellbeing*, Cheltenham, UK and Northampton, MA, USA: Edward Elgar, pp. 23–47.

Chapin, Rosemary (2014), *Social Policy for Effective Practice: A Strengths Approach*, Abingdon: Routledge.

Cheek, Timothy (2016), 'Reform and rebuilding, 1976–1988', in Jeffrey Wasserstrom (ed.), *The Oxford Illustrated History of Modern China*, Oxford: Oxford University Press, pp. 226–49.

Chen, An (1999), *Restructuring Political Power in China: Alliances and Opposition, 1978–1998*, Boulder: Lynne Rienner Publishers.

Chen, An (2015), *The Transformation of Governance in Rural China: Market, Finance, and Political Authority*, Cambridge: Cambridge University Press.

Chen, Baocheng (2012), 'Huanjie daju' (An overall view of the leadership transition), accessed in March 2017 at http://cn.nytimes.com/china/20 120724/cc24caixin

Chen, Bin (2004), 'Reforming intergovernmental fiscal relationships in China: A political economy perspective', *Chinese Public Administration Review*, 2 (3/4): 1–8.

Chen, Chin-Jou Jay (2009), 'Growing social unrest in China: Rising social discontents and popular protest', in Guoguang Wu and Helen Lansdowne (eds), *Socialist China, Capitalist China: Social Tension and Political Adaptation under Economic Globalization*, Abingdon: Routledge, pp. 10–28.

Chen, En (2015), 'Changgui zhili heyi tidai yundongshi zhili' (Why routine governance replaced campaign-style governance), *Sociological Review*, 3(5): 63–77.

Chen, Fong-Ching (2001), 'The popular cultural movement of the 1980s', in Gloria Davies (ed.), *Voicing Concerns: Contemporary Chinese Critical Inquiry*, Lanham: Rowman & Littlefield, pp. 71–86.

Chen, Fong-Ching and Guantao Jin (1997), *From Youthful Manuscripts to River Elegy: The Chinese Popular Cultural Movement and Political Transformation 1979–1989*, Hong Kong: Chinese University Press.

Chen, Jiajian (2013), 'The project system and the mobilization of grassroots government officials: A sociological study of the project-oriented operation of social management', *Social Sciences in China* (*Chinese Edition*), 2: 64–79.

Chen, Kairong (2013), *Jiasu chengshihua guochengzhongde zhengfu zuoyong yanjiu* (*An Analysis of the Role of Government in Accelerating Urbanisation*), PhD thesis, Beijing: Gradual School of Chinese Academy of Social Sciences.

Chen, Xi (2012), *Social Protest and Contentious Authoritarianism in China*, Cambridge: Cambridge University Press.

Chen, Xiwen (2006), 'Jianshe shehuizhuyi xin nongcun guanjian shi jian wuda jizhi' (The key to construct a new socialist countryside is to introduce five major mechanisms), accessed in May 2017 at http://news.sina.com.cn/c/2006-03-01/07168328201s.shtml

Chen, Xiwen (2013), 'Chengzhenhua zhong de liang, di, ren' (Food, land and people in the process of urbanisation), accessed in May 2017 at http://finance.ifeng.com/a/20130409/7880682_0.shtml

Chen, Xueyuan (2015), 'Encouraging farmers to migrate with asset', in Jiahua Pan and Houkai Wei (eds), *Annual Report on Urban Development of China 2013*, Berlin: Springer, pp. 195–214.

Chen, Zewei (2015), 'Siqunti cheng Xi Jinping yanzhong ganrao gaige "zhonggengzu"' (Four groups seen by Xi Jinping as *zhonggengzu* impeding the reform), *Outlook Weekly*, accessed in May 2017 at http://news.ifeng.com/a/20150401/43464416_0.shtml

Cheng, Chu-yuan (1982), *China's Economic Development: Growth and Structural Change*, Boulder: Westview.

Cheng, Hao (2006), 'Zhongguo liyi jituan duoyuanhua fazhan tanxi' (A study of the development of the diversification of interest groups in China), *Qiushi* (*Truth Seeking*) (Jiangxi), 4: 49–50.

Cherrington, Ruth (1991), *China's Students: The Struggle for Democracy*, London: Routledge.

Cherrington, Ruth (1997a), *Deng's Generation: Young Intellectuals in 1980s China*, New York: St. Martin's Press.

Cherrington, Ruth (1997b), 'Generational issues in China: A case study of the 1980s generation of young intellectuals', *British Journal of Sociology*, 48(2): 302–20.

Chun, Lin (2013), *China and Global Capitalism: Reflections on Marxism, History, and Contemporary Politics*, New York: Palgrave Macmillan.

Chung, Jae Ho (1997), 'Shandong: A political economy of development and inequality', in David Goodman (ed.), *China's Provinces in Reform: Class, Community and Political Culture*, London: Routledge, pp. 127–62.

Clark, Katerina (2000), *The Soviet Novel: History as Ritual, Third Edition*, Bloomington: Indian University Press.

Cooney, Sean, Sarah Biddulph and Ying Zhu (2013), *Law and Fair Work in China*, Abingdon: Routledge.

Dabla-Norris, Era (2005), *Issues in Intergovernmental Fiscal Relations in China*, Washington: International Monetary Fund (IMF).

Day, Alexander (2013), *The Peasant in Postsocialist China: History, Politics and Capitalism*, Cambridge: Cambridge University Press.

deLisle, Jacques, Avery Goldstein and Guobin Yang (2016), *The Internet, Social Media and a Changing China*, Philadelphia: University of Pennsylvania Press.

Deng, Xiaoping (1985), *Build Socialism with Chinese Characteristics*, Beijing: Foreign Languages Press.

Deutsch, Karl (1961), 'Social mobilization and political development', *American Political Science Review*, 55(3): 493–514.

Dillon, Michael (2015), *Deng Xiaoping: The Man Who Made Modern China*, London: I.B. Tauris.

Ding, Lili (2006), 'Guanyu Shandongsheng Shehuizhuyi Xinnongcun Jianshe qingkuangde diaoyan baogao' (A fieldwork report on the current situation of the Constructing Socialist New Countryside in Shandong province), accessed in May 2017 at http://nys.mof.gov.cn/zhengfuxinxi/bgtDiaoCheYanJiu_1_1_1_1_2/200807/t20080717_57866.html

Dittmer, Lowell (1987), *China's Continuous Revolution: The Post-Liberation Epoch, 1949–1981*, Berkeley: University of California Press.

Dittmer, Lowell and Ruoxi Chen (1981), *Ethics and Rhetoric of the Chinese Cultural Revolution*, Berkeley: University of California Press.

Dong, Haijun (2008), 'The weak identity as a weapon: Subaltern politics of the peasant resistance for rights', *Society*, 28(4): 34–58.

Dong, Haijun (2010), 'Shi-based game: A new explanatory framework for right safeguarding action in grassroots society', *Society*, 30(5): 96–120.

Dong, Hongjun (2007), 'Wei xinnongcun jianshe peiyang gaosuzhi "yixian zhihuiyuan"' (Training highly qualified 'frontline commanders' for the new rural construction), accessed in March 2017 at http://cpc.people. com.cn/GB/64093/64099/5336288.html

Dong, Jun (2017), '2017 Zhongyang Yihao Wenjian gongbu: Tujin nongye gongjice jiegouxing gaige' (2017 No. 1 Central Document publicised: Advance agricultural supply-side structural reforms), accessed in March 2017 at http://news.sina.com.cn/c/nd/2017-02-05/doc-ifyafcyw0282141. shtml

Duan, Peizhen (2012), *Tansuo yu Shjian: Zaozhuangshi Dishui Xitong Youxiu Diaoyan Wenji* (*Exploration and Practice: Collection of Excellent Study Reports of the Land Taxation System of Zaozhuang City*), Beijing: Zhongguo Caizheng Jingji Chubanshe (China Financial and Economic Publishing House).

Dutt, Vidya (1981), *China: The Post-Mao View*, New Delhi: Allied.

Dutton, Michael (1998), *Streetlife China*, Cambridge: Cambridge University Press.

Eastman, Lloyd (1991), 'The May Fourth Movement as a historical turning point: Ecological exhaustion, militarization, and other causes of China's modern crisis', in Kenneth Lieberthal et al. (eds), *Perspectives on Modern China: Four Anniversaries*, New York: M.E. Sharpe, pp. 123–38.

Etzioni, Amitai (1968), 'Mobilization as a macro-sociological conception', *Britain Journal of Sociology*, 19(3): 243–53.

Eyferth, Jacob (2015), 'Liberation from the loom? Rural women, textile work, and revolution in North China', in Jeremy Brown and Matthew Johnson (eds), *Maoism at the Grassroots: Everyday Life in China's Era of High Socialism*, Cambridge: Harvard University Press, pp. 131–53.

Fan, Cindy (2008), *China on the Move: Migration, the State, and the Household*, Abingdon: Routledge.

Fang, Chuanglin and Danlin Yu (2016), *China's New Urbanization: Developmental Paths, Blueprints and Patterns*, Berlin: Springer-Verlag.

Faure, David (2006), *China and Capitalism: A History of Business Enterprise in Modern China*, Hong Kong: Hong Kong University Press.

Fei, Xue (2018), 'Zuijin, Shandong weihe lianxu chuaxian minying qiyejia shiming jubao guanyuan?' (Recently, why have several private entrepreneurs publicly accused officials in Shandong?), accessed in February 2018 at http://news.ifeng.com/a/20180225/56259509_0.shtml

Feng, Lixia (2011), 'Jiquan and fenquan: Biandongzhongde lishi jingyan' (Centralisation and decentralisation: Changing historical experiences), *Academic Research*, 4: 35–9.

Feng, Shizheng (2011), 'Zhongguo guojia yundongde xingcheng yu bianyi' (The formation and variation of China's national campaigns), *Open Times*, 1: 73–97.

Fewsmith, Joseph (1994), *Dilemmas of Reform in China: Political Conflict and Economic Debate*, New York: M.E. Sharpe.

Fewsmith, Joseph (2001), *Elite Politics in Contemporary China*, New York: M.E. Sharpe.

Fewsmith, Joseph (2010), 'Elite politics: The struggle for normality', in Joseph Fewsmith (ed.), *China Today, China Tomorrow: Domestic Politics, Economy, and Society*, Lanham: Rowman & Littlefield, pp. 149–64.

Fewsmith, Joseph (2013), *The Logic and Limits of Political Reform in China*, Cambridge: Cambridge University Press.

Filipiak, Kai (2015), *Civil–Military Relations in Chinese History: From Ancient China to the Communist Takeover*, Abingdon: Routledge.

Fox, Sean and Tom Goodfellow (2016), *Cities and Development: Second Edition*, Abingdon: Routledge.

Frenkiel, Emilie (2015), *Conditional Democracy: The Contemporary Debate on Political Reform in Chinese Universities*, Colchester: ECPR Press.

Friedman, Edward (1995), *National Identity and Democratic Prospects in Socialist China*, New York: M.E. Sharpe.

Fu, Zhengyuan (1996), *China's Legalists: The Early Totalitarians and Their Art of Ruling*, New York: M.E. Sharpe.

Gan, Quan and Yuting Luo (2011), 'Shehui dongyuande benzhi tanxi' (An analysis of the essence of social mobilisation), *Academic Exploration*, 6: 24–8.

Gao, Jia (1986), 'Structural aspects of social psychological reactions and policies in the reform era', *Sociological Studies*, 4: 52–9.

Gao, Jia (1987), 'Shehui wenti' (Social problems), in Zheng Hangsheng, Jia Chunzeng and Sha Lianxiang (eds), *Shehuixue Gailun Xinbian* (*New Edition of Introduction to Sociology*), Beijing: Renmin University of China Press, pp. 359–407.

Gao, Jia (2013a), 'Fei Xiaotong (1910–2005)', in Yuwu Song (ed.), *Biographical Dictionary of the People's Republic of China*, Jefferson: McFarland & Company, pp. 80–82.

Gao, Jia (2013b), *Chinese Activism of a Different Kind: The Chinese Students' Campaign to Stay in Australia*, Leiden: Brill.

Gao, Jia (2015), *Chinese Migrant Entrepreneurship in Australia from the Early 1990s: Case-Studies of Success in Sino-Australian Relations*, Oxford: Chandos/Elsevier.

Gao, Jia, Catherine Ingram and Pookong Kee (eds) (2016), *Global Media and Public Diplomacy in Sino-Western Relations*, Abingdon: Routledge.

Gao, Mobo (2016), 'Mao Zedong', in Immanuel Ness and Zak Cope (eds), *The Palgrave Encyclopedia of Imperialism and Anti-Imperialism*, Basingstoke: Palgrave Macmillan, pp. 154–63.

Gao, Qin (2017), *Welfare, Work and Poverty: Social Assistance in China*, Oxford: Oxford University Press.

Gao, Wenxiu (2011), 'Mao Zedong and Shandong', accessed in March 2017 at http://blog.sina.com.cn/s/blog_4c3ea8090100o8ec.html

Gao, Zhili (2009), 'An experiment in radical and holistic change', in Mengkui Wang (ed.), *Good Governance in China – A Way Towards Social Harmony: Case Studies by China's Rising Leaders*, Abingdon: Routledge, pp. 14–28.

Garcia, Beatriz (2011), *Small Town China: Rural Labour and Social Inclusion*, Abingdon: Routledge.

Gardner, Daniel (2014), *Confucianism: A Very Short Introduction*, Oxford: Oxford University Press.

Garnaut, Ross, Ligang Song and Yang Yao (2006), 'Impact and significance of state-owned enterprises restructuring in China', *The China Journal*, 55: 35–63.

Gaulton, Richard (1981), 'Political mobilization in Shanghai', in Christopher Howe (ed.), *Shanghai: Revolution and Development in an Asian Metropolis*, London: Cambridge University Press, pp. 35–65.

Goldman, Merle (1981), *China's Intellectuals: Advise and Dissent*, Cambridge: Harvard University Press.

Goldman, Merle (1994), *Sowing the Seeds of Democracy in China: Political Reform in the Deng Xiaoping Era*, Cambridge: Harvard University Press.

Goldman, Merle (2005), *From Comrade to Citizen: The Struggle for Political Rights in China*, Cambridge: Harvard University Press.

Goldman, Merle and Roderick MacFarquhar (1999), *The Paradox of China's Post-Mao Reforms*, Cambridge: Harvard University Press.

Gong, Yuzhi (2002), *Cong Mao Zedong dao Deng Xiaoping* (*From Mao Zedong to Deng Xiaoping*), Beijing: CCP History Press.

Goodman, David (1994), *Deng Xiaoping and the Chinese Revolution: A Political Biography*, London: Routledge.

Goodman, David (1997), 'China in reform: The view from the province', in David Goodman (ed.), *China's Provinces in Reform: Class, Community and Political Culture*, London: Routledge, pp. 1–20.

Goodman, David (2015), 'The study of contemporary Chinese politics', in David Goodman (ed.), *Handbook of the Politics of China*, Cheltenham: Edward Elgar, pp. 1–19.

Greenhalgh, Susan and Edwin Winckler (2005), *Governing China's Population: From Leninist to Neoliberal Biopolitics*, Stanford: Stanford University Press.

Gu, Edward (2000), 'Plural institutionalism and the emergence of intellectual public spaces in China: A case study of four intellectual groups', in Suisheng Zhao (ed.), *China and Democracy: Reconsidering the Prospects for a Democratic China*, New York: Routledge, pp. 141–72.

Gul, Ferdinand and Haitain Lu (2011), *Truths and Half Truths: China's Socio-Economic Reforms (1978–2010)*, Oxford: Chandos Publishing.

Guo, Daimo and Shun'e Yang (2008), 'Zhongguo caizheng gaige 30 nian' (China's fiscal reform of 30 years), accessed in December 2016 at http://www.mof.gov.cn/zhuantihuigu/czgg0000_1/czggcz/200811/t20081 106_88263.html

Guo, Rongxing (2013), *Understanding the Chinese Economies*, Oxford: Elsevier.

Guo, Sujian (2012), *Chinese Politics and Government: Power, Ideology and Organization*, Abingdon: Routledge.

Guo, Wenqiang and Fengrong Liu (2013), 'Laiwushi gengdi baohu mianlinde wenti ji duice yanjiu' (Study on problems and countermeasure of cultivated land protection in Laiwu city), *Shandong Land Resources*, 29(1): 55–61.

Guo, Wenqiang and Xiangzhong Xu (2012), 'Laiwu jiang duoce cujin tidu jiyue liyong' (Laiwu will use multiple policies to facilitate the intensive use of land), *China Real Estate Market*, 3: 35.

Guo, Wenqiang, Xiangzhong Xu and Wenpeng Liu (2014), 'Qiantan tudi caizhengde chengxiao ji gaijin silu: Yi Laiwu weili' (Discussion on effect of land finance and improvement thoughts: Taking Laiwu city as an example), *Shandong Land Resources*, 30(1): 72–7.

Guo, Xuewang and Huize Jia (2012), 'Woguo shehuizhuyi hexin jiazhitixi xuanzhuan jizhi chuangxinde sikao' (Reflections on the innovation in propaganda mechanism of our socialist core value system), *Shandong Social Sciences*, 11: 15–19.

Guo, Yafei (2002), 'Shandong nongye you duo "Quanguo Guanjun"' (Shandong agriculture once again wins the National Champion), accessed in March 2017 at http://www.lianghui.org.cn/chinese/EC-c/100797.htm

Guo, Yingjie (2004), *Cultural Nationalism in Contemporary China: The Search for National Identity under Reform*, London: Routledge.

Haar, Barend (1998), *Ritual and Mythology of the Chinese Triads: Creating an Identity*, Leiden: Brill.

Han, Jinsong (2006), 'Quansheng Nongcun Gongzuo Huiyi zhaokai, zhashi tuijin Shehuizhuyi Xinnongcun Jianshe' (The provincial work conference on agriculture was held, and the new socialist village building will be advanced firmly', *Jinan Daily*, accessed in January 2018 at http://news.sina.com.cn/c/2006-02-25/01598295985s.shtml

Han, Sunsheng and Qianli Wei (2015), 'A new pathway to urbanization in

China? The land trading policy and practice in Yandu Xincun, Xianghe County, Hebei Province', in Tai-Chee Wong, Sunsheng Han and Hongmei Zhang (eds), *Population Mobility, Urban Planning and Management in China*, Dordrecht: Springer, pp. 275–90.

Han, Yi (2014), 'Enterprises and the social environment', in Zhixue Zhang and Jianjun Zhang (eds), *Understanding Chinese Firms from Multiple Perspectives*, Berlin: Springer, pp. 21–50.

Hao, Jia and Zhimin Lin (1994), 'Changing central–local relations in China: Reform and state capacity', in Jia Hao and Zhimin Lin (eds), *Changing Central–Local Relations in China: Reform and State Capacity*, Boulder: Westview Press, pp. 1–18.

Harding, Harry (1981), *Organizing China: The Problem of Bureaucracy, 1949–1976*, Stanford: Stanford University Press.

Harrist, Robert (2008), *The Landscape of Words: Stone Inscriptions from Early and Medieval China*, Seattle: University Washington Press.

Harwood, Russell (2014), *China's New Socialist Countryside: Modernity Arrives in the Nu Valley*, Seattle: University of Washington Press.

He Baogang (1997), *The Democratic Implications of Civil Society in China*, London: Macmillan Press

He, Baogang and Guo Yingjie (2000), *Nationalism, National Identity and Democratization in China*, New York: Ashgate.

He, Henry (2010), *Dictionary of the Political Thought for the People's Republic of China*, New York: M.E. Sharpe.

He, Hongguang (2015), *Governance, Social Organisation and Reform in Rural China: Case Studies from Anhui Province*, London: Palgrave Macmillan.

He, Qinglian (1998), 'Jiushi niandaide "Quandi Yundong"' (The 'enclosure movement' [in China] in the 1990s), in Qingfeng Liu and Siu-Chun Kwan (eds), *Jiushi Niandaide Zhongguo Nongcun Zhuangkuang: Jihui yu Kunjing* (*The Chinese Village in the Nineties: Challenges and Opportunities*), Hong Kong: The Chinese University Press, pp. 43–56.

He, Xin (2014), 'The Party's leadership as a living constitution in China', in Tom Ginsburg and Alberto Simpser (eds), *Constitutions in Authoritarian Regimes*, Cambridge: Cambridge University Press, pp. 245–64.

He, Xuefeng (2000), 'Lun banshuren shehui: Lijie cunweuhui xuanjue de yige shijiao' (On semi-acquaintance society: A perspective on understanding the village committee election), *Political Science Research*, 3: 61–9.

Heilmann, Sebastian and Elizabeth Perry (2011), 'Embracing uncertainty: Guerrilla policy style and adaptive governance in China', Sebastian Heilmann and Elizabeth Perry (eds), in *Mao's Invisible Hand: The Political Foundations of Adaptive Governance in China*, Boston: Harvard University Press, pp. 1–29.

Heurlin, Christopher (2016), *Responsive Authoritarianism in China: Land, Protests, and Policy Making*, New York: Cambridge University Press.

HKTDC (Hong Kong Trade Development Council) (2017), *Laiwu (Shandong) City Information*, accessed in March 2017 at http://china-trade-research.hktdc.com/business-news/article/Facts-and-Figures/Laiwu-Shandong-City-Information/ff/en/1/1X000000/1X0A1CND.htm

Ho, John (1992), *East Asian Philosophy: With Historical Background and Present Influence*, Bern: Peter Lang.

Hsiao, Ching-Chang and Timothy Cheek (1995), 'Open and closed media: External and internal newspapers in the propaganda system', in Carol Hamrin and Suisheng Zhao (eds), *Decision-Making in Deng's China: Perspectives from Insiders*, New York: M.E. Sharpe, pp. 76–90.

Hsiao, Kung-Chuan (1960), *Rural China: Imperial Control in the Nineteenth Century*, Seattle: University of Washington Press.

Hsing, You-tien (2010), *The Great Urban Transformation: Politics of Land and Property in China*, Oxford: Oxford University Press.

Hsü, Immanuel (1990), *China Without Mao: The Search for a New Order*, Oxford: Oxford University Press.

Hsu, Philip (2017), 'Central–Provincial power relations in the fiscal realm of China, 1980–2014', in John Donaldson (ed.), *Assessing the Balance of Power in Central–Local Relations in China*, Abingdon: Routledge, pp. 19–50.

Hsu, Robert (1991), *Economic Theories in China, 1979–1988*, New York: Cambridge University Press.

Hu, Angang (2009), 'Quantitative assessment of China's economic power and science and technology power in a comparative perspective', in Keun Lee, Joon-Han Kim and Wing Thye Woo (eds), *Power and Suistainability of the Chinese State*, Abingdon: Routledge, pp. 31–46.

Hu, Angang (2014), *China's Collective Presidency*, Heidelberg, Springer.

Hu, Feng (2015), 'Shandong Nongyeting yuanfutingzhang Shan Zengde shouhuian qisushu quanwen gongbu' (The bribery case of former deputy director of Shandong Bureau of Agriculture is published in full), accessed in March 2017 at http://news.iqilu.com/shandong/yuanchuang/2015/0215/2313003.shtml

Hu, Richard (2016), 'China's land use and urbanization: Challenges for comprehensive reform', in John Garrick and Yan Chang Bennett (eds), *China's Socialist Rule of Law Reforms under Xi Jinping*, Abingdon: Routledge, pp. 122–33.

Hua, Shiping (1995), *Scientism and Humanism: Two Cultures in Post-Mao China*, New York: State University of New York Press.

Hua, Shiping and Andrew Nathan (2016), *Chinese Political Culture, 1989–2000*, Abingdon: Routledge.

Huai, Jianjun, Xinmei Liu, Hongmei Lei and Fan Zhang (2008), 'Zhongguo fangdichan shichangzhong sida liyi jituan lianmengde boyi fenxi' (Game analysis of the collation of four [main] interest groups in the Chinese property market), *Systems Engineering: Theory and Practice*, 6: 30–37.

Huang, Jing (2000), *Factionalism in Chinese Communist Politics*, Cambridge: Cambridge University Press.

Huang, Yasheng (2008), *Capitalism with Chinese Characteristics: Entrepreneurship and the State*, New York: Cambridge University Press.

Hucker, Charles (1975), *China to 1850: A Short History*, Stanford: Stanford University Press.

Huntington, Samuel (1968), *Political Order in Changing Societies*, New Haven: Yale University Press.

Huters, Theodore (2005), *Bringing the World Home: Appropriating the West in Late Qing and Early Republican China*, Honolulu: University of Hawai'i Press.

Jeffreys, Elaine and Gary Sigley (2009), 'Governmentality, governance and China', in Elaine Jeffreys (ed.), *China's Governmentality: Governing Change, Changing Government*, Abingdon: Routledge, pp. 1–23.

Jeffries, Ian (1993), *Socialist Economies and the Transition to the Market*, London: Routledge.

Jia, Kang (2011), 'Shi'erwu shiqi Zhongguode Gonggong caizheng zhidu gaige' (China's public finance system reform over the 12th Five-Year Plan period), accessed in December 2016 at http://unpan1.un.org/intra doc/groups/public/documents/apcity/unpan049471.pdf

Jiang, Daming (2009), 'Jiang Daming zai sheng nongcun zhufang jianshe yu weifang gaizao huiyishangde jianghua' (Jiang Daming speech at the provincial conference on the rural construction project and the re-building of unsafe rural housing), accessed in December 2017 at http://blog.sina.com.cn/s/blog_59c6325c0100e235.html

Jin, Taijun and Jianjun Yuan (2005), 'Difang zhengfu chuangxin boyi fenxi' (Game theory analysis of local government innovation), *Jianghai Academic Journal*, 5: 94–9.

Jing, Yijia (2015), 'The road to collaborative governance in China', in Yijia Jing (ed.), *The Road to Collaborative Governance in China*, New York: Palgrave Macmillan, pp. 1–20.

Johnson, Chalmers (1962), *Peasant Nationalism and Communist Power*, Stanford: Stanford University Press.

Ju, Yanan (1996), *Understanding China: Center Stage of the Fourth Power*, Albany: State University of New York Press.

Keith, Michael, Scott Lash, Jakob Arnoldi and Tyler Rooker (2014), *China*

Constructing Capitalism Economic Life and Urban Change, Abingdon: Routledge.

Kelliher, Daniel (1992), *Peasant Power in China: The Era of Rural Reform, 1979–1989*, New Haven: Yale University.

Kelliher, Daniel (1993), 'Keeping democracy safe from the masses: Intellectuals and elitism in the Chinese protest movement', *Comparative Politics*, 25(4): 379–96.

Kinkley, Jeffrey (2015), *Vision of Dystopia in China's New Historical Novels*, New York: Columbia University Press.

Kipnis, Andrew (2013), 'Urbanisation in between: Rural traces in a rapidly growing and industrialising county city', *China Perspectives*, 3: 5–11.

Kornberg, Judith and John Faust (2005), *China in World Politics: Policies, Processes, Protests*, Boulder: Lynne Rienner Publishers.

Kroeber, Arthur (2011) 'Developmental dream: Policy and reality in China's economic reforms', in Scott Kennedy (ed.), *Beyond the Middle Kingdom: Comparative Perspectives on China's Capitalist Transformation*, Stanford: Stanford University Press, pp. 44–66 and 203–7.

Kung, James K., Chengguang Xu and Feizhou Zhou (2013), 'From industrialization to urbanization: The social consequences of changing fiscal incentives on local governments' behavior', in David Kennedy and Joseph E. Stiglitz (eds), *Law and Economics with Chinese Characteristics: Institutions for Promoting Development in the Twenty-First Century*, Oxford: Oxford University Press, pp. 491–509.

Lai, Hongyi (2016), *China's Governance Model: Flexibility and Durability of Pragmatic Authoritarianism*, Abingdon: Routledge.

Laiwu Bureau of Finance (2009), 'Shandongsheng Laiwushi tongchou chengxiang yitihua de jiben qingkuang, cunzaide wenti ji jianyi' (Current situations, problems and suggestions regarding the urban–rural integration in the city of Laiwu, Shandong province), in Rural Comprehensive Reforms Working Group, State Council (ed.), *Nongcun Zonghe Gaige Shijian yu Tansuo* (*Practice and Analysis of Rural Comprehensive Reforms*), Beijing: China Financial and Economic Publishing House, pp. 400–15.

Laiwu Research Office (2013), 'Nuli gongjian, ganchao kuayue, jiakuai shuaixian quanmian jiancheng xiaokang shehui bufa' (Making effort to tackle, catching up to move forward, speeding up the steps of leading to all-out construction of a well-off society), *Shandong Economic Strategy Research*, 1–2: 65–9.

Lam, Willy (2015), *Chinese Politics in the Era of Xi Jinping*, Abingdon: Routledge.

Lanteigne, Marc (2015), 'Economics and security in China', in Lowell Dittmer and Maohun Yu (eds), *Routledge Handbook of Chinese Security*, Abingdon: Routledge, pp. 40–63.

Lardy, Nicholas (1987), 'The Chinese economy under stress, 1958–1965', in Roderick MacFarquhar and John Fairbank (eds), *The Cambridge History of China, Volume 14, The People's Republic, Part I: The Emergence of Revolutionary China 1949–1965*, Cambridge: Cambridge University Press.

Lardy, Nicholas (2014), *Market over Mao: The Rise of Private Business in China*, Washington, DC: Peterson Institute for International Economics.

Lee, Charlotte (2015), *Training the Party: Party Adaptation and Elite Training in Reform-era China*, Cambridge: Cambridge University Press.

Lee, Ching Kwan and Yonghong Zhang (2013), 'The power of instability: Unraveling the microfoundations of bargained authoritarianism in China', *American Journal of Sociology*, 118(6): 1475–508.

Lee, Kuan Yew (2000), *The Singapore Story: Memories of Lee Kuan Yew*, Singapore: Marshall Cavendish Editions.

Lee, Leo (1991), 'Modernity and its discontents: The cultural agenda of the May Fourth Movement', in Kenneth Lieberthal et al. (eds), *Perspectives on Modern China: Four Anniversaries*, New York: M.E. Sharpe, pp.158–77.

Legal Daily (2012), *2012 Research Report on Mass Incidents*, accessed in March 2018 at http://www.guancha.cn/society/2014_02_25_208680.shtml

Ley, Astrid (2010), *Housing as Governance: Interfaces between Local Government and Civil Society Organisation in Cape Town, South Africa*, Berlin: Lit Verlag.

Li, Cheng (2001a), 'Diversification of Chinese entrepreneurs and cultural pluralism in the reform era', in Shiping Hua (ed.), *Chinese Political Culture 1989–2000*, New York: M.E. Sharpe, pp.219–45.

Li, Cheng (2001b), *China's Leaders: The New Generation*, Lanham: Rowman & Littlefield.

Li, Cheng (2016), *Chinese Politics in the Xi Jinping Era*, Washington: Brookings Institution Press.

Li, Feng (2013), *Early China: A Social Cultural History*, Cambridge: Cambridge University Press.

Li, Guoping and Yugang Tan (2011), 'Zhongguo chengshihua tezheng, quyu chayi jiqi yingxiang yinsu fenxi' (An analysis of key features of China's urbanisation, its regional difference and influential factors), *Shehui Kexue Jikan* (*Social Sciences Journal*), 2(193): 106–10.

Li, He (2014), 'Transforming oil-mining cities in post-reform China: A case study of Daqing', in Mark Wang, Pookong Kee and Jia Gao (eds), *Transforming Chinese Cities*, Abingdon: Routledge, pp.75–94.

Li, He (2015), *Political Thought and China's Transformation: Ideas Shaping Reforms in Post-Mao China*, New York: Palgrave Macmillan.

Li, Hui (2008), '"Shouguang moshi" qiujie zhongxiao qiye rongzinan' (The 'Shouguang model' solves financial difficulties of medium and small enterprises), 20 November 2008, *Dazhong Daily*, accessed in May 2017 at http://dzrb.dzwww.com/dzzb/dzzb-jrgz/200811/t20081120_4111337. htm

Li, Jun and Joseph Cheng (2012), 'Care performance appraisal and fabrication of economic achievement in Chinese officialdom', in Joseph Cheng (ed.), *China: A New Stage of Development for an Emerging Superpower*, Hong Kong: City University of Hong Kong Press, pp. 117–48.

Li, Lianjiang (2006), 'Driven to protest: China's rural unrest', *Current History*, 105: 250–54.

Li, Lina, Nannan Liu and Xiaoping Zheng (2016), 'Does the province-managing-county reform promote the growth of county finance and economy in China?', *Public Finance and Management*, 16(1): 25–50.

Li, Linda (1998), *Centre and Provinces: China 1978–1993*, Oxford: Clarendon Press.

Li, Linda (2012), *Rural Tax Reform in China: Policy Process and Institutional Chang*, Abingdon: Routledge.

Li, Mengzhan (2016), 'Meiti mijie Jinan yuanshuji Wang Min "luoma" beihoude fangchanshang' (The media reveals the developer behind the fall of Wang Min, former CCP secretary of Jinan), accessed in March 2017 at http://news.takungpao.com/mainland/focus/2016-02/3280103_wap.html

Li, Wenzhai and Shoulong Mao (2010), 'Zhonguo zhengfu gaige: Jiben luoji yu fazhan qushi' (China's governmental reform: Basic logics and general trend), *Management World*, 8: 44–58.

Li, Yan (2012), 'Laiwushi Laichengqu chengxiang jianshe yongdi zengjian guagou gongzuo chutan' (Primary study on increasing agricultural using land in rural areas and decreasing construction using land in urban areas in Gangcheng District of Laiwu City), *Shandong Land Resources*, 28(9): 66–8.

Liang, Heng and Judith Shapiro (1984), *Intellectual Freedom in China after Mao with a Focus on 1983*, New York: Fund for Free Expression.

Liang, Samuel (2014), *Remaking China's Great Cities: Spaces and Culture in Urban Housing, Renewal, and Expansion*, Abingdon: Routledge.

Liao, Kuang-sheng (1976), 'Linkage politics in China: Internal mobilization and articulated external hostility in the Cultural Revolution, 1967–1969', *World Politics*, 28(4): 590–610.

Lieberthal, Kenneth (1995), *Governing China: From Revolution through Reform*, New York: W.W. Norton.

Lieberthal, Kenneth and Michel Oksenberg (1988), *Policy Making in China: Leaders, Structures, and Processes*, Princeton: Princeton University Press.

Lin, George (1997), *Red Capitalism in South China: Growth and Development of the Pearl River Delta*, Vancouver: UBC Press.

Lin, George (2009), *Developing China: Land, Politics and Social Conditions*, Abingdon: Routledge.

Lin, Justin (1990), 'Collectivization and China's agricultural crisis in 1959–1961', *Journal of Political Economy*, 98(6): 1228–50.

Lin, Justin (2012), *Demystifying the Chinese Economy*, Cambridge: Cambridge University Press.

Lin, Justin (2014), *New Paradigm for Interpreting the Chinese Economy: Theories, Challenges and Opportunities*, Singapore: World Scientific Publishing.

Lin, Shuanglin (2002), 'Tax reforms and government revenues', in John Wong and Ding Lu (eds), *China's Economy into the New Century: Structural Issues and Problems*, Singapore: Singapore University Press, pp. 113–46.

Ling, Huawei (2012), 'Ruhe rang zhu shangshu' (How to let pigs climb trees), accessed in May 2017 at http://opinion.caixin.com/2012-05-14/10 0389581.html

Link, Perry (2013), *An Anatomy of Chinese: Rhythm, Metaphor, Politics*, Cambridge: Harvard University Press.

Liu, Binyan and Perry Link (2006), *Two Kinds of Truth: Stories and Reportages from China*, Bloomington: Indiana University Press.

Liu, Chengli (2008), 'Lijie dangdai Zhongguode zhongyang yu difang guanxi' (Understanding of contemporary China's central–local relations), *Modern Economic Science*, 30(5): 26–36.

Liu, Chunrong (2015), 'Community mobilization and policy advocacy in urban China', in Lisheng Dong, Hanspeter Kriesi and Daniel Kübler (eds), *Urban Mobilizations and New Media in Contemporary China*, Farnham: Ashgate, pp. 151–66.

Liu, Jianguo (2000), 'Shehuizhuyi zhenyingde ganchao langchao yu Zhongguo dayuejin yundongde fasheng' (The catch-up drive by the socialist bloc and the occurrence of the Great Leap Forward in China), *Jianghan Tribune*, 4: 75–8.

Liu, Jianhui (2010), '58nian "Renmin gongshe hao" zheijuhua shi Mao Zedong suibian jiangde ma?' (Is 'The People's Commune is good' said by Mao Zedong in 1958 a careless comment?), accessed in March 2017 at http://news.ifeng.com/history/zhongguoxiandaishi/deta il_2010_08/18/1976846_1.shtml

Liu, Kang (2004), *Globalization and Cultural Trends in China*, Honolulu: University of Hawai'i Press.

Liu, Lihua (2010), *Interpersonal Rhetoric in the Editorials of China Daily*, Bern: Peter Lang.

Liu, Qingferng (2001), 'The topography of intellectual culture in 1990s mainland China: A survey', in Gloria Davies (ed.), *Voicing Concerns: Contemporary Chinese Critical Inquiry*, Lanham: Rowman & Littlefield, pp. 47–70.

Liu, Yu (2010), 'Maoist discourse and the mobilization of emotions in revolutionary China', *Modern China*, 36(3): 329–62.

Loewe, Michael (2005), *Faith, Myth, and Reason in Han China*, Cambridge: Hackett Publishing.

Long, Taijiang (2005), 'Cong "dui shehui dongyuan" dao "you shehui dongyuan"' (From 'mobilizer' to 'mobilized'), *Politics and Law*, 2: 17–25.

Looney, Kristen (2012), *The Rural Developmental State: Modernization Campaigns and Peasant Politics in China, Taiwan and South Korea, Perspective*, PhD thesis, Boston: Harvard University.

Looney, Kristen (2015), 'China's campaign to build a New Socialist Countryside: Village modernization, peasant councils, and the Ganzhou model of rural development', *The China Quarterly*, 224: 909–33.

Lorge, Peter (2015), *The Reunification of China: Peace through War Under the Song Dynasty*, Cambridge: Cambridge University Press.

Lou, Jiwei (1997), *Macroeconomic Reform in China: Laying the Foundation for a Socialist Market*, Washington, DC: The World Bank.

Lou, Shenghua (2000), 'Shehuizhuyi gaizao he jizhong dongyuanxing tizhide xingcheng' (The socialist transformation and the formation of a centralised mobilisation system), *Nanjing Social Sciences*, 11: 33–8.

Lu, Jinzeng, Fengliang Zhao and Yuelun Fang (2014), 'Shandong nongyeting futingzhang yin shouhui yishen beipan 15nian' (A deputy director of Shandong Bureau of Agriculture is sentenced for 15 years in jail for bribery), *Procuratorial Daily*, accessed in July 2017 at http://roll.sohu.com/20140718/n402401856.shtml

Lu, Sheldon (2007), *Chinese Modernity and Global Biopolitics*, Honolulu: University of Hawai'i Press.

Lu, Xueyi (2008), 'Tuijin nongcun jingjitizhi gaige, jiejue *Sannong* wenti' (Further reform of the economic system and solve *Sannong* problems), *Zhongguo Liutong Jingji* (*China Business and Market*), 10: 14.

Lu, Yuan (1996), *Management Decision-Making in Chinese Enterprises*, New York: St. Martin.

Lü, Yuanjuan (2010), 'Jiaqiang tudi zonghe zhengzhi, tuijin chengxiang tongchou fazhan' (Strengthening the land comprehensive enhancement, advancing coordinated urban and rural developments), accessed in May 2017 at http://www.jndlr.gov.cn/lixia/tabid/62/InfoID/719/frtid/132/Default.aspx

Lum, Thomas (2000), *Problems of Democratization in China*, New York: Garland Publishing.

Luo, Chuliang and Terry Sicular (2013), 'Inequality and poverty in rural China', in Shi Li, Hiroshi Sato and Terry Sicular (eds), *Rising Inequality in China: Challenges to a Harmonious Society*, Cambridge: Cambridge University Press, pp. 197–229.

Luo, Xin (2017), 'Yiwei "Xiaosanxian" sandai wei jiaxiang paide jilupian' (A documentary filmed by the third generation of 'Minor third-liners' for her home town), *The Paper*, 9 March 2017, accessed in June 2017 at http://www.thepaper.cn/newsDetail_forward_1633138

LWTJJ (Laiwu Tongjiju) (Laiwu Bureau of Statistics) (2017), *Statistical Report on Laiwu's Economic and Social Development in 2016*, accessed in March 2018 at http://www.lwtjj.gov.cn/col/col1851/index.html

Ma, Jianbo (2013), *The Land Development Game in China*, Lanham: Lexington Books,

Ma, Pingchang (2008), 'Quanmian guanche luoshi Shiqida jingshen, cujin Laiwu jingji shehui youhao youkuai fazhan' (Fully implementing key policies of the Seventeenth Party Congress, advancing Laiwu's socio-economic development flawlessly and quickly), *Shandong Economic Strategy Research*, 1–2: 35–9.

Ma, Qiusha (2006), *Non-Governmental Organisation in Contemporary China: Paving the Way to Civil Society*, Abingdon: Routledge.

Ma, Yong (2014), 'Zhaohui ziji: Wode yiduan xinlu licheng' (Finding myself back: A part of my mental life), accessed in December 2016 at http://blog.ifeng.com/article/33983862.html

Magnier, Mark (2016), 'China's economic growth in 2015 is slowest in 25 years', *Wall Street Journal*, accessed in June 2017 at https://www.wsj.com/articles/china-economic-growth-slows-to-6-9-on-year-in-2015-1453169398

Mao, Yushi, Nong Zhao and Xiaojing Yang (2013), *Food Security and Farm Land Protection in China*, Singapore: World Scientific Publishing.

Mason, David (1994), 'Modernization and its discontents revisited: The political economy of urban unrest in the People's Republic of China', *Journal of Politics*, 56(2): 400–24.

McGann, James and Erik Johnson (2005), *Comparative Think Tanks, Politics and Public Policy*, Cheltenham, UK and Northampton, MA, USA: Edward Elgar.

Mei, Xiao (2018), *Chongqing's Red Culture Campaign: Simulation and its Social Implications*, Abingdon: Routledge.

Metcalf, Michael (2011), *Imperialism with Chinese Characteristics: Reading and Re-reading China's 2006 Defense White Paper*, Washington, DC: National Intelligence University Press.

Metcalfe, Les (1996), 'The European Commission as network organisation', *Publius: The Journal of Federalism*, 26 (4): 43–62.

Meyer-Clement, Elena (2016), 'The great urban leap? On the local political economy of rural urbanisation in China', *Journal of Current Chinese Affairs*, 45(1): 109–39.

Miller, Alice (2008), 'The CCP Central Committee's leading small groups', *China Leadership Monitor*, 26: 1–21.

Misra, Kalpana (2016), 'Curing the sickness and saving the Party: Neo-Maoism and Neo-Conservativism in the 1990s', in Shiping Hua (ed.), *Chinese Political Culture, 1989–2000*, Abingdon: Routledge, pp. 133–60.

Moody, Peter, Jr. (1988), 'The political culture of Chinese students and intellectuals: A historical examination', *Asian Survey*, 11 (Nov.): 1140–60.

Moody, Peter, Jr. (1994), 'Trends in the study of Chinese political culture', *China Quarterly*, 139: 731–40.

Moore, Scott (2014), 'Modernisation, authoritarianism, and the environment: The politics of China's South–North Water Transfer Project', *Environmental Politics*, 23(6): 947–64.

Morgan, Stephen (1994), 'The impact of the growth of township enterprises on rural–urban transformation in China, 1978–1990', in Ashok Dutt et al. (eds), *The Asian City: Processes of Development, Characteristics and Planning*, Dordrecht: Springer, pp. 213–36.

Mote, Frederick (2003), *Imperial China, 900–1800*, Boston: Harvard University Press.

Murphy, Rachel (2011), 'Civil society and media in China', in David Shambaugh (ed.), *Charting China's Future: Domestic and International Challenges*, Abingdon: Routledge, pp. 57–66.

Nathan, Andrew (1985), *Chinese Democracy*, Berkeley: University of California Press.

Naughton, Barry (1988), 'The Third Front: Defense industrialization in the Chinese interior', *China Quarterly*, 115: 351–86.

Naughton, Barry (1999), 'China's transition in economic perspective', in Merle Goldman and Roderick MacFarquhar (eds), *The Paradox of China's Post-Mao Reforms*, Boston: Harvard University Press, pp. 30–45.

NBSC (National Bureau of Statistics of China) (2000), *China Statistical Yearbook 2000*, accessed in March 2017 at http://www.stats.gov.cn/tjsj/ndsj/

NBSC (2003), *China Statistical Yearbook 2003*, accessed in March 2017 at http://www.stats.gov.cn/tjsj/ndsj/

NBSC (2006), *China Statistical Yearbook 2006*, accessed in March 2017 at http://www.stats.gov.cn/tjsj/ndsj/

NBSC (2010), *China Statistical Yearbook 2010*, accessed in March 2017 at http://www.stats.gov.cn/tjsj/ndsj/

NBSC (2013), *China Statistical Yearbook 2013*, accessed in March 2017 at http://www.stats.gov.cn/tjsj/ndsj/

NBSC (2016), *China Statistical Yearbook 2016*, accessed in March 2017 at http://www.stats.gov.cn/tjsj/ndsj/

Negro, Gianliugi (2017), *The Internet in China: From Infrastructure to a Nascent Civil Society*, London: Palgrave Macmillan.

Nettl, John (1967), *Political Mobilization: A Sociological Analysis of Methods and Concepts*, London: Faber.

Nie, Huihua (2017), *Collusion, Local Governments and Developments in China*, London: Palgrave Macmillan.

Nyiri, Pal (2010), *Mobility and cultural Authority in Contemporary China*, Seattle: University of Washington Press.

O'Brien, Kevin (2008), *Popular Protest in China*, Boston: Harvard University Press.

O'Brien, Kevin and Lianjiang Li (1999), 'Selective policy implementation in rural China', *Comparative Politics*, 31(2): 167–86.

OECD (The Organisation for Economic Co-operation and Development) (2005), *OECD Review of Agricultural Policies: China*, Paris: OECD Publishing.

OECD (2008), *OECD Review of Innovation Policy: China*, Paris: OECD Publishing.

OECD (2015), *OECD Urban Policy Reviews: China*, Paris: OECD Publishing.

Oi, Jean (1992), 'Fiscal reform and the economic foundations of local state corporatism in China', *World Politics*, 45(1): 99–126.

Pei, Minxin (2008), *China's Trapped Transition: The Limits of Developmental Autocracy*, Boston: Harvard University Press.

Pei, Minxin (2016), *China's Crony Capitalism: The Dynamics of Regime Decay*, Cambridge: Harvard University Press.

Perkins, Dwight (2013), *East Asian Development: Foundations and Strategies*, Boston: Harvard University Press.

Perry, Elizabeth (2002), 'Moving the masses: Emotion work in the Chinese revolution', *Mobilization*, 7(2): 111–28.

Perry, Elizabeth (2007), 'Studying Chinese politics: Farewell to revolution', *China Journal*, 57: 1–22.

Perry, Elizabeth (2011), 'From mass campaigns to managed campaigns: Constructing a new socialist countryside', in Sebastian Heilmann and Elizabeth Perry (eds), *Mao's Invisible Hand: The Political Foundations of Adaptive Governance in China*, Boston: Harvard University Press, pp. 30–61.

Pye, Lucian (1968), *The Spirit of Chinese Politics: A Psychological Study of the Authority Crisis in Political Development*, Boston: Harvard University Press.

Pye, Lucian (1981), *The Dynamics of Chinese Politics*, Cambridge: Oelgeschlager, Gunn & Hain.

Pye, Lucian (1990), 'Tiananmen and Chinese political culture: The escalation of confrontation from moralizing to rage', *Asian Survey*, 30(4): 331–47.

Qi, Gubo, Benjian Wu and Bin Wu (2013), 'Access to resources for farmer professional cooperatives in China: An empirical study of two cases in Shicun Village, Tengzhou City, Shandong', in Bin Wu, Shujie Yao and Jian Chen (eds), *China's Development and Harmonization: Towards a Balance with Nature, Society and the International Community*, Abingdon: Routledge, pp. 218–32.

Qian, Zhonghao and Huili Ren (2015), 'Butong liyi jituanjian huanjing xingwei xuanze boyi fenxi' (The Game Theory analysis of environmental behaviour choices by different interest groups), *Journal of Jiangsu Social Sciences*, 4: 41–9.

Qiu, Jack (2000), 'Interpreting the Dengist rhetoric of building socialism with Chinese characteristics', in Ray Heisey (ed.), *Chinese Perspectives in Rhetoric and Communication*, Stamford: Ablex Publishing, pp. 249–64.

Qiu, Jack (2009), *Working-Class Network Society: Communication Technology and the Information Have-Less in Urban China*, Boston: MIT Press.

Rainey, Lee (2010), *Confucius and Confucianism: The Essentials*, Oxford: Wiley-Blackwell.

Raman, Venkat (2012), 'Governance challenge for the Chinese leadership: Striving to affect the Great Leap from economic to social transformation', in Sujian Guo (ed.), *State–Society Relations and Governance in China*, Lanham: Lexington Books, pp. 203–22.

Rankin, Mary B. (1986), *Elite Activism and Political Transformation in China: Zhejiang Province, 1865–1911*, Stanford: Stanford University Press.

Reilly, James (2012), *Strong Society, Smart State: The Rise of Public Opinion in China's Japan Policy*, New York: Columbia University Press.

Ren, Wei (2016), 'Time to unlock rights to rural rights: China's finance minister', *South China Morning Post*, accessed in October 2017 at http://www.scmp.com/news/china/economy/article/1897830/time-unlock-rights-rural-land-chinas-finance-minister

Richman, Barry (1969), *Industrial Society in Communist China*, New York: Random House.

Rithmire, Meg (2014), 'China's "new regionalism": Subnational analysis in Chinese political economy', *World Politics*, 66(1): 165–94.

Rithmire, Meg (2015), *Land Bargains and Chinese Capitalism: The Politics of Property Rights under Reform*, New York: Cambridge University Press.

Ross, Margaret (1991), *The Post-Modern and the Post-Industrial: A Critical Analysis*, Cambridge: Cambridge University Press.

Saich, Tony (2011), *Governance and Politics of China: The Third Edition*, New York: Palgrave MacMillan.

Sato, Hiroshi, Terry Sicular and Ximing Yue (2013), 'Housing ownership, incomes, and inequality in China', in Li Shi, Hiroshi Sato and Terry Sicular (eds), *Rising Inequality in China: Challenges to a Harmonious Society*, Cambridge: Cambridge University Press, pp. 85–141.

Sausmikat, Nora (2003), 'Generations, legitimacy, and political ideas in China: The end of polarization or the end of ideology?', *Asian Survey*, 43(2): 352–84.

Scharping, Thomas (2003), *Birth Control in China, 1949–2000: Population Policy and Demographic Development*, Abingdon: RoutledgeCurzon.

Schenk-Sandbergen, Loes (1973), 'Some aspects of political mobilization in China', *Modern Asian Studies*, 7(4): 677–89.

Schlager, Jesper (2013), *E-Government in China: Technology, Power and Local Government Reform*, Abingdon: Routledge.

Schneider, Mindi (2017), 'Dragon head enterprises and the state of agribusiness in China', *Journal of Agrarian Change*, 17(1): 3–17.

Schubert, Gunter and Anna Ahlers (2011), '"Constructing a New Socialist Countryside" and beyond: An analysis framework for studying policy implementation and political stability in contemporary China', *Journal of Chinese Political Science*, 16(1): 19–46.

Schubert, Gunter and Anna Ahlers (2012), *Participation and Empowerment at the Grassroots: Chinese Village Elections in Perspective*, Lanham: Lexington Books.

Schurmann, Franz (1968), *Ideology and Organization in Communist China*, Berkeley: University of California Press.

Schwarcz, Vera (1986), *The Chinese Enlightenment: Intellectuals and the Legacy of the May Fourth Movement of 1919*, Berkeley: University of California Press.

Scott, David (2008), *China and the International System, 1840–1949: Power, Presence, and Perceptions in a Century of Humiliation*, Albany: State University of New York Press.

SEITC (Shandong Economic and Information Technology Committee) (2010), 'Guoyu yinfa 2003–2005 Shandongsheng gongye chanpin jiegou tiaozheng yijian de tongzhi' (Notification on the suggestions concerning the adjustment of industrial product structure in Shandong in 2003–2005), accessed in March 2017 at http://www.sdetn.gov.cn/articles/ch01194/201002/1265071814097117.shtml

Shambaugh, David (2008), *China's Communist Party: Atrophy and Adaptation*, Berkeley: University of California Press.

Shambaugh, David (2013), *China Goes Global: The Partial Power*, New York: Oxford University Press.

Shan, Zengde (2011), 'Tongchou chengxiang tudi guanli, cujin yitihua fazhan' (Coordinating the management of urban and rural land, and advancing the development of [rural–urban] integration), *China Real Estate Market*, 12: 32–3.

Shanin, Teodor (1985), *Russia as a Developing Society: Roots of Otherness – Russia's Turn of Century*, London: Macmillan.

Shapiro, Judith (2001), *Mao's War Against Nature: Politics and the Environment in Revolutionary China*, Cambridge: Cambridge University Press.

Shepard, Wade (2015), *Ghost Cities of China: The Story of Cities without People in the World's Most Populated Country*, London: Zed Books.

Shi, Tianjian (1997), *Political Participation in Beijing*, Boston: Harvard University Press.

Shi, Tianjian (2000), 'Economic development and village elections in rural China', in Suisheng Zhao (ed.), *China and Democracy: Reconsidering the Prospects for a Democratic China*, New York: Routledge, pp. 233–52.

Shih, Chih-Yu (1995), *State and Society in China's Political Economy: The Cultural Dynamics of Socialist Reform*, Boulder: Lynne Rienner Publishers.

Shirk, Susan (1993), *The Political Logic of Economic Reform in China*, Berkeley: University of California Press.

Shue, Vivienne and Christine Wong (2007), *Paying for Progress in China: Public Finance, Human Welfare and Changing Patterns of Inequality*, Abingdon: Routledge.

Smith, Aminda (2013), *Thought Reform and China's Dangerous Classes: Re-education, Resistance, and the People*, Lanham: Rowman & Littlefield.

Smith, Graeme (2015), 'The effects of political recentralisation on rural livelihood in Anhui, China', in Heather Zhang (ed.), *Rural Likelihood in China: Political Economy in Transition*, Abingdon: Routledge, pp. 175–94.

Solinger, Dorothy (2015), *China's Transition from Socialism: Statist Legacies and Market Reforms, 1980–1990*, Abingdon: Routledge.

Song, Changxia and Rongjun Ji (2003), 'Laiwu: Zhuangye xiehui "luanhua" nongye chanyehua' (Laiwu: Professional associations as incubators in agricultural industrialisation), *Openings*, 5: 32–5.

SPBLR (Shandong Provincial Bureau of Land and Resources) (2009), 'Guanyu tuijin nongcun zhufang jianshe he weifang gaizao gongzuo youguan tudi wenti de tongzhi' (Notice regarding the land-use issues in the rural construction and the re-building of unsafe housing), accessed in March 2017 at https://wenku.baidu.com/view/0062587301f69e314332946d.html

SPBS (Shandong Provincial Bureau of Statistics) (2001), *Shandong Statistical Yearbook 2001*, accessed in March 2017 at http://www.stats-sd.gov.cn/col/col3567/index.html

SPBS (2002), *Shandong Statistical Yearbook 2002*, accessed in March 2017 at http://www.stats-sd.gov.cn/tjnj/nj2002/03/3-8.htm

SPBS (2005), *Shandong Statistical Yearbook 2005*, accessed in March 2017 at http://www.stats-sd.gov.cn/tjnj/nj2005/2005.htm

SPBS (2006), *Shandong Statistical Yearbook 2006*, accessed in March 2017 at http://www.stats-sd.gov.cn/art/2014/8/11/art_3461_151501.html

SPBS (2007), *Shandong Statistical Yearbook 2007*, accessed in March 2017 http://www.stats-sd.gov.cn/tjnj/nj2007/new/indexch.htm

SPBS (2009), *Shandong Statistical Yearbook 2009*, accessed in March 2017 at http://www.stats-sd.gov.cn/tjnj/nj2009/new/indexch.htm

SPBS (2011), *Shandong Statistical Yearbook 2011*, accessed in March 2017 at http://www.stats-sd.gov.cn/tjnj/nj2011/new/indexch.htm

SPBS (2013), *Shandong Statistical Yearbook 2013*, accessed in March 2017 at http://www.stats-sd.gov.cn/col/col6113/index.html

SPBS (2015), *Shandong Statistical Yearbook 2015*, accessed in March 2017 at http://www.stats-sd.gov.cn/tjnj/nj2015/new/indexch_new.htm

SPBS (2016), *Shandong Statistical Yearbook 2016*, accessed in March 2017 at http://www.stats-sd.gov.cn/tjnj/nj2016/indexch.htm

Stenslie, Stig and Chen Gang (2016), 'Xi Jinping's grand strategy: From vision to implementation', in Robert Ross and Jo Bekkevold (eds), *China in the Era of Xi Jinping: Domestic and Foreign Policy Challenges*, Washington: Georgetown University Press, pp. 117–36.

Stranahan, Patricia (1990), *Moulding the Medium: Chinese Communist Party and the 'Liberation Daily'*, London: Routledge.

Strauss, Julia (2002), 'Paternalist terror: The Campaign to Suppress Counterrevolutionaries and Regime Consolidation in the People's Republic of China, 1950–1953', *Comparative Studies in Society and History*, 44(1): 80–105.

Su, Xiaokang and Perry Link (2013), 'A collapsing natural environment?', in Perry Link, Richard Madsen and Paul Pickowicz (eds), *Restless China*, Lanham: Rowman & Littlefield Publishers, pp. 213–34.

Su, Yuanyuan (2016), *Nongmin shanglou (Moving to Centralized Apartment Complexes)*, PhD thesis, Nanjing: Nanjing University.

Sullivan, Lawrence (2012), *Historical Dictionary of the Chinese Communist Party*, Lanham: Scarecrow Press.

Sun, Jie (2016), 'Shandong nongye zhanle sa quanguo diyi, Yantai pingguo zhi 105yi' (Shandong's agriculture yielded three No. 1s, Yantai apple is worth 10.5 billion), accessed in March 2017 at http://sd.sina.com.cn/news/b/2016-09-12/detail-ifxvukhx4938891.shtml

Sun, Liping (2008), 'Societal transition: New issues in the field of the sociology of development', *Modern China*, 34(1): 88–113.

Sun, Liping, Jun Jin, Jianghui He and Xiangyang Bi (1999), *Dongyuan yu Canyu* (*Mobilisation and Participation*), Hangzhou: Zhejiang People's Publishing.

Sun, Liping and Yuhua Guo (2000), 'Ruanying jianshi: Zhengshi quanli feizhengshi yunzuode guocheng fenxi' (Wielding both the stick and carrot: A process-analysis of the informal operation of formal power), *Tsinghua Sociological Review*, 1: 1–22.

Sun, Yan (1995), *The Chinese Reassessment of Socialism, 1976–1992*, Princeton: Princeton University Press.

Sun, Yongtian (2006), 'Jianshe shehuizhuyi xinnongcun yaoyou xinsilu' (Building a new socialist countryside needs new thinking), *Shandong Social Sciences*, 7: 5–8.

Takeuchi, Hiroki (2013), 'Vote buying, village elections, and authoritarian rule in rural China: A game-theoretic analysis', *Journal of East Asian Studies*, 13: 69–105.

Talas, Barna (1991), *Economic Reforms and Political Reform Attempts in China, 1979–1989*, Berlin: Springer-Verlag.

Tan, Mingzhi (2014), 'Strict control and incentive: Evolution of the policy of linking decrease of arable land with increase of construction land and its local implementation', *Chinese Social Sciences*, 7: 125–42.

Tang, Beibei (2014), 'Development and prospects of deliberative democracy in China: The dimensions of deliberative capacity building', *Journal of Chinese Political Science*, 19: 115–32.

Tang, Wing-Shing and Alan Jenkins (1990), 'Urbanisation: Processes, policies and patterns', in Terry Cannon and Alan Jenkins (eds), *The Geography of Contemporary China: The Impact of Deng Xiaoping's Decade*, London: Routledge, pp. 203–23.

Taylor, Jeffrey and Judith Banister (1989), *China: The Problem of Employing Surplus Rural Labor*, Washington: U.S. Bureau of the Census.

Taylor, Monique (2014), *The Chinese State, Oil and Energy Security*, Basingstoke: Palgrave Macmillan.

Teiwes, Frederick (2000), 'The Maoist state', in David Shambaugh (ed.), *The Modern Chinese State*, New York: Cambridge University Press, pp. 105–60.

Teiwes, Frederick and Warren Sun (1999), *China's Road to Disaster: Mao, Central Politicians, and Provincial Leaders in the Unfolding of the Great Leap Forward, 1955–1959*, Armonk: M.E. Sharpe.

Teiwes, Frederick and Warren Sun (2016), *Paradoxes of Post-Mao Rural*

Reform: Initial Steps Toward a New Chinese Countryside, 1976–1981, Abingdon: Routledge.

Terrill, Ross (2003), *The New Chinese Empire*, Sydney: University of New South Wales Press.

Tian, Xiaowen (2001), 'Deng Xiaoping's *nanxun*: Impact on China's regional development', in John Wong and Yongnian Zheng (eds), *The Nanxun Legacy and China's Development in the Post-Deng Era*, Singapore: Singapore University Press, pp. 75–97.

Tong, Jingrong (2011), *Investigative Journalism in China: Journalism, Power, and Society*, London: Continuum.

Townsend, James (1967), *Political Participation in Communist China*, Berkeley: University of California Press.

Trappel, Rene (2016), *China's Agrarian Transition: Peasants, Property, and Politics*, Lanham: Lexington Books.

Tsang, Steven (2015), 'Why China's Xi Jinping is still far from Chairman Mao status', *Forbes Asia*, accessed in May 2017 at https://www.forbes.com/sites/stevetsang/2015/02/16/why-chinas-xi-jinping-is-still-far-from-chairman-mao-status/#b8336a6a3190

Tsou, Tang, March Blecher and Mitch Meisner (1982), 'National agricultural policy: The Dazhai Model and local change in the post-Mao era', in Mark Selden and Victor Lippit (eds), *The Transition to Socialism in China*, Abingdon: Routledge, pp. 266–99.

Twohey, Michael (1999), *Authority and Welfare in China: Modern Debates in Historical Perspective*, Basingstoke, Palgrave Macmillan.

UNICEF (United Nations Children's Fund) (2015), *Social Mobilization*, accessed in August 2015 at http://www.unicef.org/cbsc/index_42347.html.

USITC (United States International Trade Commission) (2011), *China's Agricultural Trade: Competitive Conditions and Effects on U.S Exports*, Washington: USITC Publications.

Visser, Tobin (2010), *Cities Surround the Countryside: Urban Aesthetics in Post-Socialist China*, Durham: Duke University Press.

VOA (Voice of America) (2016), 'Zhongguo rijun qunti kanyi 500qi' (500 collective protests in China per day), accessed in March 2018 at https://www.voachinese.com/a/landscape-protest-20160324/3252771.html

Vogel, Ezra (2013), *Deng Xiaoping and the Transformation of China*, Cambridge: Harvard University Press.

Wagner, Donald (1998), *A Classical Chinese Reader: The Han Shu Biography of Huo Guang with Notes and Glosses for Students*, Surrey: Curzon.

Waldron, Arthur (1993), 'Warloadism versus federalism: The revival of a debate', *The China Quarterly*, 121: 116–28.

Wan, Jinghua and Changxia Song (2002), 'Laiwu nongminde "Jubaopen"' (Treasure bowl of Laiwu farmers), *Openings*, 6: 36–9.

Wang, Chang and Nathan Madson (2013), *Inside China's Legal System*, Oxford: Chandos Publishing.

Wang, Chuanhui (2016), *The Constitutional Protection of Private Property in China: Historical Evolution and Comparative Research*, Cambridge: Cambridge University Press.

Wang, Fucheng and Fuwei Liang (2012), '"Sijizhong" cuisheng Laiwu jingji sida zhuanbian' ('Four concentrations' facilitates four transformations in Laiwu's economy), *China Real Estate Market*, 7: 48.

Wang, Guihui (2014), *Tamed Village 'Democracy': Elections, Governance and Clientelism in a Contemporary Chinese Village*, Berlin: Springer.

Wang, Guoliang (2011), 'Jiating lianchan chengbao zhenrenzhi zai Shandong de queli' (The introduction of the household production responsibility system in Shandong), accessed in December 2016 at http://www.zgdsw.org.cn/GB/218994/219014/220613/14737219.html

Wang, Hui (2003), *China's New Order: Society, Politics, and Economy in Transition*, Boston: Harvard University Press.

Wang, Jiang, Lei Zhang and Weihua Lin (2011), 'Shandong nongcun shequ jianshe guihuade kunjing yu duice' (Study on predicaments and strategies of the rural community planning in Shandong), *Journal of Shandong Jianzhu University*, 26(3): 229–36.

Wang, Jing (1996), *High Culture Fever: Politics, Aesthetics, and Ideology in Deng's China*, Berkeley: University of California Press.

Wang, Jing (2008), *Brand New China: Advertising, Media, and Commercial Culture*, New York: Harvard University Press.

Wang, Lei (2016), 'Jiandingxinxin, kuganshigan, nuli kaichuang Laiwu genjia meihaode mingtian' (Firming confidence, working hard, striving for creating a better future for Laiwu), *Shandong Economic Strategy Research*, 1–2: 96–100.

Wang, Meng (2006), *Autobiography of Wang Meng*, Guangzhou: Huacheng Press.

Wang, Qishan (2016), 'Dongyuan qianbian buru wenze yici' (A thousand times of mobilisation are not as good as looking into who is responsible once), accessed in March 2018 at http://www.chinanews.com/gn/2016/06-08/7897926.shtml

Wang, Rengui (2010), 'Zhucheng "Xinnongcun" gushi' (Stories of 'new countryside' in Zhucheng), *Outlook Weekly*, 47: 20–23.

Wang, Shaoguang (1997), *Fenquan de Dixian* (*The Bottom Line of Decentralisation*), Beijing: China Planning Publishing House.

Wang, Shaoguang and Angang Hu (1999), *The Political Economy of Uneven Development: The Case of China*, New York: M.E. Sharpe.

Wang, Shaoguang and Angang Hu (2001), *The Chinese Economy in Crisis: State Capacity and Tax Reform*, New York: M.E. Sharpe.

Wang, Yu and Yangyang Liu (2016), '2016 Zhongyang Yihao Wenjian gongbu: Jiang shenru tujin nongcun gaige' (2016 No. 1 Central Document publicised: Further advance rural reforms), accessed in January 2017 at http://business.sohu.com/20160127/n436059407.shtml

Wasserstrom, Jeffery (2009), 'China since Tiananmen: Middle-class mobilization', *Journal of Democracy*, 20(3): 29–32.

Watson, Rubie (1994), 'Making secret histories: Memory and mourning in post-Mao China', in Rubie Watson (ed.), *Memory, History and Opposition: Under State Socialism*, Santa Fe: School of American Research Press, pp. 65–86.

Wen, Xiaobo (2009), 'Shilun Xinnongcun Jianshe zhong de nongmin zhengzhi canyu' (On peasant political participation in the New Countryside Construction), *Legal System and Society*, 2: 274–6.

Wen, Xiaoyi (2017), 'Cong "guojia zhudao" dao duoyuan tuidong' (From state domination to initiation of multiple actors), *Sociological Studies*, 2: 28–50.

Weng, Shiyou (2013), 'Qici zhengfu gaige nantao guaiquan' (Seven governmental reforms unable to avoid the vicious cycle), accessed in December 2016 at http://finance.sina.com.cn/china/bwdt/20130520/143315521893.shtml

Wheelwright, Edward and Bruce McFarlane (1970), *The Chinese Road to Socialism: Economics of the Cultural Revolution*, New York: Monthly Review Press.

White, Lynn T. (1998), *Unstately Power: Volume I, Local Causes of China's Economic Reforms*, New York: M.E. Sharpe.

White, Lynn T. (1999), *Unstately Power: Volume II, Local Causes of China's Intellectual, Legal and Governmental Reforms*, New York: M.E. Sharpe.

White, Tyrene (1990), 'Postrevolutionary mobilization in China: The one-child policy reconsidered', *World Politics*, 43(1): 53–76.

White, Tyrene (2006), *China's Longest Campaign: Birth Planning in the People's Republic, 1949–2005*, Ithaca: Cornell University Press.

Whiting, Susan (2000), *Power and Wealth in Rural China: The Political Economy of Institutional Change*, Cambridge: Cambridge University Press.

Whyte, Martine and William Parish (1984), *Urban Life in Contemporary China*, Chicago: University of Chicago Press.

Wills, John (1994), *Mountain of Fame: Portraits in Chinese History*, Princeton: Princeton University Press.

Wong, Christine (2000), 'Central–local relations revisited: The 1994 tax- sharing reform and public expenditure management in China', *China Perspectives*, 31: 52–63.

Wong, Christine (2007), 'Can the retreat from equality be reversed? An assessment of redistributive fiscal policies from Deng Xiaoping to Wen Jiabao', in Vivienne Shue and Christine Wong (eds), *Paying for Progress in China: Public Finance, Human Welfare and Changing Patterns of Inequality*, London: Routledge, pp. 12–28.

Wong, Christine (2009), 'Assessing the fiscal power of the Chinese state: assessing the central government's capacity to implement national policies', in Keun Lee, Joon-Han Kim and Wing Thye Woo (eds), *Power and Sustainability of the Chinese State*, Abingdon: Routledge, pp. 100–116.

Wong, Christine (2013), 'Paying for urbanization in China: Challenges of municipal finance in the twenty-first century', in Roy Bahl, Johannes Linn and Deborah Wetzel (eds), *Financing Metropolitan Governments in Developing Countries*, Boston: Lincoln Institute of Land Policy, pp. 273–308.

Wong, John (2014), *The Political Economy of Deng's Nanxun: Breakthrough in China's Reform and Development*, Singapore: World Scientific Publishing.

World Bank (1995), *China: Macroeconomic Stability in a Decentralised Economy*, Washington, DC: The World Bank.

World Bank (2006), 'Shandongsheng Shijie Yinhang daikuan chengjian huanbao erqi gongcheng: Yimin anzhi jihua' (The World Bank's loan program on the second stage of urban development and environmental protection in Shandong: Plan for migration settlement), accessed in April 2017 at http://siteresources.worldbank.org/EXTNEWSCHINESE/ Resources/shangdong2_rap.pdf

Wu, Alfred (2014), 'Selective policy implementation by bureaucracy in China: The case of civil service remuneration policy', in Bennis So and Yuang-Kuang Kao (eds), *The Changing Policy-Making Process in Greater China: Case Research from Mainland China, Taiwan and Hong Kong*, Abingdon: Routledge, pp. 171–89.

Wu, Guoguang (2005), *The Anatomy of Political Power in China*, Singapore: East Asia Institute.

Wu, Jieh-min (2010), 'Rural migrant workers and China's differential citizenship', in Martin Whyte (ed.), *One Country, Two Societies: Rural–Urban Inequality in Contemporary China*, Boston: Harvard University Press, pp. 55–84.

Wu, Jinglian (2004), *China's Long March toward a Market Economy*, San Francisco: Long River Press.

Wu, Li (2003), 'Chengshihua: Zhongguo shixian quanmian xiaokang shehuide biyouzhilu' (Urbanisation: The only path to achieve China's all-around well-off society), *Jingji Yanjiu (Economic Research Journal)*, 6: 90–92.

Wu, Xianqing and Quanlu Wu (2006), 'Qingdao Laixishi xinnongcun jianshe moshide tansuo ji duiquanguode qishi' (An analysis of the new countryside construction model of the city of Laixi, Qingdao, and its national implications), *Journal of the Party School of CPC Qingdao Municipal Committee*, 2: 46–50.

Wu, Wenyu (2014), *Urbanization and Mechanism of China: A Government Behavior Perspective*, PhD thesis, Shanghai: East China Normal University.

Wu, Yi (2007), '"Nets of the power-rights structure" and dilemma of peasants' group-rights expression: An analysis of a gravel pit dispute', *Sociological Studies*, 22(5): 21–45.

Xia, Ming (2008), *The People's Congress and Governance in China: Toward a Network Mode of Governance*, Abingdon: Routledge.

Xie, Xiaoqin (2014), 'Banzhengshi zhili jiqi houguo: Jiyu jiufen tiaojie ji chaiqian gongsi canyu de banzhengshi xingzheng fenxi' (Semi-formal governance and its outcomes: An analysis of dispute mediation and participation of demolition companies based on a semi-formal governance framework), *Journal of Northwest A&F University (Social Sciences Edition)*, 14(5): 123–8.

Xie, Yue and Kaixiong Cao (2009), 'The spectrum of collective action theory: From social movement theory to theory of contentious politics', *Journal of SJTU (Philosophy and Social Sciences)*, 17(3): 13–20.

Xing, Qingli (2012), 'Jiakuai Laiwu "Liangxin" gongcheng jianshede tantao' (Discussion of speedy construction of Laiwu's "Two New" projects), *Market Modernization*, 10: 188–9.

Xinhua News (2016a), 'Former Shandong official sentenced to 12 years in prison', accessed in May 2017 at http://www.xinhuanet.com/english/20 16-09/30/c_135725226.htm

Xinhua News (2016b), 'China unveils guideline for rural asset shareholding reform', accessed in May 2017 at http://news.xinhuanet.com/ english/2016-12/30/c_135942672.htm

Xinhua News (2017a), 'Jinnian jingji zengsu mubiao weihe xiaofu xiatiao?' (Why does the growth rate have to be lowered this year?), accessed in December 2016 at http://www.npc.gov.cn/npc/dbdhhy/12_5/2017-03/07/ content_2012472.htm

Xinhua News (2017b), 'Former Jinan mayor stands trial for graft', accessed in November 2017 at http://www.xinhuanet.com/english/2017- 03/23/c_136152264.htm

Xinhua News (2018a), 'Former provincial official expelled from CPC, public office', accessed in February 2018 at http://www.china.org.cn/china/2018-02/13/content_50512699.htm

Xinhua News (2018b), 'Policies released on China's rural vitalization', accessed in February 2018 at http://www.xinhuanet.com/english/2018-02/04/c_136948462.htm

Xu, Chenggang (2011), 'The fundamental institutions of China's reforms and development', *Journal of Economic Literature*, 49(4): 1076–151.

Xu, Chenggang (2016), 'Zhongguo Gaige ruhe jiejue guanliaotizhi jili wenti' (How China's reform has solved the issue of mobilising the bureaucratic system), accessed in December 2016 at http://comments.caijing.com.cn/20161213/4211399.shtml

Xu, Chenggang and Xiaobo Zhang (2009), *The Evolution of Chinese Entrepreneurial Firms: Township-village Enterprises Revisited*. Washington: International Food Policy Research Institute.

Xu, Feng (2000), *Women Migrant Workers in China's Economic Reform*, Basingstoke: Palgrave Macmillan.

Xu, Hua and Huiyu Cui (2011), 'The revenue system of China: Past, present, and emerging issues', *Journal of Public Budgeting, Accounting and Financial Management*, 23(4): 544–68.

Xu, Mingyi (2013), *Zhongguo Nongmin Hezuo Zuzhi Yanjiu* (*The Study on Cooperative Organisations of Chinese Peasants*), PhD thesis, Toyohashi: Aichi University.

Xu, Yan and Dali Yang (2015), 'The central government', in David Goodman (ed.), *Handbook of the Politics of China*, Cheltenham, UK and Northampton, MA, USA: Edward Elgar, pp. 76–94.

Xu, Yan, Nana Fan and Nabo Chen (2005), 'Legitimacy loading: A new explanation for the political campaign in China, 18 years of "Creating a National Sanitary City" in a Chinese city', *Journal of Public Administration*, 8(2): 22–46.

Yan, Hongliang (2017), *Heritage Tourism in China: Modernity, Identity, and Sustainability*, Bristol: Channel View Publications.

Yan, Jiaqi (1992), *The Third Republic: Political Path of China*, New York: Global Publishing.

Yang, Dali (1996), *Calamity and Reform in China: State, Rural Society, and Institutional Change since the Great Leap Famine*, Stanford: Stanford University Press.

Yang, Dali (2002), 'Reform and the restructuring central–local relations', in David Goodman and Gerald Segal (eds), *China Deconstructs: Politics, Trade and Regionalism*, London: Routledge, pp. 59–98.

Yang, Long (2004), 'Jingji fazhanzhongde shehui dongyuan jiqi teshuxing' (Social mobilization in economic development and its characteristics), *Tianjin Social Sciences*, 4: 52–6.

Yang, Xuedong, Thomas Heberer and Gunter Schubert (2013), 'Difang zhengzhide nengdongzhe shijiao' (A perspective on actors in local politics', in Thomas Heberer, Gunter Schubert and Xuedong Yang (eds), *'Zhudongde' Difang Zhengzhi: Zuowei Zhanlue Quntide Xianxiang Ganbu ('Proactive' Local Politics: County and Township Cadres as a Strategic Group*), Beijing: Central Compilation and Translation Press, pp. 4–28.

Yang, Yixin (2012a), 'Fenqiganchao, kexuekuayue, jiakuai jianshe fuqiang wenming hexie xiandaihua Laiwu' (Rising to catch up, stepping crossing scientifically, speeding up constructing a rich, civilised, harmonious and modern Laiwu), *Shandong Economic Strategy Research*, 1–2: 59–64.

Yang, Yixin (2012b), 'Guanyu Laiwushi zhuanxing fazhan de diaocha yu sikao' (Survey and analysis of the transformational growth in the city of Laiwu), *Shandong Economic Strategy Research*, 8: 4–9.

Yang, Zhigang and Bin Zhang (2006), 'Problem of government levels in local fiscal system reform: Appraisal of main schemes and current steps', *Finance and Trade Economics*, (3): 10–17.

Yantai Government (2006), *Yantai Yearbook*, Beijing: Popular Science Press.

Yao, Kevin (2017), 'China launches rural assets reforms to boost farmers' incomes', accessed in July 2017 at http://www.reuters.com/article/us-china-rural-economy/china-launches-rural-assets-reforms-to-boost-far mers-incomes-idUSKBN14N0AB

Yao, Xinzhong (2000), *An Introduction to Confucianism*, Cambridge: Cambridge University Press.

Yao, Yang (2015), 'China's juggling act with investment and debt', *The Financial Times*, accessed in June 2017 at http://blogs.ft.com/the-exchange/2015/11/07/chinas-juggling-act-with-investment-and-debt/?m hq5j=e3

Yao, Yang (2016), 'The riddles of the Chinese economy', *The Financial Times*, accessed in June 2017 at http://blogs.ft.com/the-exchange/2016/07/01/the-riddles-of-chinas-economy/?mhq5j=e2

Ye, Chuntao (2009), 'Dangqian woguo nongmin de zhengzhi canyu: Wenti, yuanyin he duice' (Present political participation of peasants in our country: Problems, reasons and countermeasures), *Journal of Chongqing Institute of Socialism*, 3: 89–92.

Ye, Kefei (2017), 'Chongman beilunde Shandong wenhua' (Shandong culture is full of paradox), accessed in May 2017 at http://culture.ifeng.com/a/20170330/50865420_0.shtml

Ye, Yumin and Richard LeGates (2013), *Coordinating Urban and Rural Development in China: Learning from Chengdu*, Cheltenham, UK and Northampton, MA, USA: Edward Elgar.

Ye, Yumin and Bo Qin (2015), 'The diversified models and outcomes of applying the urban–rural land trading policy in China', in Tai-Chee Wong, Sun Sheng Han and Hongmei Zhang (eds), *Population Mobility Urban Planning and Management in China*, Berlin: Springer, pp. 261–74.

Yeh, Anthony G. and Fiona F. Yang (2013), 'Producer services and the development of the Chinese urban system', in Anthony G. Yeh and Fiona F. Yang (eds), *Producer Services in China: Economic and Urban Development*, Abingdon: Routledge, pp. 173–98.

Yi, Xiaoyan, Yinjun Chen, Bilin Xiao and Qianqian Li (2011), 'Chengxiang jianshe yongdi *zengjian guagou* yunxingzhong chuxiande zhuyao wenti yu jianyi' (The main problems emerging from and recommendations for the utilisation of *zengjian guagou* of urban and rural construction land), *Chinese Journal of Agricultural Resources and Regional Planning*, 32(1): 10–23.

Yibaitt, WeChat (2015), 'Ruhe rang zhu shangshu' (How to let pigs climb trees), accessed in May 2017 at http://www.100toutiao.com/index.php?m=Index&a=show&cat=4&id=27303

Ying, Xing (2007), 'Grassroots mobilization and the mechanism of interest expression of peasants group: A comparative study of four cases', *Sociological Studies*, 22(2): 1–23.

Ying, Xing (2013), *A Study of the Stability of Contemporary Rural China*, Berlin: Springer.

Young, Graham and Yingjie Guo (2007), 'Managing rights talk in the "harmonious society"', in Joseph Cheng (ed.), *Challenges and Policy Programmes of China's New Leadership*, Hong Kong: City University of Hong Kong Press, pp. 97–132.

Young, Jason (2011), 'China's changing *hukou* system: Institutional objectives, formal arrangements, and informal practice', in Xiaoming Huang (ed.), *The Institutional Dynamics of China's Great Transformation*, Abingdon: Routledge, pp. 130–51.

Young, Susan (2000), 'Review of *Unstately Power*', *China Journal*, 43(1): 168–70.

Yu, Hong (2015), *Chinese Regions in Change: Industrial Upgrading and Regional Development Strategies*, Abingdon: Routledge.

Yu, Keping (2010), *Democracy and the Rule of Law in China*, Leiden: Brill.

Yu, Jianrong (2009), 'Heie shili shi ruhe qinru nongcun jiceng zhengquande' (How the evil forces penetrated the rural grassroots political system), *Lilun Cankao (Theoretical Reference)*, 4: 60–63.

Yu, Jianxing (2014), 'China's public service system', in Kenneth Lieberthal, Cheng Li and Keping Yu (eds), *China's Political Development: Chinese and American Perspectives*, Washington, DC: Brookings Institution Press, pp. 221–53.

Yue, Jun, Jiqing Pan and Deyun Zhu (2009), *Nongcun Gonggong Fuwu yu Nongcun Caizheng: 2004–2008 Shandongsheng Nongcun Diaoyan Baogao* (*Rural Public Services and Public Finance: Survey Report of Rural Shandong of 2004–2008*), Beijing: Zhongguo Caizheng Jingji Chubanshe (China Financial and Economic Publishing House).

Zarrow, Peter (2012), *After Empire: The Conceptual Transformations of the Chinese State, 1885–1924*, Stanford: Stanford University Press.

Zeng, Jin (2013), *State-Led Privatization in China: The Politics of Economic Reform*, Abingdon: Routledge.

Zha, Jianying (1995), *China Pop: How Soap Operas, Tabloids, and Bestsellers are Transforming a Culture*, New York: The New Press.

Zha, Wen (2015), *Individual Choice and State-Led Nationalist Mobilization in China: Self-Interested Patriots*, Berlin: Springer-Verlag.

Zhang, Kangqing (1998), 'Some findings from the 1993 Survey of Shanghai's floating population', in Borge Bakken (ed.), *Migration in China*, Copenhagen: Nordic Institute of Asian Studies, pp. 67–106.

Zhang, Li (2010), *In Research of Paradise: Middle-Class Living in a Chinese Metropolis*, Ithaca: Cornell University Press.

Zhang, Linshan and Fengyi Sun (2017), *Gaige Gengzu Xianxiang: Biaoxian, Genyuan and Zhili* (*The Phenomenon of the Reform Obstruction in China: The Performance, Origin and Solution*), Beijing: Social Sciences Academic Press.

Zhang, Ming (2003), 'Huabei diqu tudi gaige yundongde yunzuo, 1946–1949' (The operation of the land reform in Northern China, 1946–1949), *Twenty-First Century*, 76: 32–41.

Zhang, Ping, Chunkui Zhu and Yilin Hou (2016), 'Fiscal decentralization, flat administrative structure, and local government size: Evidence and lessens from China', *Public Administration and Development*, 36: 198–214.

Zhang, Qizhi (2015), *An Introduction to Chinese History and Culture*, Berlin: Springer.

Zhang, Quanbao and Qinghuio Wang (1998), 'Guchangcheng jiaoxia jueqi' (Rising at the foot of the ancient Great Wall), *Zouxiang Shijie* (*Openings*), 1: 60–64.

Zhang, Weiguo (2006), 'Xinnongcun jianshe: Neirongde xitongxing he moshide duoyuanxing' (New Countryside Building: Systematicity of the content and diversity of the model), 26 December 2006, *Chinese Economic Times*, accessed in May 2017 at http://www.ce.cn/cysc/agricult ure/ncjj/200612/26/t20061226_9885717.shtml

Zhang, Xudong (2001), 'The making of the post-Tiananmen intellectual field: A critical overview', in Xudong Zhang (ed.), *Whither China: Intellectual Politics in Contemporary China*, Durham: Duke University Press, pp. 1–78.

Zhang, Xudong (2008), *Postsocialist and Cultural Politics: China in the Last Decades of the Twentieth Century*, Durham: Duke University Press.

Zhao, Dingxin (1998), 'Ecologies of social movements: Student mobilization during the 1989 prodemocracy movement in Beijing', *American Journal of Sociology*, 103(6): 1493–529.

Zhao, Dingxin (2001), *The Power of Tiananmen: State–Society Relations and the 1989 Beijing Student Movement*, Chicago: University of Chicago Press.

Zhao, Shiyong (2013), 'Privatization, FDI inflow and economic growth: Evidence from China's provinces, 1978–2008', *Applied Economic*, 45: 2127–39.

Zhao, Suisheng (1994), 'China's central–local relations: A historical perspective', in Jia Hao and Zhimin Lin (eds), *Changing Central–Local Relations in China: Reform and State Capacity*, Boulder: Westview Press, pp. 19–34.

Zhao, Suisheng (2004), *A Nation-State by Construction: Dynamics of Modern Chinese Nationalism*, Stanford: Stanford University.

Zhao, Yanxia, Yi Liu and Xiaofeng Zhang (2015), 'Zhongguo tudi caizheng lujing gaige yanjiu' (An analysis of reform paths of China's land finance), accessed in May 2018 at http://www.zgtdxh.org.cn/xsjl/xhnh/2015/fhcjl/2/201512/t20151214_1391622.htm

Zhao, Yongjun (2013), *China's Disappearing Countryside: Towards Sustainable Land Governance for the Poor*, Abingdon: Routledge.

Zhao, Yuezhi (1998), *Media, Market, and Democracy in China: Between the Party Line and the Bottom Line*, Urbana: University of Illinois Press.

Zheng, Yongnian (2004), *Globalization and State Transformation in China*, Cambridge: Cambridge University Press.

Zheng, Yongnian (2006), 'The Party, class, and democracy in China', in Kjeld Brodsgaard and Yongnian Zheng (eds), *The Chinese Communist Party in Reform*, Abingdon: Routledge, pp. 231–60.

Zheng, Yongnian (2007), *De Facto Federalism in China: Reforms and Dynamics of Central–Local Relations*, Singapore: World Scientific Publishing.

Zheng, Yongnian (2010), *The Chinese Communist Party as Organizational Emperor: Culture, Reproduction and Transformation*, Abingdon: Routledge.

Zheng, Yongnian and Cuifen Weng (2016), 'The development of China's formal political structure', in Robert Ross and Jo Bekkevold (eds), *China in the Era of Xi Jinping: Domestic and Foreign Policy Challenges*, Washington, DC: Georgetown University Press, pp. 32–65.

Zheng, Yongting (2000), 'Lun xiandai shehuide Shehui dongyuan' (On social mobilisation in modern society), *Journal of Sun Yat-sen University*, 2: 21–7.

Zhong, Kaibin (2009), 'Zhongguo zhongyang yu defang guanxi jiben panduan' (Basic assessment of China's central–local relations), *Journal of Shanghai Administration Institute*, 1(3): 20–29.

Zhong, Yang (2004), *Local Government and Politics in China: Challenges from Below*, New York: M.E. Sharpe.

Zhou, Feizhou (2006), 'Fenshuizhi shinian: Zhidu jiqi yingxiang' (Ten years of the tax-sharing system: The system and its impact), *Zhongguo Shehui Kexue (Social Sciences in China)*, 6: 100–115.

Zhou, Feizhou and Mingzhi Tan (2017), *Relationship Between the Central Government and Local Governments of Contemporary China*, Singapore: Springer Nature.

Zhou, Feizhou and Shaochen Wang (2015), 'Farmers moving upstairs and capital going down to the countryside: A sociological study of urbanization', *Social Sciences in China (Chinese Edition)*, 1: 66–83.

Zhou, Guoxiong (2007), 'Gonggong zhengce zhixing zuzhide boyi fenxi' (The game [theory] analysis of [public] policy failure), *Tongji University Journal*: 18: 91–6.

Zhou, Kate (1994), *How the Farmers Changed Communist China*, PhD thesis, Princeton: Princeton University.

Zhou, Qiren (2013), 'Bichulaide "zengjian guagou"' (Imposed policy of *zengjian guagou*), accessed in March 2017 at http://www.eeo.com. cn/2013/0917/249950.shtml

Zhou, Tianyong (2009), 'Shengguanxian shi guojia zhongda zhanlue' (The 'province-managing-county' is a major national strategy), *People's Daily Online*, accessed in May 2017 at http://theory.people.com.cn/GB/49150/49152/9473017.html

Zhou, Xiaohong (2008), 'Guojia, shichang yu shehui' (State, market, and society), *Sociological Studies*, 1: 143–64.

Zhou, Xueguang and Yun Ai (2016), 'Bases of governance and forms of resistance: The case of rural China', in David Courpasson and Steven Vallas (eds), *The Sage Handbook of Resistance*, London: Sage, pp. 443–60.

Zhou, Zhihua (2015), 'Assessment of China's urbanization', in Yongnian Zheng and Lance Gore (eds), *China Entering the Xi Jinping Era*, Abingdon: Routledge, pp. 149–67.

Zhu, Yapeng and James Lee (2007), 'The coming housing crisis in China', in James Lee and Kam-Wah Chan (eds), *The Crisis of Welfare in East Asia*, Lanham: Lexington Book, pp. 223–42.

Zhu, Yu; Min Lin, Liyue Lin and Jinmei Chen (2013), 'The extent of *in situ* urbanisation in China's county areas: The case of Fujian province', *China Perspectives*, 3: 43–52.

Zuo, Wu and Longqi Chao (2007), 'The impact of evil social forces on lower-level governments', *Journal of Zhanjiang Normal College*, 28(1): 62–6.

Index

abolition of agricultural taxes, the 6
acquaintance society 158
administrative reforms 143
anti-Japanese War 10
Apter, David 9

Bai, Nansheng 4
bargaining 5, 23, 31, 43, 70, 118, 132, 141, 151, 188, 192, 194
Barnett, Arthur Doak 32
beijiu shi bingquan 35
beilun 87
Bernstein, Thomas 11
biaoda kunjing 168
binlin bengkui, or *bengkui de bianyuan* 33
blue-stamp *hukou* 4
boluan fanzheng 34
boyi 5, 21, 25, 118, 128, 132, 168, 187, 194
bumen benweizhuyi see departmentalism
bureaucratic mobilization 16

cadre assessment system 49
Caixin 79
Cameron, David 9, 10
campaign-style governance 71, 118, 196
capitalism 2
carrot-and-stick approach 153–60
CASS (Chinese Academy of Social Sciences) 163, 165, 166
CCDI (Central Commission for Discipline Inspection) 102
CCP (Chinese Communist Party) 10–12, 15–18, 25, 26, 31–9, 41, 45–52, 55, 57, 59, 61, 73–6, 79, 90–96, 98, 100–102, 111, 113–15, 124, 127, 129, 130, 138, 142–4, 147–52, 164, 170, 179, 180, 184, 185, 187, 188, 192, 193, 199, 200
CDRF (China Development Research Foundation) 4
Cell, Charles 12
Central Commission for Discipline Inspection *see* CCDI
central-local relations 17, 21, 27, 35–44, 47, 48, 77, 87, 143, 188, 191, 194
central-local relations, restructuring 37–44
chai na see forced demolition
Chen, J. 136
China Development Research Foundation *see* CDRF
Chinese Academy of Social Sciences *see* CASS
Chinese Communist Party *see* CCP
city-governing-counties *see* Shiguanxian
Collusion *see hemou*
combined-village-community model 85
Cultural Revolution, the 10, 12, 14, 16, 23, 34, 39, 65, 94, 139n2, 186, 188

danwei 110n5
de-agriculturalisation 73
decentralisation 17, 18, 24, 26, 35–7, 39, 41–3, 45, 57, 118, 187, 188, 191, 194–6
decision-makers, policy initiatives 30–60
decision-making 6, 50, 89, 144
Deng, Xiaoping 23, 34, 35, 39, 41, 43, 54, 65, 90, 93, 94, 114, 115, 128, 193
departmentalism 119
Deutsch, Karl 8
Dibao see minimum livelihood guarantee, the

dingceng sheji see top-level design of reform
dragon head enterprises 68, 135

'eating in separate kitchens' 39, 42
economic reforms 17
economic structure 121, 126, 133–5, 137
Eleventh Five-Year Plan 6, 51, 55, 59
emerging powers, invisible hand 89–110
Etzioni, Amitai 9

false or pseudo innovation 127–8
fazhan caishi ying daoli 41
Fei Xiaotong 3
fengjian canyu 34
Fengyu 147, 151
fenquan 41
fenshuizhi 41
fenzao chifan see 'eating in separate kitchens'
fiscal decentralisation 17, 39
fiscal reforms 47, 57
floating population, the 3, 4
forced demolition 108, 162, 164, 165, 168, 169
'Four Cleanups' *(Siqing)* 11
front-line roles 145–53
fushengji 68

game theory 117, 194
ganbu gangwei zerenzhi 49
'Gang of Four,' the 90
GDP 54, 55, 103, 189
GDPism 128
governmental institutional reforms 39
governmental reforms 143
Great Leap Forward 3
green-card *hukou* 4
gross output value 65, 67, 68
Guangdong 67
guanxi 110n5, 158, 161n6
guihua xianxing 82
guoce-state policy 58

heavy industry 67, 68
hemou 128
holistic-dynamic approach 20–25

household registration system, the *see hukou*
Hu Jintao 6, 51, 52, 55, 99, 100, 124, 154, 161n5, 184, 189
hukou 3, 4, 7
Huntington, Samuel 9
Hu–Wen xinzheng 52
Hu Yaobang 36

ideological legitimacy 49
imperialism 2
in situ industrialisation 5
in situ urbanisation 5
integrated urban–rural development 126, 127, 130, 133, 138
interest groups 6, 31, 70, 114, 116, 117, 119, 125, 128, 132, 137, 187, 188, 191, 194

Jiangsu 67
Jiangxi Soviet period 10
Jiang Zemin 6, 44, 45, 51, 52, 87, 95, 110n4
jianzhicun (administrative village) 85
jigou gaige see governmental institutional reforms
jigou tiaozheng 39
jinchang bu jincheng 2, 4
jiuming daocao 195
Johnson, Chalmers 8, 22

key performance indicators (KPIs) 49

Laicheng 149
Laiwu, city 27, 28, 77, 103, 112, 120–23
Laiwu, economy 121, 123, 125
Laiwu, history 121
land finance 2, 6, 7, 21, 27, 44, 48, 56, 57, 74, 77, 83, 86, 112, 122, 124, 129, 130, 166
Lao-Tzu 62
Leninist-Stalinist approach 200
liangge jijixing 42
liangshang 37
liangshou zhua see 'two-hands' approach
liangxia 37
light industry 67, 68
litu bu lixiang 2, 4
liudong renkou see floating population

liyi jituan see interest groups
local urbanisation 5
longtou qiye 135
Looney, Kristen 57

management deficit 132
Mao-style political campaign 18
Mao Zedong 33, 60n6, 63, 65, 90,
   139n1, 139n2, 139n5
Ma Pingchang 123, 133
market forces
   party-state systems 96–102
   social mobiliser 103–9
market liberalisation 90–96
media liberalisation 20
Mencius 62
middle bureaucracy 112–19
migrants 3
minimum livelihood guarantee, the 77
minjin guotui 24
minzhu jizhongzhi 37
minzhu juece 41
Mo-tzu 62
mubiao guanli zerenzhi see target
   responsibility system
multi-village-community model 84

National Social Science Fund of China
   see NSSFC
NDRC (National Development and
   Reform Commission) 119
'No. 1 Central Document' *see* 'No. 1
   Document'
'No. 1 Document' 51, 55, 56
nongcun 5
nongmin 5
nongye 5
nongzhuanfei 4
NSSFC (National Social Science Fund
   of China) 187

one village–one community model 85
Organisation for Economic Co-
   operation and Development
   (OECD) 30

pai gongzuozu 148
participatory responses 162–83
party-state systems 96–102, 199
passivity, Chinese 52, 78

peasant burden reduction 6
People's Daily 185
PLA (People's Liberation Army) (of
   China) 161n3
policy support, mobilising 111–40
political dynamics 79–87
   financial resources, coordinated
      management 86
   market forces, use of 86–7
   pilot areas, identifying and selecting
      84–5
   province-wide evaluations 83–4
   province-wide planning 82–3
   rural areas classifications 83–4
political reality 31–6
post-Mao China 1
potential losses, protests 176–82
PRC (People's Republic of China) 37,
   51, 63, 130, 200
pre-1978 social mobilisation 8–14
prefectural-level city, Laiwu 120–23
Procuratorial Daily 137
project-driven approach 27, 112,
   132–9, 156, 191
province-governing-counties *see*
   Shengguanxian
province-governing-county reform 143
provincial bureaucratic routines 71–8
   communicating documents 72
   gathering feedback 78
   holding work conferences 72–4
   leadership training 75–6
   media promotion 74–5
   personnel allocations 76
   resources, arranging 77–8
pseudo-or false innovation *see* false or
   pseudo innovation

rational correlations 169–76
'red-line' of 1.8 billion *mu,* the 73
reform period 14–20
Research Report on Mass Incidents 164
Richman, Barry 12
rural industrialisation 4, 5, 15–17, 81,
   94, 139n3
rural–urban income gap 53
rural urbanisation 1–29, 31, 41, 51–9,
   61, 65, 84, 101, 102, 109, 124–6,
   132, 135, 136, 138, 141–61, 185,
   189

sange daibiao 47
sannong wenti 5, 51–9, 189
sanzhongren 39, 59n6
Schenk-Sandbergen, Loes 12
Schurmann, Franz 10, 12
second Sino-Japanese War 8
selective implementation 119
semi-acquaintance society 158
Shandong, province 24–6, 35, 36, 62–71, 99, 120, 189
Shandong Provincial Bureau of Statistics *see* SPBS
shangao huangdiyuan 35
shanglou, nongmin 7, 81, 145
Shangzhuang 152
Shan Zengde 126, 128, 130, 133, 137, 138
shengguanxian or *sheng guan xian* 116, 143
shiguanxian or *shi guan xian* 116, 143
shiquan 43, 48, 130
shuren shehui see acquaintance society
sihua, or *sige xiandaihua* 33
small-town strategy, the 3, 4
socialism 2
social mobilisation tasks 123–32
Soviet Union, the 11, 139n5
SPBS (Shandong Provincial Bureau of Statistics) 81
state capacity 7
Strauss, Julia 11

target-responsibility system 132
tax-sharing reform 57
'three represents' theory *see sange daibiao*
three rural problems or issues, the *see sannong wenti*
three types (categories) of people *see sanzhongren*
tizhi gaige 115
tongchou guanli 78, 82, 86, 157
tongshou tongzhi 41
top-level design of reform 119
totalitarianism 25, 30
Township and village enterprises *see* TVEs
township governments 141–61
tudi caizheng 6, 7, 44, 57
tuichu sanquan 137

TVEs (township and village enterprises) 3, 4
Twelfth Five-Year Plan 51
'two-hands' approach 128

UNICEF 8, 21
urban population growth 3
urban reform 17
urban–rural inequality 5
urban–rural integration *see* integrated urban–rural development
urban–rural population distribution 48

Wang Qishan 199
WeChat 79, 88n6
Wen Jiabao 6, 52
White, Lynn 13, 14
White, Tyrene 13

xiangmuzhi see project-driven approach
Xi Jinping 55, 96, 113, 114, 127, 128, 184, 185, 199, 200
Xinhua News Agency 74, 113, 131, 154, 184

Yang Yixin 133
Yantai 35, 38, 65, 115
Ying Xing 167

zengjian guagou 7, 56–8, 71–3, 83, 105, 123, 131, 147, 188, 189
zhaijidi (housing allotment) 58, 85, 150
zhaijidi zhihuan 58
Zhang Hongliang 66
Zhao Ziyang 88n4
zhenli biaozhun dabianlun 47
zhinong zijin 77
zhizheng nengli 41
zhizheng nengli jianshe 46
zhonggengzu 16, 27, 35, 39, 48, 78, 112–15, 188, 191
Zhou Enlai 33, 128
Zhou Xueguang 162
zhuada fangxiao 95
zhua zhongdian 128
zhufang huobihua gaige 44
Zhu Rongji 6, 52
Zouping-based enterprise-style community model 85